PHOENIX

PHOENIX

a memoir

PHILIPPA MAYALL

SILVER BIRCH PRESS
LOS ANGELES, CALIFORNIA

*This book is to celebrate the lives of my brothers,
Mike and Matthew.*

*To my mum who always believed in me as a writer and
it turns out she was right about that, too.*

*To Rik and Rob with whom I have shared
some of the best moments of my life.*

*And to my little princess, Kayla,
who is a bright light in my heart.*

In order to rise
From its own ashes
A phoenix
First
Must
Burn.

OCTAVIA BUTLER
Parable of the Talents

CHAPTER ONE

❖

MANCHESTER, ENGLAND, 1988

I WOKE UP IN THE NIGHT BECAUSE MY THROAT WAS SCRATCHY AND TIGHT. My lips felt rough, like sandpaper, when they rubbed together. I ran my tongue around the inside of my cheeks and the roof of my mouth, searching for water. My spit was reduced to a thick paste so my tongue stuck to the inside of my mouth.

I wasn't sure of the time but I didn't want to wake up in case it was morning. That meant I'd be forced to get up and go to school, where I had a chemistry test. I reached my arm from under my duvet and groped the carpet with my hand, hoping to find a cool glass of water. There was no drink, but I found my chemistry book that I was revising from before I fell asleep. I think it was the cause of me falling asleep.

My throat had nearly closed up. I had to open my eyes to get up for a glass of water. I lay for a minute to focus in the dark. Although my light wasn't switched on, I was aware that something was looming.

Something wasn't right.

The air weighed heavy and I felt it pressing down on me, anchoring me to my mattress. I could taste it, too. A musty bitter taste coated my tongue with every breath. It was like a foul-tasting medicine that the doctor had prescribed. I looked across my room for the glowing red screen of my clock radio, with the time in square numbers, but I couldn't see it. I ploughed my duvet back, swung my legs out of bed, and switched on my light.

Smoke had filled my room.

It was black and had hidden the familiar horizons of my room, posters ripped out of *Just Seventeen* magazine and taped to the wall. I was only just fourteen so I hid my magazines under my bed way beyond my chemistry book.

The house was on fire.

I froze, not sure if I'd woken up at all. I rubbed my eyes but when I opened them again it seemed the smoke had gotten thicker still and I knew I wasn't sleeping, this was not a nightmare, this was real.

I tiptoed over to the sink in my room, feeling the carpet first with my toes, as if I were walking through the sea, afraid to stand on a crab beneath the seaweed. I drank from the tap and felt the crispy surface of my tongue reduce to its familiar squidge, like hardened soil turning muddy. It was cold and sent a shiver down my spine. Once I'd had as much as I could swallow, I just held my mouth under the water. Letting it run over my chin and into the sink, afraid to turn around. Unsure about what I was meant to do.

I thought of the firemen talking to us in school assembly and warning us about safety in the home and on bonfire night. I could see their faces and I heard their voices but only sounds came out, as if they were on a tape that had been chewed up in the machine, leaving the words stretched, chopped, and mangled. I wondered if Mam and my brothers were waiting outside on the grass for me. I switched off the tap and looked out my window. No one was there.

I started to feel the smoke on my chest. Like when I went to see my dad at work in the pub and sat in the cigarette-fogged room with his punters, who inhaled and exhaled with every swig of beer. *Fagging it,* Mam called it. I placed my hands on the window frame and pushed upwards, but it didn't budge. I pushed again.

Nothing.

I thought for a second of breaking it but I knew Mam would kill me and stop my pocket money forever. It was an old-fashioned window that went up and down on a pulley, so I had to have patience. I wiggled the ropes to make sure they were all loose after they'd been painted together and not opened since the summer. Then I gripped the frame again and closed my eyes and gritted my teeth. This tradition was something I'd seen in American movies, as if the closing and the gritting would give me a secret source of strength. I felt nothing spectacular. My muscles didn't tingle or bulge. But determination spread through my hands and my whole body after that. And yet unlike the movies, it still didn't open. When I let go, my fingers were cramped into a claw position and sore from the frame digging in.

I wanted to go back to bed and sleep, curl back under my duvet and ignore what was happening. But the fumes were getting thicker and when I waved my hand in front of my face I couldn't see it, a test Mam used on foggy mornings. I needed air.

I banged on the frame with my fists. I wanted to knock some sense into it. I could feel the panic seeping into my lungs with the smoke and my first ever-fleeting sensation that these could be my last moments alive. I could die right here.

I yanked at the window again. It seemed to be putting up the same protest as I'd done moments earlier about having to leave my warm bed. It groaned awake, first one side and then the other, the wood separating as if hitting the frame had been the abracadabra I'd needed all along. Goose bumps popped up all over my legs where the cold air hit them and then spread over my body.

With both my hands I gripped the underneath of the wood and forced it with all my strength to try to open it all the way. I'd developed good muscles from helping Mam carry boxes on the market and carrying my younger brothers—our Sammy, the baby, and our Mike, the older baby. It opened just enough to allow me to squeeze my face through sideways. I felt light headed, as if I'd not eaten for days. I sucked in the air as though I had a straw stuck in my mouth ready to slurp down a cool glass of Coke. I took a few more breaths and eventually I felt myself unfold and re-inflate.

My lungs filled my chest and pressed against my ribs and I could breathe properly again, my legs no longer felt wobbly and my head cleared. I stayed with my neck cricked sideways and face squashed through the gap for what seemed like a weeks worth of detention. I had to make a decision. Should I go downstairs and see where the others were or stay in my room?

I heard a voice shouting, "Help, help me," but it was faint, and I didn't know who it was. There was a pause as if they had stopped for a breath before they returned, "I'm dying." It sounded close by, perhaps Charlie or Chris, my older brothers. I wriggled my face free and crossed my room and hammered on my bedroom wall.

"Chris! Chris…are you okay?" I covered my mouth with my hand and waited for a moment, my other hand poised to bang on the wall again. There was no response.

"Chris! Chris!"

I climbed off my bed and opened my door. An angry tornado of smoke swirled outside. I stood in the doorway and stuck my head out, first looking for Chris's door about three feet away, but I couldn't see it. In the other direction no lights were on, it was empty, as if the rest of the house had been swallowed by the fire. The only reason I knew it still existed was because I could hear the signs of it dying, wood wheezing and cracking and explosions of glass. I stood back in the doorway and the fumes continued to pour into my room, choking me. I lay face down with my arms covering my head to create a clean pocket of air to breathe from and slammed the door shut with the ball of my foot.

I thought of my family. I thought about the argument I'd had with our Mike that night. I had to find him. But for a minute I stayed under the shelter of my arms where it felt safe.

When I looked up, it was as if the second coat of terror had been painted on the night. The air seemed blacker and gloopy, and when I moved I had to wade as if I was in a swimming pool, pushing the water behind me. But the darkness could no longer hide the truth—this was how I would die. I was petrified of the moment it would happen and how it would feel. I was sure it would hurt.

12

The only thing I could think to do was pray. I put my hands together like in school assemblies. I'd grown to believe that this was the microphone to God and if you didn't do this while praying the message wouldn't get through.

"Dear God, please tell me what to do. Shall I stay here or go downstairs? Please God show me what to do. Please God, keep my family safe God and if I have to smash the window, please protect me from my mam. Amen."

The lightbulb above me shattered and glass drizzled into my hair and trickled over my hands and down my neck. I was convinced that praying with my hands mimicking a microphone was the key to talking to God. Of all the unanswered prayers—a new bike, Dad to come home, extra days off school—this was the one he chose to answer. I breathed some relief. Thank God.

I stood and returned to the window for air, and I heard a voice.

"Hello...is anyone here?" Was it the voice of Him on heaven's tannoy system? "Hello. Is anyone 'round here?"

I jumped up and banged on the window to get his attention in case he tried to leave and shouted through the gap.

"Up here. I'm waving my arm out of my window. There's a fire."

I waited for some sign that he had heard me.

"Okay, love, we know. How many of you are there? Is there anyone else 'round here?"

"I have two brothers further 'round the back and another two 'round this side. Their bedroom window is above the front door."

I flapped my arms from right to left, as if I were trying to land an airplane, hoping the glow from the fire would provide him with light to see where I was pointing.

"My mam and her boyfriend are right at the front of the house."

"It's okay, love, we've got your mam. We're tryin' to find the young'uns and the other two. Hang on. Help's on its way."

He left with a mental treasure map of how to find everyone.

I heard a crash outside and high-pitched squeaking like nails on a blackboard. I hoped that this was my rescue. I wriggled

13

my face out of the gap and stood up to see what was happening below. Ladders had been set next to my window and I could see the reflective armbands of a fireman's jacket moving closer towards me. With every rung he climbed, he grew into the window and was framed as if he was on a TV set. I wished I could switch him and this whole nightmare off.

He wore an oxygen mask that covered his face and made him sound like Darth Vader when he breathed with a deep rumble in his throat. He tried pushing on the sash of the window but he didn't manage to budge it any more than I did. His densely padded hand reached around his waist and returned with his axe.

"Move away from the window, love."

"No...no! I can't go back in there. I can't breathe...I can't breathe!"

I looked behind me into the deep cavity. Heavy globs of soot swirled around me carried by the torrent of the fumes. They did laps of my room spreading their poison and feeding off the ash that continued to rise into the air as the fire burned.

I think I can see within them the ashes of our lives. Photos of each year we were alive, Biro marks on the kitchen door from Mam measuring our heights every month, spare cushions under the stairs for when Dad peed on the sofa, Charlie's hidden report cards found by the flames under his secret floorboard, blue handprints from my day of painting, Sammy's dent in the lounge door from charging at it full speed in his baby walker, crayon marks graffitied on the playroom wall by Mike and his mischievous friends, and Chris's love letters stashed under his mattress. It all swirled around me. It was everywhere.

I took small, shallow breaths and stood with my fists clenched, as if they had all my courage wrapped in them and if I were to open them it would all escape and I'd die.

"Please don't make me go back."

"Step away from the window! I said step away from the window!" He paused a moment before raising his axe like in a real horror movie. I backed away and watched him hack at the frame, pulling his arm back and driving the blade in. The glass from the window shattered into my room on first impact. The smoke stopped swirling around me and gushed through the hole and I raced towards him.

"What's your name, love?"

"Flip."

"OK, Flip, do you think you can climb down the ladder? Or shall I carry you?"

I looked down. I wasn't overly fond of heights, I would only ever look over the edge of a cliff if I was lying on my stomach. I thought about how I would be hanging headfirst and my body would swing like a pendulum in a grandfather's clock. If he dropped me, I'd have bad eyes like our Charlie because Mam says Aunty Helen dropped him as a baby.

"I'll be fine," I assured him but not myself.

He'd removed the jagged edges of the glass from the wood, but as I climbed through the frame, I caught the sleeve of my favorite yellow pajamas and tore it.

"Careful love. Take it slow."

Black bullets of rain started to fall. I felt the cold slimy first rung of the ladder beneath my feet. I couldn't tell whether it was wet from the rain or the hoses. The air was freezing and I shuddered. I held onto the ladders tighter, afraid I'd wobble off them. The fireman started to move, and I followed. I reached down, feeling with my big toe for the next place to land before placing my whole foot down. I did the same for each rung and the journey down seemed to last for ages.

I never looked down but glanced up to my bedroom window to see that it looked like one of the derelict houses on the estates by the market where Mam worked. I could hear the flames raging and pounding against the wind.

I stopped and strengthened my grip on the ladder. I heard explosions of glass from behind the flames. Probably Mam's ornaments, and the deep sighs of our belongings collapsing inwards, melting and giving in.

As we got farther down I glanced sideways and caught my first sight of the demon that visited us that night that made

15

Tony's fighting and swearing seem like a dream. I had a homemade security system that stopped him barging into my room when he was angry. A piece of string tied between my bedpost and the door handle with cups hanging from it. If he tried to get me while I was asleep, the cups would smash at the point of attack. Mainly he attacked Mam though.

This demon was even more monstrous. Pouring out of windows and doors, as if it had tentacles, long and floundering like an octopus. The steps up to the back door were still standing as strong as the memories we had created every time any of us walked in and out of the door. We used to drop from the kitchen window onto the steps and run through the back and into the kitchen again when we played tag. Our friends knocked on every morning to walk to school. When Sammy was born he made his grand entrance into the family through the back door.

In fact, if anyone came to our front door, Mam told us to keep down and be quiet because it might be someone wanting money. She was usually right. Only the milkman, the Avon woman, the rag and bone man, and Jehovah's Witnesses rang the front doorbell. The postman would ring for his tip but that only happened as often as Christmas.

When I felt the concrete, bumpy and uneven, under my feet from when Mam had the driveway resurfaced, I felt a lump in my throat rise but I swallowed it back, not wanting them to think I was a baby. A policeman wrapped a blanket around my shoulders. I grabbed the edges and pulled it tighter. I looked at the fireman and he turned around—I wasn't sure whether I was supposed to shake his hand or curtsy. So I smiled as hard as I could, just managing to raise a lopsided half-smile. The policeman spoke into his radio.

"Got her, Sarg," I heard him say.

I was led up the path as if I was a stranger who didn't know the way. Even though I'd spent years walking, skating and cycling up and down it, I probably would have got lost at that point. I passed the front door and looked up to Mike's and

Sammy's room above. It looked empty and soulless. I was used to hearing their giggles and gurgles as I passed under their window. I was positive they must be waiting at the end of the driveway. Sammy will have been carried out of his cot and Mike would have enjoyed the climb since his latest ambition was to be a fireman. He'd had a visit to the local station and his photo was printed in the newspaper for being the first under-age visitor allowed. He was with the Captain of the white watch and was leaning out of the cockpit window wearing a helmet and a huge grin.

As we got closer to the front of the house, the firemen shouted orders to each other and glass layered the driveway. On the front lawn, I saw a figure lying still on the grass underneath the lounge window. At first, I wasn't sure who it was. I didn't recognize the whimpering. But as I got closer her features became more familiar. I stood over her.

"Mam, are you okay? What's wrong, Mam?"

"I'm okay, love," she paused for a moment. She screwed up her face, as if it were being pinched together. "I've broke my back. Get into the ambulance, love. Go on," she spoke in a low whisper and ushered me with her eyes towards the ambulance.

I looked around to see where it was. What seemed to be the whole street was stood in front of me—faces that I passed on my way to school but didn't speak to, neighbors from across the road that Mam gave Christmas cards to but never saw afterwards, the doctor and his wife who didn't own a video player. I was never so happy to see Abdul. He stood at the end of the driveway in a black silk dressing gown and slippers.

Abdul lived next door and had fancied Mam for years. He was as wide as he was tall, six-foot at least, and had all sorts of smells wafting from him, *Because he's an Arab and eats weird food,* I'd always thought. Any chance he had to speak to Mam, he did—bringing a bowl of pungent food that flavored the frosty air. Scariest of all was his glass eye that stared from his skull like a dead fish eye.

"It'll be okay, young princess," he whispered to me as I stepped into the back of the ambulance.

Chris and Charlie were waiting in the back when I climbed in. It stank of hospitals and TCP that Mam put on Charlie's gashes and scrapes when he somersaulted over his handlebars or off the end of his skateboard. But for a minute it reminded me of home as if nothing had happened. I sat next to Chris on a side seat instead of facing ahead, like my favorite seat on the bus in the morning. The windows were blacked out but the inside was bright.

Chris had cream on his face and arms and bandages around his hands. He wore his red dressing gown that he'd got one Christmas years ago and refused to throw away. It had a new tear at the shoulder but I knew he'd probably ask Mam to sew it like he had done with half a dozen other holes. Our Charlie was half naked in his boxer shorts. He looked like he'd attempted suicide. Half-dried streaks of blood dripped down his arm from his wrist and mixed with the dirt to look like volcanic lava. He held a large white pad to it, and his blood had soaked through. He showed me his watch that had a deep gash across the strap—if he hadn't worn the watch he would have slit his wrist and bled to death. None of us said anything. Our faces read the same thing.

We waited.

I felt like I was in some sort of time warp. It seemed that on the outside of the ambulance time was moving at ten times the normal speed, as if it were set on fast forward. On the inside, it was as if time was stopped dead.

A new ending about to begin.

After what seemed several more light years, Mam was carried in on a stretcher. She was dirty, like our Charlie, with a sooty face, apart from where she'd screwed up her face, and that left white wiggly lines across her forehead. She didn't talk or try to joke like she usually did to make us feel better, and I knew that meant she was really sick. The doors were still open and there was another ambulance parked behind us, I assumed for the others to get in but I didn't see them.

"Where is everyone?" I asked.

Nobody answered.

"Mam?"

"They're dead...they're all dead."

Her words spun around in the air. It took them a few minutes to reach my brain. When they did, I didn't believe her. How would she know? I saw our Mike sleeping only a few hours ago. But then I looked at Mam and my brothers and how dirty and bloody they were, like a scene from a battlefield. I cried because none of it seemed real. I looked at the ambulance behind us looking for a flicker of life.

"Put your arm 'round your sister."

Chris put his bandaged fists around my shoulders and the ambulance doors were closed.

After waiting hours at the hospital, I was unhooked from the oxygen mask and wheeled into a room. My brothers were already there, our Charlie lying on a gurney and our Chris in a wheelchair, same as me.

A doctor stood in front of us. He, too, was unable to make eye contact.

"I'm Dr. Brunsmith, I treated your brothers and stepfather when they arrived at the Emergency Department. We tried everything we could...their injuries were severe...I'm sorry, we couldn't save them."

He carried on talking, but by then it seemed his words were like treacle dripping from his mouth, the whole scene slowed down. The single tear dripping down our Charlie's cheek stopped dripping, whereas droplets of Chris's tears suspended in midair. I could feel the pop of my insides as my heart broke and the foundations of my spirit crumbled, taking everything I knew with it.

CHAPTER TWO

❖

LOS ANGELES, CALIFORNIA, 2002

THE RADIO CRACKLED TO LIFE ACROSS MY ROOM. I was awake but it startled me back to earth from my thoughts. I was strapped—the torturous limbo between being awake and asleep, hangover and recuperation that happens after a night of martinis and cocaine.

I knew I was dying and I knew I was killing myself. It would be a long slow death that no one noticed, especially not Mam. My organs would erode, the way saltwater erodes the coastline, until there's nothing left.

It wasn't how I'd planned it. I'm not sure I had planned it. It just seemed the natural thing to do given the circumstances. Why would I possibly want to live? Is it even feasible to live with this amount of heartache for another fifty-plus years?

I'd tried suicide before but the other methods were more instant. When I was seventeen I tried to make myself bleed to death with a dull shard of glass, but it didn't even draw blood. When I was twenty-three, I took my month's supply of Prozac with most of a bottle of wine. I thought I'd end up really happy or really dead. Both were fine with me.

My fear of dying seemed to be outweighed by my misery at being forced to live. So nothing worked. I thought of a new plan. I decided, after I'd been taking drugs as a recreation for years, that this would be the way to do it. Drugs were a feasible way I could top myself and hopefully it would be after Mam died. Reducing my life expectancy seemed to be a good compromise. Just in case I changed my mind, maybe.

I listened to the tail end of the radio report.

...and finally, the bodies of two children were found by the Coast Guard today, two days after their boat capsized. The father of the children and his other son, who were also involved in the incident, are recovering at Daniel Freeman

Hospital in Marina Del Rey. Thanks for listening. This is Doc on the Rock for KROQ.

They'll never recover so long as they live, I thought. I wondered what I might say to the father. How I could explain that, even after years, the loss can still feel like it was yesterday.

Dear Father of Three, I wrote in my head. *Nobody will tell you this, please allow me to enlighten you. Trust me it will save you years of anguish and pain if you can just realize these simple facts. Your surviving child might be young but he will feel the loss of the others like you. It might be a different feeling but he will hurt for his siblings. You will probably feel guilt and think it's all your fault and you should have saved them, so will your child. They say time heals, but it really doesn't, it only recycles. The air is always stale. And when you think you're having a good day, all of a sudden a memory will be lanced into your brain for no obvious reason. Maybe it was a scene from a movie, a song that you all used to sing, an expression, someone who looks like them.*

No matter what, you will notice the loss and it will spread to your heart and lungs and you will feel like someone is strangling you because you won't be able to breathe. This is the truth and I hope you don't mind me telling you.

Yours truly,
Flip (Fellow Survivor)

My brothers and stepfather hadn't been the only deaths. The fire seemed to be a roaring catalyst and people I knew and loved popped out of the universe as suddenly and as shockingly as balloons bursting. First it was granddad, just three hundred and sixty-three days after my brothers—his liver exploded after years of guzzling alcohol. Then Aunty Liz, Mam's best friend from childhood whom we lived with after the fire. She had a thrombosis and died in a hospice.

Dad didn't die so much as disappear. He got married to an alcoholic, like him, and after the ceremony we never saw him again. I was sixteen at the time. For the first six months, it didn't seem odd whatsoever. Dad often took off for months with promises to return, and out of nowhere a postcard would drop through the letter box from Bournemouth, London, Skegness, all over England. Or there would be a slurred message on the answer machine.

"Errr, kidssss, ssss yerr errrr, Dad. Whatssss goin' on?"

Click went the phone. The kitchen, where we listened to messages, would be silent again. The sound effects of clinking glasses, raucous laughing, orders being shouted, ended with his phone call.

Dad never had forgotten my birthday. Never. I might not see him all year, but my birthday—the one day of my life he contributed to—was marked every year.

The first time he forgot was my seventeenth birthday. I excused him, "Probably out with his new missus," I said. *Getting fucking plastered out of 'is mind,* I thought.

Ten days after the event and two driving lessons later, I got the call.

"'Appy birthday, love," he slurred. The pedestal I had him balancing on started to crumble. All the times Mam had told me "he's a good-for-nothing-drunk!" became real. There was no longer a foundation for me to cling to. The rubble from my dad's pedestal crushed me that day. I lay suffocating in the dark for a long time. *I'm never gonna end up like 'im,* I thought.

"Flip…are you awake?" The voice came from my bathroom next door. It was Gina, whom I'd been out with until just a few hours earlier. I didn't think I'd see her until the evening dawned again.

I pedaled my sheets back with my feet and sat up, eyes still closed.

There was another knock.

"'Ang on," I shouted.

Through the mesh screen and the wrought-iron bars, Gina stood smoking a cigarette. She was wearing all black as usual, *It's just how I feel,* she'd told me. Her hair was whipped up in a butterfly clip with black curls that slopped over the sides. Her dark Dolce and Gabana glasses disguised the signs of the night before. But I knew she hid red rubbed eyes that were probably sunken into her skull. I also knew they hid much more. The baggage of her past—an absent father, an alcoholic mother, and from princess to pauper when her mother's business collapsed—those were like a chain around her ankles. It forced her to move in a slow, slouchy stroll, even though her favorite expression was *carpe diem.* She approached the bars and we spoke like an inmate and a visitor at a prison.

"Hey, I've been trying to get a hold of you. You wanna go to TJ?" She said spitting the dregs of her fumes over me.

"TJ?"

"Tijuana."

"Hell yeah."

"Okay, well, I'm gonna go get Scott and we'll swing by for you on the way back to the freeway. Sound good?"

"*Si, si.*" Which was the only Spanish I knew apart from *mas papas por favor* (more fries please) and *batido de fresa, ahora mismo!* (strawberry milkshake, immediately)—essential language to communicate with the bus boys where we worked.

I met Gina when she applied for a job at Rock 'n' Rollers, a '50s diner. I'd recently been fired from, what I decided, was my last position in public relations and was only my second. I'd flown six thousand miles from Manchester and risked everything to try my luck in LA. I'd since discovered I could make as much money with half the stress just by serving people malts and fries, much to Mam's dismay.

"All that education down the spout," Mam's words pinballed through my mind but were just as easily dropped into a pocket of my subconscious when I had a bundle of cash

23

scrunched in my hand. I knew she was right on some level but I was also determined to make it on my own.

Gina bounded up to the counter with the energy of a puppy and a Hollywood smile that leapt off her face, pearl white teeth that looked like they'd been cut out of a magazine. She handed me her resume, which I took into the back office for the manager to review, all the while scanning the page for information about her, twenty-three, good experience, Libra and that's as far as I got before reaching the office door. I knew I'd see her again.

As with all new servers, I took an instant dislike to her. She was a threat to my already dwindling section that got chiseled away with each shift. I expected to come into work one day to find my section out by the bins in a heap of rubbish, serving leftovers to roaches.

All the servers were supposed to "turn and burn" or "burn and turn," some crazy American expression that meant to get the customers out of there. Without giving them a chance to wipe their mouths and watch their grimacing, greasy faces as they were churned out with a friendly goodbye and a hearty dose of indigestion. Years of watching Mam chatter on the market and giggle with customers was a genetic disposition for me. I didn't notice as I fell into a black hole of conversation, triggered by people's responses to my accent. I'd developed a whole tip-winning script.

"Scottish or Australian?" I was asked maybe twenty times a shift.

"English. From Manchester," I would pause and raise my eyebrow as if I was thinking and count on my hand. "Two 'undred and twelve miles north of the Queen and thirty miles east of The Beatles."

Throwing the Queen in was usually worth a giggle, and I felt better that, at last, her role as a figurehead was having a direct benefit for one of her subjects—me.

"Really? That's a thick accent. How long have you lived here?"

"Two years."

From there, the conversation could branch out to, "How are you coping with the death of Princess Di/George Harrison?" Or, "I went to London once. I can't believe they really drink warm beer!"

I took my time to entertain my "guests," throw in my rendition of the cabbage patch dance, and they tipped me handsomely, returning only to sit in my section.

I was pulling a double the first time I worked with Gina. Steve had called in sick. I knew that was a hoax. In a new wave of his gaydom, he'd started to dress in drag and call himself "Stef." As Stef, he scored a hot date with some gorgeous bloke with peachy skin. I agreed that I'd take his shift if he called in a sicky.

I was a veteran of four weeks and felt I could pitch myself against the new staff, show them what I was made of when I made the most tips and enjoy a dreaming moment of revelry. But I watched my daydream unravel in a few spins that left me dizzy and feeling drunk as Gina's bouncing puppy energy turned into that of a vicious pit bull. She jetted from behind the counter, juggling customers' orders, balancing burgers and malts, and slapping tomato ketchup "happy faces" into a cardboard tray.

My competitive nerve was struck, and I started gunning from table to table collecting orders and tapping them quickly—and incorrectly—into the computer that would spit the order out on a printer for the cooks, Carlos and Jose. They couldn't speak a word of English and could only read diner words like "hamburger," "cheese," and "fries" that came with the orders. If I had to communicate with them, I had to use fingers and thumbs and contorted expressions to explain the words I didn't know.

Gina witnessed my attempts to get my starving customers the correct order from the cooks. They nodded, laughed, wrote something down on a napkin, gave each other high fives and the script to read with the new burger, an apology I assumed.

She was at the next table taking an order when she overheard me read the script off the napkin. She tapped me on the shoulder and whispered something in my ear. What she told me stopped me asking my Hispanic customers if they'd like a side of erections with their burgers in Spanish. It was too late for the table I was at and who knows what untold damage I did to the kids?

At the end of the shift, we sat in the same booth at the back of the diner. It was dark and empty of customers, my section. I didn't usually like to count my day's takings in front of other staff, embarrassed by my comparatively slim stash. But I was grateful Gina had stepped in to help me out.

"You smoke 'erb?" she asked, leafing through a wad of cash.

"Erb?"

"You know, 'erb. Weed."

I burst out laughing, "'Ang on, wha'd'ya call it? 'Erb? What about the aitch? Herb."

"What was that? H, h-erb?"

I laughed so hard I slammed my hand on the shiny surface of the table, leaving a sweaty hand print. Gina's neat pile of money fanned out like a deck of cards. She quickly scooped it back up and weighed it down with the salt shaker.

"I 'ave to say that's the funniest thing I ever 'eard. You can't say herb, but vee-hicle is right? Are you barmy?"

She'd been studying the money, counting and recounting, but a smile flickered across her face and I knew if she could take my sarcasm, our friendship was certain.

❖

I opened my windows and stood for a moment allowing the sun's rays to energize me before scanning my bedroom floor for anything to wear, not necessarily clean, just cool. I'd not unpacked my suitcase for the two years I'd lived in Los Angeles, part laziness and part because I had been sat on a bi-coastal seesaw since the plane had touched the runway.

One moment I craved the chippy and wanted to be in the

pub with my mates drinking Stella and in the next minute I would be at Venice Beach scheming how I could stay once my visa ran out. Technically, it was already void since the public relations agency that had applied for the work visa on my behalf had fired me.

My room doubled as Grandma's storage ever since I'd shown up unannounced with suitcase in tow. Before that it was her daughter Ali's room, but that was forty years prior to my arrival.

I'd met Lillian years earlier when Emily, my friend from university, and I flew to LA to take a break after writing our dissertations. I struck up a friendship with Lillian, whom I called Grandma by the end of the trip, instantly even though she was six decades older, nearly to the day. Her husband had died and she was back in the dating game at the age of eighty-eight. We spent hours in her bedroom talking into the night about the pros and cons of her latest troupe of toy boys. (It was hard to find any men remotely sane past the age of eighty-five, Grandma claimed. *For all the years it takes 'em to mature, it only takes a night for 'em to get undone again).*

Sam took her only to the 'early bird special' at Norm's so they had to eat at 4.30 p.m., which she thought was cheap. Lincoln—*bless him,* she would say—was a terrible driver and she couldn't risk it because he veered to the wrong side of the road. *Not at my age, honey,* she told me.

She settled on Mort, who didn't drive. That meant she could and he was happy to indulge her every whim. He would get up and down all day to fetch her ice cream and peanut butter on toast, each followed by a cup of tea with sweetener but no milk—American style. The fact he managed all of this with a hernia, Grandma and I decided, demonstrated his dedication. But her sometimes-wicked sense of humor drove her to tease him. *Who's been your greatest lover, Grandma?* She would look at me and wink across the table before responding, *I didn't meet him yet, sweetheart.* Mort would pull his face and hang his head, and so she would take hold of his hand and make him smile.

A mishmash of faded tastes from decades past layered each surface of my room. Everything was frosted in dust that was never disturbed. Nothing new seemed to have been added since the sixties. An incense burner was on a small table by the window and a tie-dye headscarf was wrapped around a mannequin head. I laughed thinking of Grandma back in the day smoking pot. *No way,* I thought, *she was just trying to be in fashion.*

Paintings with garish gold frames were stacked against walls, leaving dusty shadows from where they'd settled. Some were tipped to one side as if leaning on a walking stick, others had settled into a recline as if they were in a favorite armchair. Paintbrushes were crammed into old coffee jars and left on top of the dresser and hidden in boxes.

In the middle of the room was my mess. I picked up my jeans from the night before by the belt loop and frisked the pockets for any baggies of unfinished cocaine. There were just a couple with powder stuck in each corner. Gina usually dipped her finger in the bottoms of the bags and after licking the snowy peak of her finger and she would speak as if her tongue had swollen too big for her mouth.

Last night she'd forgotten about them. I inspected each bag to see if I could get a decent line from putting all the bits in the corners together. I tried tearing the plastic down the seam so I could empty the coke onto the dresser, but the bag snapped out of my hand and the flakes drifted to the carpet and I accidentally flushed the other bag. I unrolled the notes we'd used—a fifty, a couple of ones, and a five—none of them more valuable than the other when it came to function.

We went to the same place every time, PF Chang, where we were guaranteed a good night. We sat at the bar and Don and RC shook apple martinis for us laced with a comedy act from behind the bar— they were both aspiring actors—and lines of coke in the toilet. We never paid for the martinis and in return when they visited Rock 'n' Rollers they got an extra patty on their burgers, a helping of fries that broke all the portioning rules, with a tomato ketchup happy face to dip them in.

The aftermath of the alcohol thudded inside my head. I tried to rewind my mind to the beginning of the night so I could calculate how much I'd had to drink. As if it mattered now. My head spun and vision wobbled. The booze never totally knocked me out. I'd lie in bed awake for a few hours until morning. This was the worst part—the comedown.

Every single time, I thought about home and Mam and my brothers, dead and alive. I couldn't believe I'd not walked down the stairs. At least tried. Mike and Sammy had been dead fourteen years and I'd still not forgiven myself or God. He had answered my prayer on the night of the fire by giving me the heart and legs of a coward. I was alive; they're dead. It was my fault. And His.

What would they think if they saw me lying here dealing with the effects of coke wearing off? I cursed myself for what I'd become—my father's daughter for certain. Exactly what and who I didn't want to be.

My friends at home told me not to worry, *it's only coke*. I couldn't stop myself and no one else seemed to think I needed to.

One night, after working for six months at Rock 'n' Rollers, four of those with Gina, I slipped in a puddle of water and ended my waitress career with a bone-shattering crush of my wrist.

It had been a night of celebration. Excitement sizzled in the air and burgers on the grill. The Grove, another new shopping mall, was opening. Grandma was fuming about it. Every time we drove past, she pointed and sighed, longing for the good old days of streetcars and nickel ice creams. But the servers stood to earn two hundred dollars a night in tips, even me. Grandma's nostalgia evaporated to cold hard cash.

My section was brimming with customers and my apron looked like an abstract ice cream painting from making my own malts and shakes.

29

"Go and change your apron," my boss told me in the middle of a crush of customers. I thought she was kidding but apparently not as she reminded me with a glare moments later. I went into the back and never came out again. I was carted off in my boss's Mercedes after slipping in the water and landing on my wrist. I wasn't heavy, but eight-stone was enough to turn my bones to powder.

It was a straight shot to Cedars Sinai Hospital but even with the fancy Merc suspension it didn't stop me yelping every time we hit a pothole.

At the hospital, I was petrified because I had no insurance. The NHS didn't seem like a bad idea at that moment, the wait times reasonable compared to the bill I would get stuck with at this point. *Thousands, no millions,* I thought. *At least thousands though.* I wondered if giving birth was as painful as crushing bones?

"Workers comp this one," the nurse pushing me into the x-ray room said.

I didn't know what that meant. I allowed them to feed me morphine through an IV before I decided I could think about it. When I woke from my delicious morphine dream, I found myself with a lawsuit (me suing Rock 'n' Rollers), an attorney, and weekly disability checks to compensate the use of my favorite limb, my writing hand.

Gina's exit was more dramatic, and I should have taken it as a sign of things to come. It was New Years Day, and of course we'd been out the night before. Celebrations started early because we had to be at work by seven. We didn't sleep all night, but I at least rested. The morning was slow, to the point of empty. At midday during a mini rush, she was hollering at the top of her voice at a customer who had apparently left her a stingy tip.

"Happy fucking New Year, dude!" I heard her shout. I turned around and looked in the direction of the turned heads. Her apron flew like a snowball across the counter and she left before she was fired. I didn't see her for a few days, and after that I couldn't shake her.

It meant me and Gina had lots of time to get wasted, and we did a few times a week and when we weren't doing coke we'd be parked up at the beach or a supermarket car park smoking pot. Sometimes we'd go back into Rock 'n' Rollers, with glazed pink eyes, giggling and with a severe munchie attack. We sat at the counter, put nickels in the mini jukeboxes and ate apple pie with a huge scoop of vanilla ice cream without any conversation until it was finished.

My favorite part of getting high with Gina was talking. She was the first person I'd met who seemed to understand the predicament of requiring the drugs to be able to blot out the past and function on a daily basis. But also the drugs were killing us. We sat in her car for hours chatting about our families, consoling each other.

"After my brothers died, I didn't know what to do or 'ow to cope. The Brits don't talk about much, so we all just sat there as if nought 'ad 'appened. Me mam was always angry, always kickin' our Charlie out. Chris 'ad already left to live with 'is girlfriend cos 'im and Mam 'ad a fight.

"When I met Emily at uni, you remember me mentioning 'er right?"

She nodded.

"Right. So when I met 'er she was already into taking ecstasy. I didn't even smoke cigarettes! I can't even imagine not takin' summat now. I drank a few times, but that made me sick. A whole crowd of us went out on New Year's Eve and everyone was taking E. Then I wanted to try it to see what everyone was talking about. That was back in the day when ecstasy was MDMA, not rat poison and speed," I laughed. "'Ere, give us your bowl so I can pack some herb."

"Well, of course you ended up on drugs! How else would you cope?"

"I just remember how miserable I'd been. I didn't understand why. I thought I should be over my brothers' death at that point. One ecstasy took all that away, and my accent apparently! I spoke in an Irish accent for six hours straight. My

Irish friends thought I was taking the piss," I said in an Irish accent—*M'Oirish friends tought oi was taking te piss.*

"I could talk about how I felt, I could think about my brothers and remember them without feeling their absence. It freed me completely. Until they started cutting the ecstasy with other shit and it stopped working. That's when I got into coke! Coke always worked. Instantly. I thought LA would give me a break, but it turns out the coke is waaaay better out 'ere," I smiled.

"Sweetie, you came to LA to get off drugs? Now I know you're either insane, ultra sarcastic, or both" she laughed. "But who can blame ya for taking drugs? What did they expect?"

What did they expect? I thought.

"I started taking coke when I was eleven," she told me.

"Eleven!" I thought back to that age. Dad had been officially moved out of the house and Mam got a divorce. Tony had moved in, but Mam wasn't quite pregnant so he hadn't started to be violent.

"Yeah. My parents were using, and I used to take theirs. My grandfather was loaded. He owned a magazine. I used to take a limo to school with my friends and we'd get high the whole way, or drink from the bar," she laughed. "Then the magazine was sold and we were out of money. I had to sell my horses and buy this car, drive myself to school. My parents kept using and I kept stealing from them. Rich one day, poor as fuck the next."

❖

When I opened my bedroom door, I could instantly smell the bacon. My stomach rumbled and mouth salivated for a split second before the nausea lurched back up my throat. I stood for a moment in my doorway listening to the bacon sizzle in the pan.

It spat the same tune as Mam's on a Sunday morning. I wished I could go back to the times before Mam had met Tony. It was just her, me and my brothers—Chris the eldest, our Charlie ten months older than me, and our Mike who was the youngest at the time. Sammy came later, compliments of Tony.

Sammy had to be the sweetest angel in heaven, I thought. He wouldn't've existed had Tony not come into our lives. But Tony had also destroyed us. Killed the family with his cigarette, that's what the official cause of the fire was—one cigarette and one manic depressive drunk. I sometimes wished Mam and Tony had never met, but felt immediately guilty that that would mean no Sammy either.

I felt my body start to close down section by section like the machinery in a factory being switched off for the night. Heart first to stop pumping blood, next windpipe stuck together to cut off oxygen, and eyes shut as if the lights were going off. I saw everything through my mind's eye and like an old projector movie, the film was scratched and the sound quality poor. I could only vaguely recall the sounds of their voices—our Mike saying my name and Sammy's laugh because he'd not said his first word yet. What else had I forgotten about them that I'd never remember again?

I took a deep controlled breath, as I'd learned to do, and filed the thought in my subconscious, along with a million more like it. *File it,* was all Mam had said after the fire. It's all she could manage.

I knew Mort had to be out of the house. He was Grandma's latest boyfriend and Orthodox Jewish. There was no way he would have any type of pig meat at a breakfast table or any other type of table he was at. Grandma was Jewish, too, but a plate of bacon, extra crisp because it's been fried, was too much for her to resist.

Mort knew when we'd *forced her to sin,* as he put it, as she never quite removed her greasy smile and she'd have a satisfied look on her face. Then he would refuse to kiss her for eight hours, which is how long it took for her to be cleansed, he told me.

I passed through the dining room on my way to the kitchen. Grandma was at the kitchen table picking at hissing, sizzling strips of bacon. She would try to convince me that that was the way they talked and they were begging to be eaten. *Begging*, she would repeat. Who was I to criticize her vices? Her daughter, Ali, would throw a fit if she knew, but she was only interested in herself and waterskiing. The only reason she ever showed up was for a loan.

"Morning, Grandma," I leaned in and kissed the top of her head knowing that would make her happy the whole day. She would think of her son, who'd moved to England thirty years ago, Emily's dad.

"Hi there, sweetheart."

I looked into her turquoise plastic mug—one of those stolen from the hospital each time she was admitted. She had a whole collection in pink, blue, and beige, too.

"You want more tea?" I asked.

"Always, honey. Always."

From the kitchen, I could hear Fe pelting out distorted notes and words of a tune. It wasn't until I heard the words that I could recognize the song.

"...and Venus was his name. He's got it, yeah baby he's got it..."

In the seven years she'd been in LA, she'd learned English, kind of, she still couldn't pronounce 'th,' 'f,' or 'w.' One morning when she bounced into my room with the phone shouting, "Plip, Plip, is de pone por you!" I almost fell out of bed laughing and she shouted, "Bloody Dude!" And that's what she called me from that point on.

Fe existed in stereo. She moved in as Grandma's live-in care assistant because Grandma had slipped and had a small stroke. At the time, I was in hospital waiting for surgery on my wrist. Her presence made the walls of the house bulge. Everything about her was loud, from her clothes to her laugh. Even her cooking, the meals had gone from 99c Store specials and chicken water with noodles made by Mort, to homemade Chinese and Thai food, better than at any restaurant. After The Folks—my term of endearment for Grandma and Mort because they reminded me of the grandma and the grandpa on the *Waltons*—went to bed, I sat in Fe's room talking and drink premixed Long Island Ice Tea.

It smelled as if she were cooking another of her delicacies from the Philippines. My stomach lurched, and I poised for a moment ready to run to the loo. But it sank back down again. Everything she cooked was drowned in fat, and although she read a dozen women's magazines every week warning of the dangers of animal fats and sugar, she lived in her own happy oblivion.

Her right shoulder propped her mobile phone up to her ear, and she chatted to a friend, "Sing, you look bery pat last time I see you," Fe would say to her plus-sized friend, "der will be no honey por you." Sing would reply with something equally as cutting. And where at first I was shocked by their open brutality to each other, I later understood it as part of the culture. Like when Angelinos say "sick" or "bad" to mean a good thing. Where I lived, I had to get used to people from three different cultures and they had to get used to me.

I poured water into the coffee machine and waited to hear it gurgle. I got the peanut butter and chocolate ice cream from the freezer and scooped out a large bowl for breakfast, lunch, and dinner. When I first got to LA, I was considered "chunky" by Hollywood standards. A bowl of ice cream represented all my food for the day and supported my hundred and ten pound frame, which in my language converts to seven stone, twelve pounds. Pretty average for Hollywood standards. I stood in the kitchen to eat so Grandma didn't see and want a bowl, too.

Fe laughed, "*Oh ziggy,*" she said, which always ended her conversations, and she turned to me. "You were out last night?" She stirred the thousand tiny sardine eyes around the pan.

"Er...yeah, why? Did I bother you coming in? It wasn't that late I don't think?"

"No, dude. I just ask you where you go? Martinis, dude?"

"Totally, mate. Hey, listen, I won't be home for dinner tonight I'm off to Tijuana for the day."

"Okay, but you'll miss a good dinner. I make pork ribs. Your grandma's paborite." She turned and looked at Grandma. "Right honey? Pork rib, your paborite, right?"

Grandma nodded back, chewing her bacon at the same time.

"You gonna bring us a Mexican hunk back? Por me and one por your grandma?" She looked at Grandma smiling. "You want one, right, honey?"

"Sure. Why not?" Grandma turned to me, "Get me two, sweetheart."

We all laughed.

"Actually, Mexican men are like this." Fe held up her little finger and wiggled it up and down. "Bery small."

Grandma was shaking her head and her red lips spread across her face into a smile. Her eyes always twinkled like she had diamonds set into her pupils. Fe couldn't help laughing at herself and she stuffed rice into her mouth at the same time.

The phone rang and I ran out of the room to answer it.

"I'm outside. Bring your bud."

A last scan of my room ensured nothing was visible that shouldn't be. No doubt Grandma would poke her head in the doorway on her way to the toilet and remark how disgusting it was and that she was going to throw me out.

I closed the door and left the house.

CHAPTER THREE

❖

MEXICO WAS NOTHING LIKE I EXPECTED AFTER SEEING
EMILY'S HOLIDAY PHOTOS FROM CANCUN. She'd stayed in a
fancy resort and had a different six-foot tall, half-naked bloke
every night. Her favorite was a stripper who wore white pants
(that tore off in one snap of the wrist, she confided), a sailor
hat, and that's all. It was his washboard stomach and steel
buttocks that sent her head over heels, but when he never
replied to her e-mails she was devastated.

Stepping across the border was like walking into a football
stadium with a full-capacity, roaring crowd. Everyone was
shouting, trying to sell, con, or beg. A recipe of instruments
only used by the Mexicans—five pounds of acoustic guitar,
two cubes of harmonica, a dash of tambourine, and add
trombone and trumpet to taste—played in time all around us, as
if the whole of Mexico was playing from the same sheet music.

We followed a stream of tourists toward *Avenida
Revolucion,* rumored to be *the* place to go in TJ. We kicked
wrappers and crunched dropped taco shells on the bridge that
crosses the Tijuana River.

They made the same noise as the autumn leaves Mam used
to pile up in the back garden. Me and my brothers would fly
through them—Mike with his arm forward and a cloak, really a
red towel, tied around his neck. Sometimes, Chris would pick
him up and launch him from his arms. Mike splattered through
the padded landing, giggling all the way. Mam would fume and
we would have to spend an hour raking them all back into
piles.

On the other side of the bridge, there was an explosion of
color that was noticeable before anything else. It was as if
they'd tried to paint over the Third World grime and dazzle the
tourists. The bridge opened out into a huge square and my eyes
brimmed with everything I'd heard.

Gifts from the souvenir shops crept out onto the pavement. Hammocks swayed between stands that had sombreros piled one on top of each other. Stripy ponchos were strung up above entrances against a bright canvas of pink, orange, red, blue, or green paint. Mini-acoustic guitars and maracas were suspended in the air, as if being played by invisible musicians.

Workers sat on the cold concrete and slouched back into the doorways drinking beer and smoking cigarettes. There wasn't a spare square inch of space that wasn't displaying something that could be sold. The only empty space I could see was the sky and even that was filled with noise: horns, music, and shouting.

Mexican women were dotted around, under the shade of an umbrella, behind their tables that they draped with a blanket to sell their wares. Children hid under the tables, using them like forts, and ambushed us the moment they saw a foot with shoes pass by. A pair of feet with no shoes means the person is a local. The kids held up boxes of Chiclets chewing gum and wooden snakes that slithered when held at the tail.

"*No mas dinero,*" I said, repeating what Gina had taught me in the car park. But within seconds, I was reaching into my pocket and handing out change to the dirty, hopeful faces looking up at me. I put my head down and marched through the crowd like a movie star on a bad hair day, caught by the paparazzi. The strong scent of *churros* dragged me out of the begging zone as I raced towards the cart that sold the long doughnut sticks dipped in cinnamon. Gina got the worst munchies of us all and Scott was feeding one to her by the time I caught up.

"Dude, we've got another mile to go. You need to be more of a hardass or we'll be broke before we get to *Revolucion*," she said, rolling the 'r' off her tongue. Spanish was Gina's first language, since she was raised by her housekeeper instead of her mother. Scott, her boyfriend of four weeks by that time, stood next to her with his arm clamped around her shoulder, shaking his head. He held a cigarette to his mouth between the only two fingers he had on his left hand.

He'd arrived at Venice Beach from Austin, Texas, wearing a red plaid shirt and Wranglers with a guitar strapped to his back. I half expected him to be chewing grass, but he just smoked it and sold it. He was in a hurry to leave and sold his Stetson for the bus fare, but he never said more than it was because he was bored working as a farm hand.

His farm boy background was disguised by his shaved head, with a few tufts teased into spikes down the center of his skull. He wore a black T-shirt, dark blue Dickies long shorts, which revealed his shins poking out like two mop handles, with black Converse pumps attached to the end. His ears had pierced holes lined with metal rims big enough that I could see straight through them. The first night I met him, he talked me up his arm explaining all the tattoos that sleeved his forearms. He had a half-naked woman that his pop needled onto his arm when he was thirteen as a Texan rite of passage into manhood.

"Yis Ma'am," he'd said. "Pop did this fer me at my birthdi party, said he'd disown me if I shed a tear. An' when I have a son, it'll be the same for him, too."

One night after eating hash cakes that I'd baked while Fe had taken Grandma and Mort to the seniors dance on Melrose, Gina decided that he wasn't the guy for her. She drove to his commune where he had one of the four bunks in a room. There were two straight couples and one gay man—who made himself a couple most nights—in the other three. She followed him into his room, where the metal frame of one bunk rattled as if an earthquake had cornered that part of the room. The Bob Marley tapestry that hung across the bed frame fluttered from the huffing and puffing coming from behind it. But Scott said the three words every girl wants to hear, *I dig you,* and somehow won her over.

Cheap booze and tacos were the main purpose of our trip, according to Gina. I had a more cultural purpose in mind. I supposed all those outings with Mam and my brothers on a Sunday afternoon to the museums had had a greater influence on me than I'd imagined. *Avenida Revolucion* was crowded with rubbish bags that overflowed on one side and vendors on the other shouting to potential customers, "Best price Señor, what's your best price? I geev you better."

We walked on deciding to avoid the tourist epicenter, shuffling through the McDonald's wrappers that stuck to my shins with two-day-old mayonnaise. I was too stoned to care where we went and followed the Vans logo on the heel of Gina's trainers. We were stopped by a gaggle of publicity staff standing on a corner. When I looked up, lights flashed the names *Havana, Meditarano,* and *Miami,* above a row of girls that stood in the road. Their sequined clothing glittered, and I guessed we'd made a wrong turn into the strip club district.

We stayed anyway and were led downstairs into a dark cavern where a neon thong danced around a pole. We were welcomed by men dressed in *serapes* offering us Vicodin and ketamine. Scott spoke to one of them, and I saw him hand over money. I didn't want to know what for. At the bar, Gina ordered margaritas for our free drinks, and we found a booth to smoke a joint.

On our second round, while Scott was using the loo, an older man in a suit who'd been standing at the bar drinking shots walked up to us.

"Excuse me, beautiful ladies, my name is Hector," he smiled. "Can I ask you a favor?"

"I suppose," I said.

"Depends what?" Gina said.

"You are both so beautiful, most beautiful breasts. I wonder would you perform on the stage for us here today." Our shocked silence encouraged him more. "You have all the free drink you want…and tips. Very good tips," he said puffing on his cigar and winking out of his left eye. We looked at each other, wondering if he was joking, but as usual Gina decided to err on the side of caution. She stood up and pushed his

40

shoulder. "You fuckin' pervert, get outta my way. We're leavin'," she said and barged past him.

The bloke stared at me as if I were going to jump up and get *my* kit off. I took a long drag of the joint still burning between my fingers and blew out a trail of smoke as I dashed to catch Gina. When we told Scott what had happened, he wanted to go back and get the guy with the penknife he used to cut the string on bales of hay.

The shops by the border were open late to catch the last of the passing trade. Those who didn't have the luxury of a real shop set blankets on the pavement to spread out their goods. Those without a blanket or a shop pushed a cart through the bumper-to-bumper traffic. Those with nothing but silver, draped it over their arms and around their necks, and weaved between the cars while peering through windows.

To get back into America, we followed pedestrian traffic through the double doors into a dimly lit corridor. There were FBI wanted posters of seventy-nine men suspected of document forgery, drug smuggling, and murder. Above our heads, a sign read "NO ARMS OR WEAPONS AND NO NARCOTICS OR MARIJUANA ALLOWED INTO THE US." The lights above began to feel like spotlights beaming on my face, and my mouth went dry. Ahead, a couple of Border Patrol officers stood behind tables. The silver gun handle and crescent of the shiny handcuffs glinted against the dark uniforms, as if they were winking at us.

The crowd slowed into a queue that zigzagged around a barrier. One by one, each of us approached the desk with a guard behind it and showed our ID. Scott and Gina went ahead of me.

"Next, please."

"You're next," a voice came from behind me.

I handed over my passport. He turned to the back of it and looked at the photo and then at me. He flicked through the rest of the pages, stopping at a couple.

"Excuse me, Ma'am, where is the visa in your passport?"

41

My heart dropped like a brick into my gut.

"Eh? What d'yer mean?" I knew exactly what he meant. I knew exactly where it was. But I'd forgotten it. I felt the alcohol start to drain out of me like a petrol tank with a leak. Each gallon feeling like I was turning a new shade of white.

"I need to see your visa that you used on your first entry into the U.S. Without that, I cannot allow you back into the country, Ma'am. Please step to one side."

I stood by an empty desk watching a party of people file through. White teeth against tanned faces, clinking bottles of tequila and perfumes, the fresh smell of leather. Hundreds more followed behind them, a multicolored current of sombreros bobbing down the corridor.

Another more official-looking guard approached me. He wore a shiny shield attached to his shirt and underneath his name badge read SGT. HELLAND.

"Ma'am, you will not be allowed back into the United States of America without the correct documentation..."

"But..."

"Please do not interrupt me, Ma'am. We do require your visa and until you can provide us with that, you will have to remain in Mexico. You may speak now."

I was silent. I held my head in my hands as if rummaging around in the top to find a solution in my brain. A door slammed and a man shouted behind me. When I looked around, he was being led, with his hands handcuffed behind his back, through a door that read "Interrogation Room."

"But how can I get my visa if I'm not allowed back across the border? I just thought I needed ID."

"Photographic ID is only permitted if you are an American citizen Ma'am. Are you alone?"

"No, my friends are over there," I pointed and Helland waved them over.

When Gina heard the news she started crying like a child, unable to catch a breath and trying to talk in between sobs.

"But...but..."

I looked back into the tunnel. It was getting darker and emptier and the current of sombreros appeared to have slowed into a trickle.

"My visa's in my room. Hold on, let me find my keys." I patted my pockets down. Her eyes started brimming again as I handed them to her so I blurted out the rest of the instructions before she had chance to start bawling.

"I'll...I'll never find it. Oh shit...your room is such a mess. I told you...told you to fuckin' clean it. Where...where will it be?"

"It's in a carved wooden box on the dresser in my room. I'm positive."

The officer stared through us with a brainwashed gotta-go-by-the-book expression. Not a glimmer of emotion. His mouth was straight and tight, as if it was on his face to underline his nose.

"Ma'am, can you step over here please," he said.

I tiptoed towards him keeping one eye on the interrogation room.

"Your passport is a disgrace to your Queen and country. How did it get into this condition?" He held it in front of my face the corners tattered and dog-eared. I couldn't believe he'd brought the Queen into it. Why did she give a shit about the condition of my passport? I felt the anger swelling through my body, my teeth started jackhammering together.

"You should have more pride. I'll let you through on this occasion but you need to replace..." He kept talking but I slipped into my own space. I was so happy I wanted to get high. My body felt light and airy I wanted to buy a bag of cocaine and stay up all night kissing the roads and the sand and the sea. Gina pinched my arm in her excitement and I snapped back into reality and heard Sergeant Helland finish his lecture.

We ran back to the car. When the engine was switched on, Eminem blared from the CD player, "America...we love you, how many people are proud to be citizens of this great country of ours? The stripes and the stars..."

My pulse didn't stop racing for a few songs. I sat in the back with the window open taking gulps of air to try and slow my heart. I wanted to bang my head against the window to try and knock the craving out of myself. I rolled my head around my shoulders and tried to stretch the tension creeping into my neck. I chewed a piece of gum to try and stop grinding, a habit I'd copied from my gran, who still did it with her false teeth. Every nerve in my brain felt like it was screaming, *Feed me! Feed me,* and banging on the sides of my skull to make sure I heard. *I fuckin' heard you,* I wanted to shout back.

I sat on my hands and clenched my teeth and thought about getting home and taking a couple of Vicodin with a glass of wine to knock myself out. I went to light up another cigarette but my pack was empty and there was still ninety minutes before we got back to LA.

Gina drove to Scott's to drop him off. He'd taken whatever he'd bought at the strip club and was comatose until further notice. We grabbed an elbow each and dragged him up the steps into his commune.

"Drop him right there," Gina said pointing to an armchair. His head hung down into his chest and his top lip drooped from chewing it when he was stoned.

We got on the 10 freeway and headed east towards my house. I didn't speak and Gina had the volume high, which I knew meant no talking anyway.

"I'll take you home. I'm going somewhere else but I'm not sure you'll want to come."

"Well, where you off? Maybe I want to."

"Downtown," she paused. "I need to get high, dude. The situation back there fuckin' freaked me out."

I smiled to myself, "Let's go then. Take me with you."

"Are you sure?"

"Totally, mate. Totally."

I leaned back in my seat and watched the street names flash by for every exit: La Cienega, Fairfax, Western, Vermont.

We left the freeway at Alvarado and stopped at a traffic light. A man pushed a shopping cart across the road. Plastic bags were tied to the outside of it from grocery stores and Rodeo Drive exclusive boutiques. He stared ahead as he crossed and the headlights revealed the abuse like a forensic laboratory torch. Two pouches under his eyes swung like hammocks and his cheeks had cigarette burns branded into them. His beard was thick and matted with something slimy. The tip of his nose was pointed towards me and his skin looked like a hardened field of mud that had cracked in the heat of the sun. A bottle of scotch leaned in the corner of the child seat. *For all I know that could be my dad,* I thought.

I thought I recognized the area from when Emily and I had got lost in downtown looking for Olvera Street, a reconstructed Mexican market, when we came on holiday. We took turns getting out of the car at petrol stations outfitted with bulletproof glass to ask for directions. It took us two hours to get home and we never went back.

Gina turned onto a street called Bonnie Brae.

"Here, get your money out. We're close. I'll talk," she said.

We turned into an alley up the side of an apartment block. Four men who had been standing on the corner, ran up to the car next to my window. Gina powered it down with her controls. One of the men, whose name I later found out to be Jorge, spoke for the others. He was small and chunky with slicked-back black hair and a thick mustache. When he spoke, he sucked his lips into his mouth and out again and around his teeth.

Gina nudged me. "Get the money out and hold out your hand." I did as I was told. Jorge put his thumb and his forefinger between his gum and his top lip. He placed small white rectangles, like teeth, into my hand. They stuck together in a clump because of Jorge's spit and he kept going back into his mouth for more, each time adding to the pool of saliva gathering in my palm.

"Count them. Quick," Gina said.

I moved my hand to a light shining through the window and nudged the clump around from side to side. They had a yellow tinge like nicotine-stained smoker's teeth.

"Seven."

She said something else and Jorge reached into his mouth one last time and placed another tooth in my hand, bringing with it a tightrope of dribble.

The headlights shone on a black woman at the end of the alley leaning on her hands against the wall. She looked from side to side and pulled one of her hands out to wave us on. Her toothless smile was camouflaged by the night. She wore a headscarf and a crocheted blanket that on her bony shoulders looked as if it were draped over a wire coat hanger. The blanket had lots of dropped stitches, which was my gran's polite way of saying something was full of holes.

"You know her?" I asked.

"Yeah sure, Flip. Me and that chick are always kickin' it together. No, course not! They pay her in crack to sit there and check it's okay for clients to move on."

"Crack?"

"Yeah. That's what we just bought."

"No way! That's what it looks like?" I looked at it in my hand. The recreational drug line didn't include heroin or crack.

That was a firm rule.

But I was starting to look at it through beer goggles. It didn't seem like it was any worse than coke and it didn't need to be injected. *Maybe I should just not inject,* I thought. *Maybe that should be my new rule?*

"Hold on...'ow long 'ave you been doing crack?" I asked.

"Here, put that in something. Don't drop any of it." She took the cellophane off her cigarettes and handed it to me. "Remember I told you about going to rehab?"

"Yeah."

"Well this is sort of my relapse. I've been on it again for eight months."

"No fucking way."

The moment she said it, the unanswered questions in the back of my mind found simple answers: her moodiness, times

46

she went missing for days, not returning calls, and she was always broke and hitting me up for a loan.

We pulled into the Viking Motel car park and drove to the back where it was deserted. Gina reached into the side pocket of her door and pulled out a glass tube streaked in white on the inside.

"See this thing here?" She pointed at a black disc that lodged at one end of the tube.

"Yeah."

"That's the brillo. Not the soapy kind, you don't wanna smoke that. It acts like a filter or the rocks would just melt onto your tongue," she explained. "But you gotta be careful 'cos it can slide up the tube and you'll suck it right into your mouth."

She pulled out the cellophane wrapper and took out one of the teeth.

"Put the rock on the brillo like this, see? You might need to break it, but that's okay." She inspected the rock in her hand. "Looks like this is an old batch, it's a bit yellow."

She held up the tube, so no crumbs fell out, and held the flame at the end. There was a sizzle like a mini-firework display and the white streaks started to melt and the brillo glowed. Smoke filled the pipe and she inhaled it into her lungs. When she exhaled I could smell burning plastic or some type of chemical. Her head slammed back into her seat and fell to one side. Her eyes were open but it was as if she'd stepped out of her body and left me with her shell.

After a minute, she rolled her head across the back of the headrest to face me.

"You wanna go?"

Nerves cartwheeled in my stomach, my foot turned clockwise and anti-clockwise, up and down. I needed a hit—I had since TJ. Smiffy came into my mind, a friend from home who had gone from poppers to crack and once he started on crack rumors spread about him being on it and off it, in rehab, in custody. While I was thinking, Gina was busy loading and she handed me the pipe. *It isn't a needle,* I reminded myself. *I*

47

need a hit. I held up the pipe and lit it like I'd seen Gina do. I held my breath and exhaled after counting to ten.

With the first hit, I saw splinters of myself flying off in an explosion: self-worth, dignity, pride, and hope. I didn't seem to care. What took its place was completely alluring. Mesmerizing. At last.

The world had stopped.

My feelings were dead.

I was looking but not seeing, listening but not hearing. It felt like I was floating for hours.

Reality crept back like a migraine and when I looked over at Gina she was checking her mirrors from side to side. I wanted to do it again, I wanted it to become my reality. The ability to be pseudo-dead for my sake and yet pseudo-alive for my mam seemed an even better compromise. Without reloading the pipes, she pulled away.

"There's someone at the window. I saw 'em looking through the blind," she said.

Apparently the high only lasted five or ten minutes, but it just feels like forever. The rest of the night was spent going back and forth picking up hits and finding somewhere to park. At first, I bought into the paranoia, believing that the curtains and blinds were twitching. But after a couple of hours, I just wanted her to stay still.

Before we ran out of money for the night, we stopped at my house and sat in my car that I couldn't drive because of my wrist. I was happy that smoking crack didn't seem as bad as everyone made out. I don't know what I really expected, *What's the big deal?* I thought.

CHAPTER FOUR

I COULD SEE GINA'S PUPILS FLICKERING BEHIND HER
EYELIDS LIKE FLIES KNOCKING AGAINST A PANE OF GLASS.
She lay in my bed, her eyes closed, but not really sleeping. At
least, I didn't see how she could possibly be sleeping. I'd never
experienced a comedown like this from speed or coke. I sat on
the floor rocking back and forth like a child being comforted in
the arms of her parents.

"Damn, damn…No crack, no heroin. That was my fucking
rule…I can't believe I smoked crack…I can't believe it. I
fucking hate myself. Why did I do it? I hate myself. Why the
fuck did I do it? I'm just like Smiffy now. Maybe I should tell
one of my friends. Who, though? Who'll understand? My mam
best not find out. She'll fucking kill me. I'm just like my dad.
Why did I have to be like him? I know I'm only like this
because Mike and Sammy died. I know that's the reason I do
this. I'm such a coward. I should have tried to find them. Damn
me. Fucking, damn me. I should have at least died with them so
they weren't alone. I'm such a fucking coward. I hate myself.
Hate myself…"

I avoided Gina for a week after that night and took nothing
more than the doctor's prescription of Vicodin and my
prescription of cocaine. Even when she was rapping on the
bathroom window and shouting my name, I ignored her.

I knew Grandma and Mort wouldn't hear her above the din
of *CNN* and that Fe would be performing her favorite hits at
full pelt on her karaoke machine until the next mealtime. I
wondered if she had noticed that I'd become a drug addict now
instead of a recreational drug user? As if I'd just lost my
virginity and had a glow or a secret smile of a person in love.

Fe knew I smoked pot, or Mary Jane as she called it, but she
didn't notice when I was high on coke jabbering away. My

mind spinning with all the conversations I wanted to have but couldn't speak fast enough. The words became backlogged and every time I tried to talk I sounded Dutch or German, maybe Chinese. Sometimes she responded in Tagalog, her native tongue, *"Pooh tang in ya,"* which she told me meant "motherfucker" and then her whole body shook in a fit of laughter.

Even though I was able to avoid Gina, I still had to wake up with myself every day. I called Emily and told her what I'd done. I said it casually as if I was talking to her about the latest scandal in *EastEnders*, "I was smoking crack with Gina the other night."

Emily, of course, was horrified, and even started calling me Philippa.

"Philippa, are you mad, babe? It's dangerous, hon. It'll kill you. Just stick to coke." Emily wasn't one for religiously calling me, not even when I first moved to LA and was at my most homesick. For that week, she called me a few times a day to check I was just doing coke.

I distracted myself, kidded myself, ran from myself, but there was no escape from my mind. That was the purpose of the drugs. I could hear the sizzle of the rocks when the flame hit them, smell and taste the chemicals, envision Gina dissolve into a disheveled heap behind her steering wheel. It all seemed so real I felt I could reach out and touch it. I wanted it. I wanted to slump out of life and rekindle the dead feeling.

It's not a needle, I thought.

The knock came, and I opened the bathroom window. I don't know why. But the moment I saw her, the craving came stomping through my body, hitting every nerve and blasting every neuron into a frenzy. The light shone on Gina like a spotlight and she stood in a cloud of smoke through which I could see the tip of her cigarette glowing. She looked as if she were about to perform at a jazz club in New York.

"What's up? Why you avoiding me? You screwin' around with someone?" she asked.

"No. No. Not bin feelin' an 'undred percent, though. Know what I mean? Probably everything the doctor keeps giving me."

"Oh, I'm sorry. Here let me in, let's talk."

"Go 'round the back, mate. The Folks are still up, and you'll 'ave to go home by the time yer can shake 'em off. Yak, yak, yak. You know 'em."

The Folks had taken a shine to Gina because she stopped for Christmas dinner with us and charmed them. They both glugged back a jug of homemade Bucks Fizz between them, together with medication that wasn't supposed to be mixed with alcohol.

We played charades after dinner and laughed as Mort pranced around the den imitating a shark. We already knew it was *Jaws* but we let him carry on for the full three minutes and took photos. Grandma shook and coiled in her armchair, tears rolling down her cheeks with laughter. Now they only have a vague memory that the Christmas of 2002 was fun, and when I show Mort the photos he thinks it's something I made up on my computer.

Gina wasn't wearing her dark glasses and I noticed how murky her eyes appeared, like a polluted sea with hidden depths and secrets.

"So are you okay? You know, after…"

"Yeah I know what you mean. Could 'ardly forget now coulda?"

I leaned against the counter with my arms folded. My body felt like a hot piece of glowing coal. My heart revved up and slowed down, the noise vibrated around the cavity of my chest, bouncing from rib to rib. I took slow deep breaths counting to ten and holding. Nothing seemed to be able to break the fever of obsession.

It was the same when I thought about coke, and I was close to scoring and racking up the first line. I'd think of all the obstructions between, my dealer Ron's house and home, and how I would overcome them. Each move choreographed, the chosen route to his house rehearsed and timed. How impatient I was to cut it up into a fine powder so it would shoot easily up the straw or rolled note. I would taste a bitter trickle down the back of my throat, quick at first and then slow drops. That was the cue to run and get more.

I was one of Ron's best customers—every week had slowly turned into every other day and quickly into every day. He waited for me to show up. We'd slurp down apple martinis, snort lines. Ron only used meth. "I don't use that stuff," he said about coke, and he gossiped about his other clients. Who owes him money, who's tried to hop into bed with him to buy their stash from him—men and women—who buys what from his menu of uppers and downers. Once he called and swapped me twenty Vicodin for a gram of coke so he could add a special to his selection for Thanksgiving.

If The Folks were in the lounge or their bedroom, I went around the back. But if they were on the front porch and awake I may have to discuss the latest coupon savings at Sav-On for fifteen minutes. When I first arrived in LA, coupon clipping was a Sunday morning tradition for us all over a feast of *chremslach* pancakes—matzo crackers crushed and blended with water and egg and then fried and sugar sprinkled over the top cooked by Mort. After that, they would go out shopping and forget the coupons and now there were stashes of them wrapped in elastic bands, like bundles of cash, in drawers, on counter tops and fallen under the sofa cushions.

But Saturday nights had overtaken in popularity and I'd become more like a guest at breakfast the next morning. If I did get up, Mort would rush to set the table. Like an outfit for church, the best napkins were laid out next to the polished silver, and we sat for hours poring over double discount Wednesday at Ralphs and buy one get one free at Rite-Aid.

Without realizing it, Grandma and Mort entered into a subliminal competition, sat across from each other lobbing and slicing prices across the fruit bowl. I sat between them and was relied upon like a Wimbledon umpire for the deciding vote. Both fixated their stares on me while they waited. I didn't want to hurt Grandma and sometimes it paid to be strategic and I'd find in favor of Mort. Then I could look forward to a day of peace and Grandma would get a refilled bowl of ice cream because Mort thought he'd won. So now they let me know about the savings whenever possible.

"Flip, Flip," Gina snapped her fingers in front of my face. "Zoned out there for a minute, dude."

"I'm fine. But…"

"But what?" she jumped in.

When I looked at her, images throbbed in my mind. Instead, I looked at a fly that had just had a happy death in the vat of alcohol that was my glass.

"Well if yuv gotta go, that's not a bad way to do it," I said.

"Go where? Whadda ya talking about?"

"Ah, nothin'…it's just that I can't stop thinking about it," my fingers curled over my collarbone. "I don't know what's more addictive, crack or the sizzle. All I ever hear is sizzle fucking sizzle. Light a cigarette—sizzle, smoke a spliff—sizzle. It's doin' my 'ead in, mate. An it's proper physical, too. Tight chest, clammy 'ands. Know what I mean?"

"I know, sweetie. But it's okay. The comedown is a bitch at first, but it gets better. You saw me? No problems, right?"

I rolled back on my heels leaning against the counter. I took my eyes off the fly and looked up at her. The explosion happened the moment our eyes met, like the drunk, dead fly I was moving into another plane.

It was only a block to Third Street from home and, once there, Gina drove east, as if possessed, to Bonnie Brae. I knew the bus route from trips into downtown with Fe when we went to arrange an ID card for her. She had a contact for everything; Jimmy at the Department of Motor Vehicles could get fake drivers licenses, a cleaning lady at the hospital who sold "quality" jewelry. Ramon provided her with a social security number and the mention of his name turned her natural olive complexion a foreign shade of white.

I imagined that one of the seventy-nine faces wanted by the FBI that I saw on my way out of TJ had a connection somewhere along the supply line. She even managed to enter the country with somebody else's passport that had her photo stuck in it.

"Here, open the ashtray," Gina told me. Inside was a shiny dishwasher-clean pipe with a ribbon tied around it but stuck in a scrap yard of fag ends all piled on top of each other.

"Oh yeah, sorry. Don't wanna get busted if the cops shine a light in."

"You got a new one?" I asked

"No, dumbass, it's for you."

"For me? Erm...'ow did you know?" She didn't answer.

"Well...thanks."

"It won't pack itself, chop, chop."

At the lights, she rummaged by her feet, rolling back carpet, lifting lids and pulling out compartments. She handed me the brillo to ball into a filter and the tools for prodding it to each end. A snapped-off radio aerial and an alice band that was turned out at the end like a foot and the plastic coating was stripped off. Her pipe was worn and cracked off at one end, leaving a black, jagged edge where the flame was held. I pushed the wire filter against my thumb with the radio aerial. It was hard like a stone.

"Careful, careful. Don't break my pipe more than it is. I'll have nothing to smoke out of," Gina said. "Melt the resin and push it out. But not too much. I don't wanna lose anything."

I was no longer like the new girl at school who's led to every lesson on the first day. The initiation was over, and I was just another pair of hands to make the first hit happen quicker.

"It looks clogged." She kept turning around to check I was doing it right. "I think you'll have to cut some. You need some for yourself anyway."

I picked up the brillo scouring pad that still had the packaging attached to it. I read the label and it was supposed to be most effective for burned on residue.

"Got any scissors?" I asked.

"No, sweetie, I'm not a freakin' stationery store. Figure it out. Just pull a bit off. Can't you just pull some off?"

I held it tight and hacked through the sharp bristles string by string with my house key. By the time I'd finished, my hands had tiny slices all over them. Sweat seeped into them and my whole hand stung. At the end of the night, each cut would be filled with black resin from my pipe.

From the moment the decision was made to go back to Bonnie Brae, it took forty minutes to load the pipes. Gina took the first hit, driver's privilege or some bollocks. I was jealous that I wasn't already with her. I wanted to climb out of my skin, too.

Instead, I looked ahead and into the wing mirrors, ready to shout *TJ* if I spotted the police or if someone was walking or driving nearby. I heard the lighter flicking around, then the sizzle, and the thud of her head against the leather headrest before a cloud of smoke filled the car. Just as I'd fantasized for the past week. The smell made my stomach soften into a squidge, as if the aroma of an ex-boyfriend's aftershave was in the air, and I'd fallen in love all over again.

I grabbed the cellophane with the stash in it and loaded my pipe while she was wasted. I made a record-breaking sizzle until I felt the glass get hot on my lips. Gina had revived to the point where she could talk.

"Let up on the flame. Dude, put it down."

My body slumped towards the window, and I knocked my head on the glass.

"Here, watch your pipe on the seat…watch it," she continued.

She was killing my joy.

We drove back to Bonnie Brae five more times to score, promising to each other that it was the last visit. Gina ran out of cash after the second visit and my eighty-dollar budget was blown. I pounded on the cash advance function of my credit card, doling out money to dealers and Gina. Every time I thought of stopping, we turned around.

At first, we'd stay for forty-five minutes to an hour in one place. But Gina's progressive, chronic paranoia kicked in, and she thought we'd been spotted by police that turned out to be post boxes, or snipers were following us that turned out to be a cat. When we took off, she was certain the car behind was tailing us. Then she would insist we leave the car and walk to a deserted area in the Hollywood Hills, cracking shins on rocks and dragging flesh through thorns.

Scott called every hour. "Babe, ya comin' over? I'm fixin' a go ta bed." His thick Texas drawl gave the impression of a tall, muscular cowboy with a bristly chin that a bulldozer would have trouble running over. Not the wimpy, whiny dip-shit he turned out to be. He couldn't even deal pot without fucking it up. He gave out wrong-size deals and lost money or he forgot where he left his stash because he was too stoned. Then he had no money to buy more. So instead of getting a job, he just went nicking in the local shops to feed himself.

"Sweetie I gotta watch my sister at the Irish dance festival. I told you that already."

I remembered calling her one night after my shift at Rock 'n' Rollers to see if she wanted to housesit in Hollywood with me for the weekend, but she'd given me exactly the same excuse.

"Sucker," she said looking at me.

"Yeah, right."

She switched off her phone after a dozen calls but had about twenty messages waiting when it was back on.

Until five in the morning, it was easy to park and smoke. After that, on every street we drove to there was some type of enthusiast: joggers, dog walkers, and cyclists. The sprinklers fired up in the front gardens, sounding like gunshots to my sensitive hearing. We watched and waited for people to go by and then Gina started the engine and we drove off again.

"Do you think they saw us?" she'd ask.

"No. Calm down will yer. I'm sick uv all yer bleedin' paranoia."

By nine in the morning, we had driven to every nook and cranny of LA county looking for somewhere safe to hit our pipes: motel car parks and apartment blocks, dead end streets. But normal life was unreeling itself before us as if the sun was raising the roof on it as it rose into the sky. We ended up in the wooded area of Griffith Park where we could hide from normal life behind the bushes. We hopped from tree to bush when a ball was kicked and the thud of footsteps came shuddering towards us. I lay back in the leaves where the ground was cool and just a few rays shone through the trees.

Gina hit her pipe. Nothing. Again. Nothing. Again. Nothing. She refused to believe it was over for the night. Then I heard her scraping the glass with the alice band and trying to remove the brillo which had hardened into a stone. We knew it was over, no cash, no energy. But we lay for a while in silence.

Mourning.

On the way home, we stopped at Ralphs car park, where I was able to recall most of the coupon deals they had running just from seeing the logo. Gina threw me a plastic bag for the jumble of evidence that had collected in the footwells and stuck to our seats.

"You gotta pick the brillo out of the carpet. And get that glass out. Shit if my mom had any idea she'd fucking shoot me," she said.

"Yeah, right, cos mine 'ud give me a fuckin' medal."

"There's that sassy mouth again. Yours isn't gonna be lookin' into your car any time soon, smartass."

Yep! I thought. *A total bitch when she's smoking crack. Hope I don't end up like that!*

"Damn, we smoked a lot last night." I said looking into the back of the car at the empty cigarette packets and bottles of water thrown onto the back seat.

"Keep your voice down."

I wiped my face with my T-shirt and tried to untangle the ropes of matted hair. Gina rubbed a finger across the front of her teeth in the small mirror of the sun visor. We smoked a cigarette and a joint with our feet up on the dashboard as if we'd just finished a long night shift and were relaxing. I scanned the floor and doors for fallen rocks, just like Gina said I would. I felt no comedown. No need to cry and rock. Just the throb of guilt that crack was the wrong thing to do. *At least crack stopped me drinking*, I thought.

When she pulled up outside the house, The Folks were on the front porch holding hands with their heads leaning against each other like two glasses clinking. Her, a well-rounded wine glass and him a tall, thin champagne flute. They didn't turn or wave so I knew they must be sleeping. I slipped down the side of the house and in through the back door.

CHAPTER FIVE

IN A FEW WEEKS, MY ADDICTION CAUGHT UP WITH HERS,
AND I STARTED TO LOOK AND SOUND LIKE A CRACKHEAD.
Cheese-bubbled lips that burned every time Mort tried to make
me eat his chicken water, which was exactly as it sounds, water
flavored with chicken bones. I had a hacking cough, crack
lungs, as I was later told. I was trapped in a sticky film of my
own toxic sweat from hot-boxing in crack fumes. I sometimes
caught my reflection on a shiny surface and would spin around
thinking I was being followed. Dark circles ebbed under my
eyes like rings on a tree trunk, each representing a point of
decline in my life.

My bank account corroded in tune with my body. The
disability check Rock 'n' Rollers sent me—over six hundred
dollars—lasted a few days only. Gina got pocket money off her
mam and that never lasted more than a night. We stopped at her
dad's too, in a grungy part of LA, mid-Wilshire. He appeared
briefly in the doorway, and she would either climb the stairs to
his apartment or they would part at the front door in seconds.

"He's totally off his face," was often her first comment.
"But I got the green. That's what counts."

I could see where Gina got her stocky, short body, and
although I'd not seen her dad up close, I was pretty certain her
face was a reflection of her mother.

While we waited for money to roll in, Gina stayed with
Scott at his commune. The only bargaining power he had for
his rent anymore was squatters' rights. He had been working
at a headshop on the boardwalk in Venice, but was fired for
stealing. He walked past his boss with the sound of glass
pipes clinking against each other and a two-foot bong. He
limped home with challenged vision because of swollen
eyelids, and he was seeing double of everyone and
everything.

"I looked at my hand," he said and stared down at his hand with two fingers and a thumb. "And I thought I had six fingers outta nowhere!"

I covered the smirk on my face with my hand.

I used the waiting period to knock about with Fe—QT (quality time) the Americans called it—and switched my addiction to a boozy night smoking spliffs and listening to Rick Astley. If only Rick Astley knew how he contributed to the progression of my addiction. He was only bearable after a stiff cocktail when it sounded like his words were slurring together. In reality I was probably the slurrer.

Fe became even more lewd when she was drunk, the Philippines' answer to Bernard Manning.

"It's all about dem dude, no sushi, sushi por me!" she complained one evening after a date as the guy didn't reciprocate the oral sex she gave to him. "No sushi, sushi, no orgasm, right, dude?" She held one hand high waiting for me to high five her and cackled throwing her head back to reveal her rotting, cracked teeth. But her contagious laugh had me squealing along to her racist and sexual remarks.

Time was becoming an unbearable enemy. First the days and now the seconds between each hit were torture. I never imagined there was a drug that could infatuate me this much. Coke was a tease, a flirt. Crack had me enchanted. This is when I started to feel like a crackhead, too. Craving had swollen inside me. I felt like a skinny person with a huge three hundred pound monster raging to get out of me. Squeezing out of my pores, making my eyes bulge and ears ache. Everyday it was gaining ground, gaining more weight, sucking me in from the inside out. I didn't have any idea what it would look like, what it was that was about to take my place on earth. What it would look like in future family photos?

I woke up one morning with still a few days before my cheque arrived and read a text message from Gina. It said, "911 CRAKMERGENCY!" I felt like I had insects crawling under the surface of my skin, and I wanted to claw my flesh off. I didn't know what she expected me to do with our current predicament.

Within minutes of the text, literally, Gina was rapping on my window. *She must have been parked outside or around the corner*, I thought. When she walked into my room our energies collided into an explosion. No words were necessary. Three hundred and fifty pounds.

We scoured my bedroom for items of value and hauled them out to her car—a stereo, a lamp, a coffee machine, electronic scales. If I could have bottled the dignity and self-worth I had left and exchanged it for crack, I would have.

We made one last stop at a pawnshop to pawn some of Gina's jewelry from an ex-boyfriend. Her face lit up into a fiery comet when she heard they were only plated gold and she parted with her last memories of him for twenty dollars.

"I'd rather have the cash anyway that miserable son of a bitch. Just wait 'til he tries crawling back to me," she said.

When we arrived, we joined a queue of shopping carts as if we were doing nothing more than waiting at the drive-thru. They were overflowing with TVs, stereos, computers, standard currency for crack. I imagined most of the goods were a compilation of local burglaries, and I felt surprisingly embarrassed about our offerings. As if I wasn't a real crackhead because I couldn't pull off an armed robbery or grab a purse from a pensioner.

We pulled up to the first window and ordered and paid Jorge. Then his accomplice wriggled his finger around the inside of his gums to provide us with our order accompanied with a gummy smile. At the next window condiments were available and I heard *"una pipa por favor"* shouted to the next man down. I later discovered I could buy the same thing from Melrose for just a dollar and it was new. For five I got a used, cracked pipe with no idea whose mouth had recently been squeezing the glass.

We didn't even leave the Viking Motel car park before we were out. We were up to three or four rocks per hit. The first time we did it, I jumped out of the car and puked up in the gutter of some ritzy neighborhood. Gina's paranoia was furious with me and barked orders to get back in the car before anyone noticed. I was half in the car when she revved down the street as if that would solve the attention issue.

I needed more.

Four hundred pounds.

We went home to Grandma's house and through the front door. To the right was another front room, not a "den" like the room with the telly. This room was filled with was antiques but probably none of which would be recognized by Jorge. I stopped and gave the room a once-over. Two huge six-foot sofas, shelves crammed with photos of Emily when she was young, with the same color hair that Grandma dyed hers, with her sisters and brother. There were crystal or glass bowls filled with ancient sweets I was never tempted to eat. A musty smell of stale memories lingered and were only dusted off when Grandma entertained Fe and me with a tale of one of the grandkids smashing something to the ground or Ali showing up with a toy boy. *Like mother like daughter,* I thought. I knew if I took anything, I wouldn't be able to look her in the eye and she would know something was wrong.

In my room, we stripped our clothes, certain that a rock had fallen from the pipe and lodged in our underwear. When we didn't find anything, we crawled on my bedroom floor in case while we were taking our clothes off, something had dropped on the carpet. The dark green color was like a spotlight for white paint chips, old dried pasta and plastic. We smoked them all, hoping.

Gina suggested we use a checkbook from a closed account that she just happened to have in her car and had worked. It was a way of buying credit, and if we never came back with the money they could just cash it. So they thought. We sat in my room with a blank check deciding how much to make it out for as if we were millionaires.

"Here's a couple of mill, darling. Have yourself a good night out now," I joked in my most refined aristocrat accent.

"Three or four hundred," Gina said.

"We can't take the piss, mate," I argued.

I couldn't believe Jorge accepted a check for two hundred dollars. Gina rattled on to him in Spanish. I knew she could manipulate after what I'd witnessed in Mexico, I assumed she was using the same tactics. I thought that would set us up for the day. But after a few hours, the stash was low.

I looked at Gina, wondering if she had taken some without me seeing. I'd never thought of it before but it became an obsession to take some without her seeing, after all I did pay for most of it. The cellophane wrapper from the cigarettes was usually left on view, so stealing rocks wasn't an option. But I got out of the car three or four times for water and petrol so she could have snatched some then.

We stopped on Third Street at Western where there was a 76 petrol station. I knew the area was dodgy, Salford market dodgy, where Mam worked. Low income housing, bloomers drying in the wind on balconies, high crime and drug addicts everywhere. I got out of the car and paid for ten dollars on my credit card. There was a young lad at the next pump and I approached him.

"Ai'ight mate!" I said, startling him. "If I pay for your petrol on my credit card can you give me the cash, only I forgot my pin number."

The idea popped into my head without any thinking. The bloke drove off and I stood on the concourse of the petrol station and waited for the next few drivers. I even offered them an extra ten dollars in petrol but nobody was interested and the manager moved us on threatening us with jail and cops.

People were looking at me like I looked at the tramps who slept in shop doorways and on park benches. I knew Mam would have a heart attack if she saw me right now. But if I smoked enough, I could forget her and the looks and sometimes the smell that floated from my body in toxic little clouds.

Before it got too late, I knocked on Fe's bedroom window to ask her for a loan. She knew my knock and rarely did we speak during the transaction. I looked at the stars winking as if to seduce the oncoming daybreak back into the sky. I felt naked, as if all my innermost thoughts were reflected by the moon. But I was grounded in swampland created by sprinklers but no drainage. Mort forgot to switch them off.

Slit-eyed and still breathing cocktail vapors, she robotically reached for her bag and doled out some cash as if I were standing at the cash machine. The next day, she asked me why I needed the money but never really listened to my response.

While we were running through ideas of how to get money, I was thinking about Ryan, a lad I'd been seeing before I'd met Gina. He was a photocopy delivery boy at the office where I worked. On our first date, he bought booze with his prison ID.

"I forgot my driver's license," he said.

I was coked out of my mind and had a bad case of the sniffles to pay too much attention. I needed the booze to bring me off the coke. We had a long night ahead of us in a cheap motel. *Is that when I got pregnant?* I thought. It could have been any of the nights I was too messed up on coke and booze, trying to hide my coke habit from Ryan. He couldn't smoke weed because he was drug tested by his probation officer every month.

I called him to ask him for money for his half of the abortion. I was the one who had lined up at six in the morning for the free clinic, peed in a cup and called through the list of doctors I was given by a nurse. I was left with the agonizing decision of keeping it or getting rid. I wondered if it would get me a visa to stay, but I had to shake the idea from my head as lines of coke kept me awake to talk to my friends back home. I quit smoking for a couple of days, though.

"Keep it..."

"Adopt it..."

"You don't 'ave to give up drinking just cos your preggers, love, but maybe you should ease up on the coke."

In my heart, I knew it would be wrong to consider a baby. Where would we live? How would we survive? What problems

64

would it have from everything I'd done? The day I went to the clinic I had my dream of a family surgically removed.

When we showed up at his house in the middle of the night, he didn't have any abortion money. He'd lost weight and his two front teeth. I remembered the day he showed up to Grandma's with one of his front teeth missing.

"Skating accident, babe," he'd said. I cringed at the thought of him calling me "babe." I asked him for money for the abortion then.

"I lost my job, I don't have any cash," he said.

Ryan, too, was a crackhead. Just like when I found out about Gina, I made sense out of nonsense.

"My mom died, and I got an inheritance. All I'm planning to do now is smoke crack 'til I die," he said. "I smoked my rocks for the day, too, so I got nothing to offer. Hold on though..." He got up and searched the sofa where he was sitting and pulled out his crack pipe that still had a white resin coating on the inside. He started scraping and then heating the pipe. After a minute he lit the end and took a long slug before passing it to me. *You can't even give me first hits,* I thought. I got a teasing hit, not near good enough to satisfy my needs, but enough to make me need more. My head raged.

On the positive side, I learned how to scrape a pipe, which made each rock last five times longer. Now nothing could stop me. Gina nicknamed me Resinator for my abilities to mould the resin into a hit on the end of the brillo. Still, we mourned all the lost resin, all the wasted highs.

We had run out of all our options. We would just have to wait for my check to arrive. I would go home and try to sleep. It was like considering torture. Seconds dripped by.

"There's only one other thing we can do," Gina said.

I breathed a sigh of relief. Gina always seemed to have an answer. She had all day and night.

"What?"

"Sex," she mumbled.

"What?" This wasn't the answer I was looking for.

"I've done it before," she said and waited for me to react. "I got six rocks. Three each."

I didn't know what to say. My mind and body were screaming at me, desperate for more. Desperation was one of my new states of being. I was either fucked up, or desperate to be fucked up—and there wasn't much in between. It was another barrier I had to cross, only it wasn't as high when I was high.

"Really? Fuck...Six rocks, though, not bad," I tried to seem deadpan. *That's about thirty dollars' worth. Shit, I got that much for my stereo, and I only paid twenty-five dollars for it in the shop. Fuck it, it'll do, it'll have to, I told myself. Hold on, though. Hold on. Does that make me a prostitute?* I chewed the word in my teeth like a piece of gristle. *Do I have a rule for this? Isn't it no needles and no shagging around? Well, shit, it's all I have, and I need my fucking rocks.*

"It's okay. It's not like real sex. All you gotta do is drop your pants and let 'em do it. They use a condom, there's no kissing. It's just sex."

"Do we both need to do it?"

"I don't know. We have to decide. Do you want to?"

I didn't know what the criteria were for deciding whether I wanted to do that or not. How was I supposed to weigh the pros and cons? I heard the sizzle. And now the drip, too.

"Let's go," I said.

Neither of us spoke, and the stereo was switched off. I looked out of the window at women lining the streets, some dressed like drag queens, waiting for their next trick. I looked down at myself: dirty bony knees, hands sliced up from the brillo and filled with a black sticky resin, like treacle. It'd been a few days since I could last be bothered to take a shower and a sweaty stench evaporated from my skin. I realized that thirty dollars was probably what I was worth, since this was LA and even the prostitutes on the street looked good.

❖

I listened to her speak, trying to make out the words I imagined she would have to say: *el sexo, el shaggo, el fucko.* Instead, Jorge looked at us both before speaking.

"He'll do it with me because he knows me. Your turn next time," she told me.

"Thank you, thank you, thank you. " I said under my breath.

"Here, come with me. Let's lock up the car."

We followed Jorge in silence through the darkness of a courtyard. Above us, laughter and music danced out of open windows, lights flashed and conversations rumbled behind closed doors. I stumbled after them up two flights of concrete steps. She turned to me. "Wait here. I'll just be at the top with him. It won't take long."

"Okay, I won't move."

I heard the sounds of belts unbuckling and zips being undone, jeans scraping against the concrete. After that there was nothing. I sat on the step and waited. It stank of the cellar at home and piss. I looked down at my feet and I thought I could see something crawling on the steps. I jumped up and leaned against the wall. I thought I could feel something on my neck. I stood away from the wall and turned around. I couldn't see anything, but I was certain something was there.

I didn't like to admit it, but paranoia had started to eat my brain. I noticed Grandma's worsening condition since the stroke—fading memory, atrophied muscles—and I could sense what she was feeling. Reality was atrophied for me, memories weakened by intensifying paranoia.

I stood on the top step where a light shined from a window, and I could see. No one came out of front doors to see what was going on. No one stared out of windows. A minute later, I heard the rustle of clothes and footsteps and Gina's face came out of the dark shadows.

"Let's go," she said. "Back to the car."

I waited at the passenger-seat door and watched her collect payment.

"Seven. Awesome," she said.

The next day, my check arrived, and we went out for two more days, deciding to stay in motels so we could have complete peace to smoke. Scott came with us so he wouldn't bother Gina with phone calls every five minutes or turn up at my house. Gina had been sneaking out with Scott and picking up crack on credit, leaving me to pay it off before I could even get some for myself.

We sat in the bathroom scraping our pipes. Scott was sleeping on the bed. The creeping paranoia had us imprisoned in the safety of the bathroom, me on the closed toilet seat and Gina in the bathtub.

"Scott is asleep, we could run out right now and get more," she said.

"I'm not buyin' any fuckin' more," I shouted.

She looked shocked. I felt shocked. "I'm tired of yer tryin' to get me to pay for the lot." I grabbed my bag from the room and headed for the door. Gina grabbed my shoulder, but I shrugged her off.

Outside, it was still dark and the cold was punching through the remaining warmth of summer. My thin frame was burning like a match, it seemed, and my head felt like it was on fire. In Manchester, they would have called me an anorexic. Mam was always on my back about my weight. I was six when we first moved into Victoria Crescent and Mam put me on my first diet.

Charlie and Chris, our Mike was still a huge lump at that point, picked on me for all the extra vegetables they had to eat. I timed Charlie once and it took him two and a half hours to eat three sprouts, and if he hadn't they would have been his breakfast. Our Mike grew up exactly the same and the only difference between them in looks were Charlie's Joe 90 gigs. Out of Mam's earshot, my brothers hummed and sang, *Nellie the elephant packed her trunk and said goodbye to the circus, off she went with a trumpety trump, trump, trump, TRUMP!* On the last trump, they made their armpits fart. Then they made sure they taught Mike, too.

Gina's car screeched out of the car park and she pulled up next to me.

"Sure you're not gonna come with?" she asked.

"No! Leave me alone. I'm tired of yer tryin' to always get cash outta me." It was as if the monster had finally cocooned my body and mind. Whatever was left of me had been sucked in and there were just dregs of my former self in a puddle at my feet. I lit a cigarette and walked to the closest bus stop to catch the bus that would take me down Third Street. A man lay across the bench under the shelter. I felt guilty looking at him that I had money clutched in my hand that could feed him. *Food my arse,* I thought. *That bloke'd be smoking something, same as me, or he probably wouldn't be on that bench now. Better in my lungs.*

The bus was half full, mainly Mexicans coming back from late shifts dressed like penguins from serving food or dressed in white from cooking and cleaning. A tramp sat at the front belting out a chorus of "Born to Be Wild" and no one stopped him. The bus was his temporary mobile home. He used the bus fare like rent and accompanied the driver across town and back again so he didn't have to be outside. I sat away from anyone so I wasn't drawn into any conversations that would then reveal my accent and then the same dialogue that I'd been having for the past few years, but always starting with: *Are you Scottish, Irish or Australian?* For the one person who did guess Manchester, I awarded a free portion of fries and an extra happy happy face.

I got off the bus at Alvarado and walked farther on to Bonnie Brae. I didn't care about the imminent danger—the hookers checking me out, being white in a racially charged neighborhood, the cops flying ghetto birds above and shining lights on the bums in MacArthur Park. I just cared about scoring what I needed. Before I turned into the road, I checked to see if the dealers were standing on the street corner. I mimicked everything Gina did so I didn't get caught. If they weren't on the corner, it was possible that it was hot on the block—too many cops driving around. But I could see figures moving in the dark, so I walked on.

69

Jorge recognized me and greeted me with a gold-toothed smile. I repeated what I heard Gina ask for.

"*Cuarante, por favor.*" I handed him a fifty dollar bill, hoping to get change. He ripped me off, too, because he knew I wasn't about to argue with him. I tipped it into an empty Vicodin container, zipped it into my rucksack and started to walk home. Without getting any change, it was going to be a long walk so I scanned the alleys and car parks for somewhere to take a hit. I heard a voice behind me.

"How much?" a man said.

I carried on walking. A hand grabbed my shoulder, and I spun around preparing to be knifed or shot—pissed off that I'd not yet taken a hit and I'd die sober.

"How much," he said again.

"Yer what?" I replied.

"How much do you charge?"

His accent was thick. Not American, not Mexican, not really anything I recognized. It took a minute for it to register what he meant. About as long as it took me to get one of our Charlie's jokes.

"I think yer barkin' up the wrong tree, mate. I'm not into that."

I turned and walked on. I thought: *What the hell must I look like?*

I walked on for another block before he was back at my side. During that time, I thought about the long walk home and how I'd blown everything I had because my bus fare was supposed to come out of the change I was supposed to get. Gina's words ran through my head, *It's not really like sex, just take your pants off and let 'em do it. They wear a condom anyways.*

"You sure, lady? How much? Come on, I'm not an asshole."

I stopped and turned.

"'undred dollars." I heard the words come out of my mouth, but I didn't think it could be me. I finally looked into his eyes trying to see if his soul was good. He had soft brown curls that framed his face but his eyes were shadowed by the peak of his baseball cap.

"Hundred dolla. Okay, we do it three time."

"No. No way. Two time," I said, mimicking the way he spoke. "But no blow job, and we use a condom. Oh yeah, and I want the money upfront."

"We go back to my place. I pay you there."

I thought about going to his place and how many hacked up corpses there could be. Maybe he mounts the heads of his victims on his wall like a moosehead? But it was worth the risk.

After leaving Hannay, I flagged down a cab to get home. I stayed up the rest of the night and slept all day. Taking his money had felt good. Almost as if I was stealing it from him. Money for nothing. But when I had to face myself the next day, I was disgusted. I reached out to the reflection facing me and traced my finger around the outline of the face. Tears choked out of my eyes. I didn't recognize this person.

I stood in the shower, allowing the scorching water to run over my skin. The night came back in flashes. Hannay's room wasn't the cesspit I'd imagined. It was a graveyard for computers, not hacked-up corpses. A plain white room without furniture except for a bed. Nowhere for him to hide anyone. He seemed normal but for the fact he'd picked me up off the street.

I reached for the shower gel Fe had given me from her collection. I flipped open each lid to find the one that smelled the least like a bunch of flowers, but still it was overwhelming. As I rubbed the shimmery soap on my body, I remembered his hand on my arse and caressing my skin. He'd tried to kiss me but I turned away, that was too personal it seemed. I reached for the loofah and scrubbed its abrasive surface on my skin. Scrubbing and scrubbing. *Stop thinking, stop thinking*, I told myself.

I stopped. Breathed. I allowed my thoughts to roll up to the popcorn ceiling of his room, where I'd let my vision roll after catching a glance of his bloodshot pulsing eyes and face puddled in sweat.

The little bathroom collected the steam quickly, and I was soon showering in a sauna. It was refreshing, as if I were being wrapped in a blanket of renewed life like a phoenix that crashes and burns only to rise from the ashes. The steam spaced me out, and I felt a natural high. Like a sign from above, I thought I was being shown how the simplest pleasures can make you happy without drugs.

By the time I got out, my skin was a deep pink, the color of a Venice Beach sunset in the summer, and water was evaporating off my skin, making me seem like some mystical creature of the ocean or from outer space. I decided I felt so good about being alive at that point, and, better than that, I was invincible. So when Gina called, I answered.

"Hey so you wanna come out tonight?" she asked.

"Nah, I'm takin' a break, mate."

"Don't be a dumbass. Come outside."

"Yer outside?"

"Just come on."

Sometimes I imagined being shackled to a slab and having a doctor transfuse my blood until it was all pure. Pure goodness like the day I was born. I wished there was a reset button that allowed me to be returned to factory settings. I wished I could just stop.

The moment I stepped outside the house, my mystical natural high wore off and my super-powers were left like a trail of blood and guts behind me. Instead shame and guilt returned. Even more guilt than what I had. Now I was a junky and a prostitute as well as a coward who let her brothers die.

Scott was with her which made my decision to stay at home easier. I leaned on her door and she blew a puff of smoke in my face.

"That's for not answering my phone calls. So where've ya been?"

I looked at her. She was parked under a street lamp that lit up her eyes.

"Damn it, Gina. Yerra to'al wanker at times. I know yer 'igh. Look at yer. Is he, too?" I asked, pointing to Scott. He turned to me, and I could see they'd been out together. They were like crack androids—they looked human, but once I looked into their eyes and was reciprocated with a plastic glazed look, the game was up.

"Do you have any cash?"

"No, I don't need to smoke. We need to quit. We're gonner die. I've 'ad chest pains, I'm not kiddin'—"

"Sweetie, you're freakin' out. That's just crack lungs. Everyone gets 'em. Did you go out last night? Are you having a bad comedown? And you didn't call me?"

"So what. It was last minute. And you just went out without me."

"You didn't answer your goddamn phone. Now get in the back and let's go. We can talk about this on the way."

I hopped in the back, "Do I need to stop by check cashing?" she asked.

"Yeah."

CHAPTER SIX

I STASHED HANNAY'S PHONE NUMBER IN THE BACK OF MY PURSE, AS IF IT WAS A MAGIC NUMBER TO UNLIMITED CASH. I never told Gina, I was somehow too ashamed, but it was there just in case. "Just In Case" was a state of mind I'd lived in for the past fourteen years. A condition married to "Anything Can Happen at Any Time" that I caught like a disease after the fire.

In my rucksack, I carried my passport (just in case I need to flee the country), a defunct credit card (just in case the credit card company increased my limit and I could buy a flight home), a book (just in case I got stuck somewhere for a long period of time), photos of my past life (just in case I forgot the source of my misery, once the source of all my happiness). I added to my collection all the necessary paraphernalia (just in case I got a score).

Gina could see the depth of my addiction before I could. She saw me falling. She didn't try to save me or pull me back. More like, when I was teetering on the edge she didn't just let me fall, she pushed and tied the ball and chain from her own ankle to mine to make sure I fell quick and hard. But the landing was soft—that was the illusion of crack—into a puddle of quicksand that I sank into and glugged myself to the bottom.

She had been calling me at two or three in the morning asking me to go out with her to score. When I first started smoking crack with her, I didn't know she would call me at such ridiculous hours. I picked up the receiver about to blast the enthusiastic telesales person from New York who was awake three hours earlier than me. I could have unplugged my phone but just in case I changed my mind, I never did.

"Hey, waddaya doin'?"

"Gina! It's..." There was a pause while I dropped the phone trying to find the time through the dark and squinted vision.

"Flip, Flip," I heard her shout and pointed my hand in the direction of the squeaky voice.

"It's fuckin' two forty-three. I *was* sleeping."

"And now you're not. Get dressed and come out."

Why would I wake out of a perfectly good sleep to go out and get high? Shouldn't that kind of activity be started during the misery of waking hours? When the day became far too poisonous to cope with?

It wasn't long before silent torture racked me in the darkness. I gripped the roots of my hair and pulled, wanting to yank it out which would be less painful than not smoking crack. I picked up the phone to make sure there was still a ringtone. Why didn't Gina call me? What was so fucking important that she wasn't picking me up?

In rare moments of clarity, I'd stare at the phone not wanting to answer, knowing what would happen. Not wanting to answer, but knowing I would. The clarity passed like an eclipse. But in that instance, I saw possibilities, a future with a home and a job and maybe children.

Ever since I'd turned sixteen, Mam had been urging me to hang around behind the bike sheds at school, hoping I'd maybe meet someone and she could have grandkids. I wasn't quite sure whether she was joking or not. Mam's sense of humor is sarcastic.

April Fool's Day was traumatic in our house. We all climbed into her bed first thing in the morning leaving no room to move resulting in either a knee, an elbow, or a nappy in my face. One year, Mam promised me extra piano lessons with the piano teacher, Mrs. Matthews, who scared me to death with her one leg longer than the other. She clomped like Frankenstein through her house and her shadow stretched into an eight-foot monster. Mam would pick us off one by one with her "fools." Only our Chris didn't cry because he realized it was April Fools by the time she got to him.

The ringing would continue. Tears rolled down my cheeks as I would reach for the phone and clutch the handset, the images dissolving.

I was infected with guilt and saw no value in continuing to live. None at all. God had let me live as some kind of sick torture, but I was going to show Him. *I will top myself, Goddamit*, I thought.

Every time I imagined the night of fire, instead of turning from the smoke and barricading myself in my bedroom, I thought of walking down the two flights of stairs to another flight where Mike sat dying on the top step. I learned that from the news reports. *If I couldn't save him, at least we could have died together*, I thought.

Gina knew I was home, knew I was dealing with the sizzle and drip. And now she added a ring.

I never saw endings coming. I never thought my brothers would die, and I never thought my dad would leave and not return. I never thought life as I knew it would ever end.

The phone rang at seven in the morning. It couldn't be Gina. It was too late to be safely smoking crack without interference of the police and too early to just be knocking around. But where was she? Why isn't she calling? I was ready for my next rock.

I turned over and felt the cold sheet on my cheek. A fresh set of thoughts sprang to mind about how I'd made it through the night on a bottle of wine and a couple of spliffs. I tossed and turned, wrestling myself. I thought the ringing was in my head. Another hangover. I picked the phone up just in case I was mistaken.

The sound of her voice deflected my anger. Something was wrong. I sank into anxiety waiting for her to unleash disaster into my life. Not stopping to think my worst day had gone by, nothing could beat the fire.

"Listen," she said. "I've been talking to Scott about you. I'm worried..." Her voice cracked into a whimper.

"I find that hard to believe, but go on."

"You. Sneaking out. Going to Bonnie Brae on your own. It's gone too far. We gotta quit."

It felt like my body turned to lead and sank deeper into the mattress. I never thought I'd hear *those* words out of *her* mouth. I was also furious. Scott was part of the decision? That worthless prick. Everything on her terms, again. Picking me up when she needed a hit, quitting when it suited her. What about when I wanted to quit? What about when I was gagging which was pretty much all the time. She gave me the answer to my problems and now she wanted to take it away.

Fuck her.

"Wha' are you talkin' about? So wha' I go on my own? So do you."

This was Scott's way of messing with me. I knew it.

"I never meant for it to go this far. I never wanted to turn you into a crackhead and now I have..."

I didn't really know what she expected would happen. Crack would help me turn into an Olympic athlete or a movie star? Crack turns people into crackheads.

A piercing cry came out of the phone, directly into my ear.

"Fuckin' 'ell, Gina!" I shouted holding the phone away. "Only dogs can 'ear you now, luv."

She carried on. I lay the disturbed noises on the bed. But they continued inside my skull. Screaming thoughts. Attacking memories. Mam. My brothers. My dead brothers. I wanted to live, and I wanted to die. I didn't know what I wanted. I didn't want to be me.

Maybe I had gone too far. It was almost a complement to my personality. I had always been thorough, or obsessive compulsive, however you choose to phrase it. I never left a task until it was completed to the best of my ability. I had become the Resinator, and I considered that to be an accomplishment alone.

I thought about what it meant to complete the task of crack. Empty smile. Blank face. Bankrupt thoughts. Homeless. Soulless. Broke. Death. I remembered the woman at the end of the alley with a black hole smile and coat hanger shoulders. And that was my life and my future death.

"You can't just do this to me..." I stopped. Contemplating another end, even though it would be a good end, it seemed like a loss. It woke my fears that ran like a herd of elephants, crashing through my fragile glass mind. Loss was still a fresh wound even after so many years. I spent that time massaging it with different substances, and for a second it wasn't so raw.

I had wanted to quit at one point, but I'd gotten over that weeks before. It was impossible while Gina was devoting her energy into getting me to smoke. She showed up at the house one sunny afternoon to ask me to go and get loaded with her. I was livid with her for feeding me the thought, for reminding me that I was a crackhead and needed it like oxygen. I gave her forty dollars to get high without me. She only needed my money, not me.

"Get the fuck out of here! I want to quit. Quit!" I shouted.

She sped off and returned a few hours later. I'd not been able to shake the images of her smoking without me. The feeling she was experiencing, while I paced in real life. I cursed myself, feeling I was now more worthless than Scott, as I got in the front seat.

We got high until the next morning. For seven of those hours, we were trapped in a car park that belonged to a block of flats. Car parks were one of our favorite non-paranoid places, right up until we were locked in, then motels became the only "safe" place.

We followed a car in at two in the morning and the gate clunked shut behind us. This wasn't usually a problem, as we would pull up to the gate and it opened automatically. This time, it was remote control and the weight of the car failed to trigger the sensors to allow us to escape.

It was nine the next morning before anyone left, despite Gina's angry rantings when her bipolar demeanor tipped into the manic side. The moment we left, we scored four rocks each. Paranoia was disguised in desperation and for a moment it was like the good old days when we just got high, with the occasional peep for cops.

Some nights, I did coke to get off crack. Gina would show up with pupils like black suns. I hopped up to her car window and instead of looking at her I swiped and punched the air with karate moves I learned as a kid.

"Will you stop that!"

"Mate, look at me. Does it look like I need to take anythin' else?"

"Maybe some liquor to calm you the fuck down!"

I shook my head at her with a bizarre pity that I didn't think applied to me.

"Aagh, I gotta do stuff inside," I told her, anxious to pace around, clean my room, anything that didn't require me to be still. "Laters, mate."

I was still wide awake at three in the morning when she called me. I was gagging for drugs. I ran outside, and we spent the rest of the day going back and forth to Jorge.

It never worked. We had to stop together.

"You need to take me to get summat. You can't just order me to give up. I need one more. You know it."

I held the chemicals in my lungs for as long as possible. I didn't want this one to wear off, knowing the moment I breathed out, it was over. I was scared. What would it be like? My desire to become a full-time prostitute to finance my habit was weak.

After the crack funeral, we drove straight to the Clare Foundation on Pico Boulevard, still high. Gina had told me about drug recovery meetings. It was where she'd spent her twenty-first birthday, apart from her mam picking her up, taking her out, and knocking back shots of Grey Goose.

"There's a lot of religious crap in it," she'd told me.

"Oh! I'm not really interested in that then. Fuck God, not like He did me any favors."

Now, we were approaching, at crack-speed, a location where God might be, and I felt myself tense. I was ready for battle. Or was I?

A swarm of people lingered on the corner outside the crab-colored building we were headed towards. They seemed to have been magically summoned by the puff of smoke they appeared to be in. We parked behind an old Ford truck only the 'F' had been painted over as an 'L' to read Lord. *Oh God,* I thought.

It turned out to be a cloud of cigarette smoke and steam from polystyrene coffee cups that were the call signs for the drug recovery meetings. We were at a narcotics recovery group meeting but there were groups for alcoholics, cocaine, overeaters, sex, and smokers.

People smiled, laughed, and hugged each other. I didn't understand what they had to be so happy about without any drugs or booze. I smiled back because Mam taught me to be polite, especially with the customers on the market. I didn't feel like smiling, I was nervous and really wanted a hit. Just one more before we give up. *And at least now I know what to expect,* I thought. I stopped before we got to the smiley, laughy people at the door and clutched Gina's arm.

"Come on," she said.

She dragged me still grasping her arm into the room, past a man and woman at the door who welcomed us. *What do they want?* I thought. They reminded me of the staff at the malls who were always prepared with a "hello" and a comment to sell you an outfit that made you look like a donkey. *I won't fall for the donkey crap,* I told myself.

Inside, the chairs were set out in a horseshoe and linked by a podium behind which stood a tall black man with a tattooed face and head. He called the meeting to order, his smile bright as the sun glinting off his gold canine teeth.

"Hey y'all, Tank addict alcohawlic..."

Half the people were still milling in the back of the room. I smelled coffee. They stopped and turned around to say, "Hi, Tank." I'd let go of Gina and she joined the group at the back and was stirring coffee and eating cookies by the time I got there. Just like crack, it seemed like a good idea because everyone else was doing it and I helped myself, too. I stirred and sipped. The warm liquid trickled down my throat and into my empty, cold belly. I was soothed instantly.

When we were ready to sit down, there weren't two seats together so we sat across from each other in the horseshoe. People were introducing themselves, "Pat, addict, sixty-three days," and the rest of the room replied, "Pat."

He looked like he was out of a rock band, black spiky hair with red tips and tattoos creeping up his neck from under his black sleeveless T-shirt. There was only one more person before I had to talk. I looked to Gina for help, hoping to catch her eye, but her focus was centered on the speaker.

The room went silent.

My turn.

Staring eyes. My mind went blank. *Say your fucking name,* I screamed at myself. *Say it!*

"Flip, er…erm…"

"How many days Flip? Welcome!" Tank shouted.

I blushed at all the attention, "A day, or part of."

Clapping flooded my ears, and I was taken aback thinking it was gunshots or ghetto birds. Hours ago, I was still in downtown scoring crack. Now I was by the ocean in a room with people who had been there and done that. Businessmen and jocks, people I would have never thought in an eternity would use drugs.

When the introductions were over, I decided my favorite drug addicts were Pineapple Head and Vanilla Bean. I bit a hole through my polystyrene cup and blistered lip when the hippies said their names—they used to be Kevin and Jemima. *Maybe they were on acid?* I laughed to myself.

And realizing how long it had been since I had laughed, my body rippled in delight. I understood then that any time anyone introduced themselves as an alcoholic the whole room responded to them. I nearly choked when some bloke, Walter, declared twenty-eight years sober. *He's fucking mad,* I thought. Tank stood again.

"We will now observe the seventh tradition," Tank announced.

The group started shoving hands in pockets and diving into handbags. The confusion had me scared and I wondered if I was doing something wrong? A basket was handed around and dollars were dropped into it and a handful of change that came from the businessman. *So this is the deal*, I thought. *They brainwash you and make you hand your money over! Where the fuck did Gina bring me? Religious pricks!*

The meeting started and ended with prayer. Nevertheless, I sat amongst this pack of junkies and listened to them share their stories. There was a lot of God talk, just as Gina had told me. I squirmed in my seat thinking of the last time God and I had talked. In my bedroom, on my knees, the house wrapped in flames like a gift from the devil. Since then I'd removed bibles from my room, stopped going to church. Maybe I was following Mam's example?

Before Mike and Sammy died she took us to church every week, belted our Charlie if she caught him with his Walkman, and then pelted out a chorus of "All Things Bright and Beautiful." Then as if hymns weren't enough in church she lalala-ed the whole day through laundry and a Sunday roast.

Me and my brothers were never serious about church. We went to so many—Evangelical, Methodist, Church of England—that we weren't totally sure what religion we were. I just knew it wasn't Catholic because they had to make the sign of the cross with holy water before they even sat in a pew.

We went for free sweets and to find someone to knock about with afterwards. When we were confirmed, it was all about the free booze given with a wafer at the altar by the vicar. Maybe it was church that triggered my addiction. It was my first taste of wine, after all.

The fire changed our church-attending habits, too. At first, Mam couldn't go anyway because she had to recover from her broken back, and that took months. When she regained her ability to walk, I realized from her snarling comments that church would be the last place she would step into.

"What kind of a God would do this?" I'd heard her say. When people from the congregation stopped by to see if we needed help, she wouldn't open the door, and if they left a note or a stew on the front step she referred to them as interfering busybodies. It seemed to me she might have a point. After being fleeced of money, people raised their hands and Tank pointed at a young lad, a blond version of Scott, who rolled his skateboard back and forth under his chair.

"Robbie, addict," he said.

"Robbie!" the room responded. I shielded my head from the noise.

"Man, dude! I'm in love!" There were chuckles around the room. I didn't find anything funny. *Man, dude*, I thought. *Man, dude! What kind of English is that?*

"This is the first time I've had the hots for a girl without bein' loaded."

More laughs. Still not funny. *Man, dude!*

Gina's laugh was like a wrong note. I heard her distinct, forced noise. Robbie carried on, and on, it seemed, about this girl and stopped when a buzzer sounded. *How the fuck is that supposed to keep me off crack?* I thought. He looked around the room. I wondered what was happening.

Everyone appeared completely normal but for the tapping feet and fingers, twisting and chewing hair or gum, twitching limbs only cured by incessant smoking, which was only cured by absurd amounts of drugs.

Robbie pointed to a woman in her twenties.

"Melissa, addict," she paused for response. Obviously a frequent visitor to these rooms. She wore a sleeveless T-shirt with tight-fitting jeans and heels. I distinctly hated that look. For me, it was an abomination to remove jeans from ranking casual into a more upscale arena. They were designed on a foundation of casualness but some people, Melissa, wanted to uproot that idea. I had an instant dislike towards her for that reason.

"The cunning of this disease is shocking to me. I don't even have a reason to be an alcoholic. I had a loving, attentive family. But I'm reminded on a daily basis..."

83

Doesn't even have a reason to do drugs? That nailed it for me with Melissa. *Try losing half your family. Then come back and whine about the needle in your arm. At least I have a reason.*

Crack was still bobbing in my bloodstream and my head was like a pile of soggy ashes on acid. Words darted out at me and colors bounced in my vision. Robbie was annoying but Melissa and her perfect life story had me boiling mad.

Gina thrust her arm into the air, panting for attention. I ducked, thinking a torpedo was being aimed at me. Melissa chose her.

"Gina, addict. I just quit smoking crack. This was the first place I remembered to come. I smoked it for nearly a year this time around, but I was in rehab before that for crack, too." Her voice cracked, and I knew she was about to cry. She was hardly intelligible, as if she had a mouthful of muffin.

"Fwa myo shrw poom," it sounded like to me. But the group nodded sympathetically and as if they understood. After listening to Melissa and her reasonless drug addiction, I felt a wave of sympathy for Gina. I could see how she might want to mess herself up after all.

The speakers carried the same theme of dead spirits and sunken souls and had similar American-Feel-Good-Factor endings of having discovered God and serenity and they loved everyone in the room.

Pineapple Head and Vanilla Bean had stopped loving each other and appeared to be having a lovers spat across from me.

"Shh! Shhh!" the group hissed.

"Tank, addict," he took to the podium when the bickering continued. "Y'all need to leave the room if you can't respect it," he said to the couple. They rose and left.

The last speaker was a bloke called Frank. I remembered him because he said, "I'd like to qualify myself as an addict." He continued with his story, drank this, snorted that, injected everything in sight.

I was distracted with the qualifications required to be an addict. Was there a certain number of grams you had to have snorted? Does it matter if you've never injected? Can you still attend? Who would answer all my questions?

"Aaron, addict/alcoholic."

I thought the meeting was over!

"I am your literature dude. If you have any questions, if you're not sure you're an addict, if you need to find more meetings, if you need a Big Book, I have everything you need to know right here," he said as he sashayed around his table like a game show glamour girl. "Thanks for letting me be of service."

I beelined for the table after we'd finished praying in a circle holding hands. *Can this get any worse?* I thought. *Self Test for Cocaine Addiction,* one read. I looked around to see if anyone was watching before I scanned down the list of questions that covered both sides of the paper. *Do you make excuses to friends and family about your drug use? Yes,* I thought. *Do you use drugs at work? Yes.* Out of the twenty-two questions I answered only one with a no. *I could be in worse trouble than I thought.*

All the love, crying, and hugging made my British stiff upper lip tremble. I was angry He had helped my worthless atrophied soul and taken Mike and Sammy. I wasn't so bothered about Tony. I tried. It just wasn't natural. I was glad he was dead, even though he seemed to have gotten the easy end of the bargain. If he'd lived, Mam would have found a way to get rid of him anyway. She had a group of scary mob "friends" at the market that she and the rest of the traders, paid protection money to. Vinegar Vera was our favorite.

When Mam pulled the car into the driveway, all our activities ceased. Even our Charlie, who could usually be found sleeping somewhere, unplugged his thumb from his mouth. We congregated in the kitchen, and Mam told us tales of Vinegar Vera. She lived on a housing estate behind the market that we dubbed "Beirut." So named because it was like entering a war zone that represented Beirut at the time. There were young kids with shaved heads—like a stereotype you hear about only much younger—trampolining on the roofs of cars that had either been abandoned by the owner or were in the process of being stolen. The older kids were "drug runners," earning pocket money by delivering marijuana and "billy whizz" (speed) to Vera's customers on the estate. Because of the protection racket that was near enough everyone and anyone who didn't pay suffered the consequences.

She earned her reputation after giving birth to her twin boys, Rhino and Rudy Junior, first of the sixth, sixty-six— Lucifer's children. It is rumored Vera suffered major postnatal depression and lost her mind. One evening, the babies were screaming and so were Vera and her husband, Rudy Senior, which was nothing unusual in the Vinegar household. But, at some time during the night, Rudy Senior's cries were heard echoing across the estate, through every smashed window, in every derelict house. The myth goes that he made such a din that for a moment people froze in what they were doing. Each one of them remembering where they were at the time, as if John Lennon or Kennedy had just been shot: dealers and junkies mid-way through exchanging drugs and money, matches with frozen flames pinched between the fingers of arsonists, a husband with a raised fist and a wife with a knife edge to her lovers throat. It was worked out by one of the kids on the estate, who had a GCE, that had the police arrived at that minute, the collective sentence for all those flaunting the boundaries of the law would have exceeded two hundred years.

Rudy Senior was never seen or heard of again. He may have just run away, but those who have been to Vera's flat (and left again) say there is a locked closet with contents not even known to Rhino and Rudy Junior. It is rumored to have Rudy Senior's remains.

Pickled.

In vinegar.

Some people on the estate have only two or three fingers per hand, branded by Vera, and they're the ones who say they've seen inside it. It is dubbed the *Vinegar Pickling Hall of Fame.*

"He's up there," they'd say. "I recognized one of his eyes in a jar right next to my finger."

Mam would mimic Vera's walk and impersonate her "scallyness," using a pen as a cigarette. Vera raved on like a lunatic for an hour, before Mam became dizzy with trying to distinguish Vera's bust from her midriff from her hips. She appeared to be made up from a series of bulges all stacked on top of each other, as if she were storing rolls of carpet under her sweater. All this was topped off with a small head and a boyish cropped hairstyle. Vera would have surely de-limbed Tony for Mam, if only because she enjoyed doing it. But Mam was grateful when Derek the rent collector for the market stalls showed up and Vera scarpered, as she did when anyone with an official-looking title showed up.

I woke up the morning after the meeting with a blinding light in my eyes. *Shit, I really did kill myself,* I thought. Then I heard a familiar footstep, but without its usual bounce— nevertheless the rhythm of the walk, in all its somberness, let me know it was Fe. Her head poked around my door.

"Bloody Dude, are you awake? I must talk to you."

She came in my room. I was by now standing in the open window allowing the sun's rays to energize me like solar power before scanning my bedroom floor for anything to wear, not necessarily clean, just cool.

"What's up, mate?" I asked.

She said nothing but stood and tried to squeeze her hands into her snug-fitting pants that she insisted on wearing. When that didn't work, she inspected the junk in my room.

"Look at me, dude."

I was digging through a pile of clothes, but the tone of her voice, just like her walk, seemed different. I stopped to face her. She placed both of her hands on my arms as if to steady herself.

"I care aboud you a lot," she said, pausing. "Have you been taking drogs? Cocaine or crack?"

I sucked in a sharp breath and gulped down the air. It was like drinking razor blades. She wasn't looking at me anymore. I looked at her, studying her face for any sign that this was an April Fool. Mam's face had subtle clues that took me years to notice. And it was only after she embarrassed our Chris in front of his latest girlfriend that he sat me and Charlie down for a "birds-and-bees" style heart-to-heart about how to outwit Mam. He tried to tell Mike, too, but Mike kept waddling away.

Fe's eyebrows hugged together and she got a twitch in her eye. Most noticeably, and I'm shocked I didn't realize for as long as I didn't, she belched her words out like a frog, deep rumbling vowels that rolled up from the deepest caverns of her gut. Fe seemed "normal." Her soft, sorrowful eyes managed to pierce into me.

I responded instinctively. I couldn't lie to her.

"Yeah...yes...I have." I paused, waiting for her to respond. The silence encouraged me, and I reached under my bed and grabbed a handful of paper. "But, look, I'm getting help, I'm going to a narcotics meeting." I showed her the leaflets clutched in my hand. "It's cos of my brothers dude, I'm sure it is..." I made a final attempt to explain myself, but it seemed pointless to explain to someone whose English isn't even fluent. "How d'you find ou'?" I asked.

"I receeb a pone call last night, er, was Gina's honey, what name?"

"Scott?"

She nodded. "He try to search por Gina and den he tell me dat you bote out in downtown smoking de crack."

"Yer sure it were last night? I saw him after the mee'in'. That's where we were, not smoking crack. I fuckin' 'ate him. He never said anythin'."

She looked distraught, but said nothing more. Before leaving, she hugged me.

I panicked. I called Gina the moment Fe left my room.

"Hey can you come get me, I need to bust out of 'ere. Fe knows."

"What does she know?" Gina asked.

I mustered all my sarcastic venom to respond.

"Well apparently 'your honey' called 'er last night and told 'er everythin'. Well actually, he told 'er a pack of lies cos we weren't even doing what he said we were. Which makes him a total wanker cos we were with him last night for hours."

I gauged her reaction, tried to read her voice and silence like I could her face. Suspicious that Scott had confided in her and that she'd known all along.

"I don't think so, but if he did, that's fucked up, man."

"Call me when yer on yer way over, I've got another call."

As usual, I cut the caller off. Call waiting always got the better of me. Grandma answered when it rang again.

"Hello, hello, hold on, I can't hear you…Mort switch that down honey,"

"Vat hone-y?" Mort's accent was a mixture of Polish and Russian. He'd fled to America sixty years ago. Like Fe, he had some peculiar pronunciations, and sounded like the vampire from Sesame Street.

"Turn it down!"

The call was my attorney.

"Sweetie, I've been getting calls from your Mom in England. She's worried you're taking drugs. Are you?"

I wasn't sure I'd heard her correctly. I thought she just said my mam knew I was taking drugs. That couldn't be true because Mam didn't even know I smoked fags. At first I could only stutter letters. "W, w, w…" Then words. "The, the…" Then a whole sentence. "What the fuck?" I told her the same as I'd told Fe. I considered lying, but the story tumbled off my tongue. We arranged to meet at her office, and as I hung up the phone rang again. This time it was Ali, Grandma's daughter who collected my rent.

"Honey, your rent checks have bounced, eight hundred dollars. Is there a reason?"

I told her I'd check with my bank and get back to her. I called Gina.

"Gemme out of 'ere!" I said.

I didn't know peoples' lives could implode over and over. But mine just had again.

Later that day, I got a message off Ali.

"Flip, honey, don't come home tonight. It's detrimental to come home. Call me."

Detrimental, I thought. *She knows.*

And again.

CHAPTER SEVEN

WE ROLLED UP INTO THE "CAGE," A CAR PARK AT
VENICE BEACH SURROUNDED BY TEN-FOOT-HIGH WIRE
MESH FENCING. This was my new home. The back of Gina's
car, a Ford Explorer, my new bedroom. With the seats folded
down I could easily stretch out and for an instant forget that
this was what I'd amounted to.

I used to dream of being a glamorous actress, and getting to
Hollywood became an obsession. *The Waltons, The Cosbys,
Little House on the Prairie* were the perfect families I yearned
for, and *The Red Hand Gang* seemed to have the most fun. I
wiggled my first front tooth out watching *Chips,* drooling
blood and saliva down my chin and T-shirt. Right after, Mam
announced we were going to the caravan for Easter.

"Aww, Mam! Can't we go to America? Pleeeeeeese?" I
pleaded to Mam as if the tooth was a sign that I was meant to
go.

Mam bought the caravan in Anglesey after we moved into
Victoria Crescent. It was a cheap way to keep us occupied for
the summer and usually she stopped at Beaumaris Castle on the
way there and the way back. We ran around the ancient,
crumbling walls firing pretend arrows and launching imaginary
cannonballs at each other. After our energy was exhausted and
we were putting along, we stopped at the chippy. Mam told us
the fish was the freshest we'd ever eat, straight from the
Atlantic. It tasted just the same as Joe's chippy to me, but it felt
better eating it on a mossy wall with the wind whipping around
us.

Mike was still a baby and his antics had us in stitches.
Running around in his nappy and tickling our feet calling them
mouses while we lay in bed. One of the times Dad came with
us, Mike dropped his gold watch out of the front window into

the jaws of Farmer Jones' tractor that he was using to cut the grass. Dad's watch was sprayed out in gold flashes looking like a mini-firework display.

I could fill a castle the size of Beaumaris full off happy memories from the caravan. But it didn't seem that much fun when Mam was picking dead rats out of the storage under the seat, of course we called it Roland, and it didn't remove my passion for America.

Gina gathered her necessities to stay at Scott's commune. She rummaged through her bag, talking to herself and making a mental checkmark under her breath for her pipe, psych meds, and cigarettes—all the essentials. She never left me the keys, probably thought I'd drive to downtown the moment she'd turned on Speedway.

"You sure you won't come and stay at Scott's? He won't mind."

"I do. I know he told Fe. He's a total prick. I'd rather freeze out 'ere."

I knew that wasn't going to happen. I had always thought what an ideal place LA is for a tramp, at least the sun shines all day and there's no shortage of entertainment. Now it seemed I was living out a self-fulfilling prophecy.

"Whatever! He says he didn't say a word."

By night, Venice wasn't the exciting tourist venue that it was during day. It became anonymous. The dealers lurked and the addicts and alcoholics lay slumped in shop vestibules and on benches—strung out. No one knew who they were or cared—they were just Drunk or High. No cops or lifeguards raced across the sand in their trucks to save people and stop crime.

Out of the windscreen I watched two bums fight over who got the bench to sleep on, *Those poor bastards,* I thought as I sat in my comfy back seat. On the radio, I listened to "Loveline" on

KROQ and smoked a joint so it looked like a cigarette, my new evening ritual. All the emotional screw-ups called in to "Loveline" and I found myself empathizing with "patients" of Dr Drew and Adam and filling in the blanks of my own life with the advice they offered.

I've been using meth for the past few years and my boyfriend wants me to quit. I told him I have, but I can't do it," the caller would say.

"Did your parents use or did you suffer a traumatic experience when you were growing up?" Dr Drew asked.

Ohhh, I thought.

Between "Loveline" and the drug recovery meetings, I patched together a Picasso-style image of what my brain might look like. Distorted and twisted like the thoughts and actions that came from it. The only other clue I had was from a few years earlier, before Gina even existed to me. I snorted coke just because I was watching the telly on Saturday night at home. I couldn't possibly consider not snorting coke—some people eat popcorn with a movie. My thing just happened to be a gram or two. Which seemed normal at first. The part that seemed slightly abnormal was when my gram ran out, and I drove around the streets trying to find the club Ron would be tramping around at.

That's when I started to wonder if I might have a problem. I would still be up at five in the morning. Bored. Paranoid. I called my friends at home in England.

"Coke's nothing," Em said. "Just don't do it more than once a week, sweetheart."

"But I drink, I do coke, I do something everyday. You don't think I have a problem? Maybe?"

"Maybe you need to lay off the weed cos it seems to be making you paranoid, darlin'."

Lay off the weed?

Once a week was impossible. I went in search of an answer. For years, I'd thought the problem was being a Scorpio. I read my horoscope everyday and every month so I knew what to expect. But I'd met many Scorpios who didn't seem to have the same drug and insanity issues. It had to be something else.

In LA, self-help was a huge market. I headed to the self-help aisles of Barnes and Noble. In bold, black print, a book called *Grief and Addiction* stood out at me. I flicked through it and read about a condition, Post Traumatic Stress Disorder. It occurs when the brain is exposed to an experience humans aren't designed to be able to process, like war or the loss of half your family in a night. It explained about flashbacks, panic attacks, hyper-vigilance and how these symptoms often lead to drug and alcohol abuse.

I sighed with relief. I felt real. Possibly sane. I pinched myself and it hurt, my flesh red and sore. *I'm real, I'm real!* I wanted to shout. I couldn't afford the book plus pay for my coke, so I went back every day to read a new segment.

Knowing why I did it didn't stop me. I was relieved to realize I wasn't a complete nutter and used the information as an excuse to carry on.

❖

The first few days after I was kicked out of the house were spent lolling on glorious Venice Beach, avoiding confrontation with anyone—including Scott, but especially Mam.

I remembered back in the days when me and Em had been tourists, so long ago Grandma was still in her eighties and swearing at the telly when George W. Bush came on, *That lousy-son-of-a-bitch! What? He thinks his shit don't stink, too!* The boardwalk was a circus of activity and excitement. We stopped at all the shops and gawked at the acrobats. We spent full days sunbathing topless on Venice Beach, sucking in the sun's rays and the unexpected attention. When we were topless on the beach in Tenerife nobody cared that much. I didn't know it was illegal until I met Gina years later. But then I didn't know about crack either.

Now, I mused at a similar cavalcade of tourists pounding the boardwalk. Filtering through them was a circus of familiar characters entertaining the crowd to earn a living. Fortune tellers babbled out the same horoscopes to different unsuspecting faces, dancers limboed to the crowds while juggling fire, and Larry Carry skated up and down strumming his red and white guitar, dressed all in white like an angel. It was his turban and a shirt that flowed behind him as he moved in a swift gliding motion that made him seem that way. He'd been hustling on the boardwalk for twenty years, an icon of Venice. Gina introduced me to him, and I curtsied as if I were meeting Venice royalty. The same day, I saw him eating pizza, ropes of hair straggling down his back, shorter because he was wearing flip-flops not his roller blades with oversized wheels. The only reason I recognized him was that his eyes were like crystal balls bleeding into the crystal sky. On this night, I noticed they lit the darkest caverns of the soul, like a human x-ray. He was a magical being.

I searched Larry's eyes for my answer whenever he stopped for a chat in between tourists. He somehow sensed it and turned in the direction I was and either nodded or waved. As Gina was walking away, he said: "I'm not your answer. Look to yourself and you will find it within." His comment stunned me, when I realized he was talking to me.

During the first days of cracklessness, I noticed the order of my life changed from night to day. Color flooded into my vision so it started to look like one of the vivid abstract paintings that were sold on the boardwalk. The sky smiled down on me all day and the smell of the exotic flowers tickled my nose. From its rosy glow at the break of dawn, through to sunset where it looked like a delicious, giant peach—that I would have liked to taken a bite out of—slowly falling behind the Malibu Mountains, the sun gave my soul the kiss of life. I felt alive. I could feel my pulse and hear my heart. This life I was in hadn't been a dream. Or a nightmare. It was real.

There were moments, though, when the craving raged through me like the fire had raged through the house—gutting my insides, leaving a toxic anger to swirl out of me. It rose from unplumbed depths only Larry could witness and gripped me around my throat trying to choke me into submission. *Get high, get loaded, whatever! Just get something.*

Shadows crept into sunny areas of my life. But I found myself chasing the dragon, trying to find more new things that would keep my pulse racing and heart throbbing.

Sometimes I felt as if I were dying and my life kept flashing before me in a loop: me, Chris, and Charlie all dressed in the same tracksuits—me with albino blond hair, Charlie with Joe Ninety glasses, and Chris with his signature flick covering his right eye. Mam was there, Dad was there. Me and Charlie—him ten months older, me ten centimeters taller—holding hands and asking Mam to have another baby. Mike's birth at the house. Him screaming and Mam lying on the floor in a pool of her blood. Dad was still there—on and off. Mike learning to walk in his baby walker. Chris starts kissing girls. We're happy, Dad or not. Sunday morning breakfast, Sunday afternoon museum. Summer at the caravan, where we spend midnights at the cemetery bat hunting, picking up a bag of chips that were sprinkled with chunks of sea salt and vinegar that stung our eyes. Christmas, birthdays, hugs, giggles.

Dad's not been home for a while; we get the odd postcard. Tony shows up, Mam is pregnant again (I pray for a sister, which didn't happen. Probably my first experience of losing faith). Tony gets violent, hitting Mam when she is eight months pregnant with his kid. Friday night chippy stops. Sunday breakfast and museum stop. Dad's gone. Chris's still kissing girls. Charlie's started too. Mike doesn't like girls—he's too young. The baby is born. It's *another* boy! He doesn't know what a girl is. Tony more crazy, more drunk. The baby so cute. My brothers, my heroes. My mum, my heroine. Tony, a psycho. Violence. Alcohol. Fire. Death.

Death. Death. Death. Death.

It echoed at me. Attacking my heart and my mind. A picture of crumbling happiness torturing me in a loop. I wish I had a drink, I wish I had some crack. Something. Anything.

What happened? I asked myself. *What happened? How can we have gone from total happiness to this?* And the loop repeated itself—and I tried to pinpoint the moment happiness had started to slip away and the moment it had left completely and we were left with its ghost.

I had to fight the craving. I imagined myself wrestling with this invisible force, this feeling, turning over and over in my skin. We eventually got tired and then stoned and it became more of a stinging than a raging.

❖

A couple of days into my life as a bum, I still woke up excited by the novelty. Unless I got up early enough, the car would be baking inside. I sweated in my clothes and now they and I stank. I wasn't quite at the point where my own rancid body odor didn't bother me and I could rummage through rubbish to eat—trashcan surfing.

I felt like more of a high-class bum with a nice car to sleep in and weed to smoke. I felt a sudden urgency to collect my clothes and disability check. That would mean going home and facing Grandma and Fe. I would have to call Ali for permission, too. I became frantic about making the arrangements.

"Just call. Want me to call for ya?" Gina said. I knew she was only bothered about getting her hands on the money.

On the morning I was to collect my belongings, I woke up suffocating in the heat. I thought I'd learned my lesson after my first night, but obviously not. I heard something crawling in the back of the car and when I sat up to see what it was, I smashed my head on the back of the reclined passenger seat. The back of the truck had mysteriously filled with blankets and clothes during the night. I couldn't think what the opposite of being robbed was, but I knew it was too early for Father Christmas.

When I turned to look at the sunrise my vision was blocked by silhouettes of Gina and Scott. I was horrified to find they were asleep in the front seats, looking as peaceful as the

Nevada desert. Gina's stumpy legs draped easily over the steering wheel and her head rested against the seatbelt. Scott had tried to relax with his legs stretched out in the footwell. I scrambled out of my comfy recline, grabbed my rucksack and opened the door to escape to the car park.

The brightness of the sun stung my eyes temporarily but the breeze in the air let me breathe again. I heard a slam behind me, but I carried on walking anyway.

"Flip! Where ya goin'?"

I stopped and turned around.

"I dunno, but I'm not staying with 'im in the car. What the fuck are yer doin' 'ere anyway? Don't yus 'ave a perfectly good bunk at the commune?"

"I had an argument with Brian. He called me a crackhead, and I got mad and got my stuff and left. I'm not going back there, he's an asshole."

Brian was Scott's bunkmate who slept on the top bunk. I only ever recognized him upside down when he swung his torso over the edge of his bed or was doing handstands on the beach.

"Okay, first off, we *are* crackheads. Second, I'm not going to be near him so I need to know what's going on. Are we all supposed to live in the truck now?"

"Flip, he didn't say that to Fe. She already knew. Why won't you believe me? She's the one who told everyone and had you kicked out, not Scott. Why would you think I'm against you. We've been friends a long time already"

"But why would Fe hurt me? She's been my friend too. She wouldn't have done anything if he hadn't called her. Not just that. He could have told me the other night. He could have warned me."

"Now come on, Flip. If you had an opportunity to screw him over, are you telling me you wouldn't take it? You two have a brother-sister type relationship."

I glared at her.

She ignored me. "But I'm tellin' you, sweetie, Fe already knew. She did this to you."

I didn't answer, I couldn't, I had no idea what to believe, but I knew the sad reality was that I had nowhere else to go. I silently followed her back to the truck but stood outside and smoked a cigarette to collect my thoughts.

Gina rolled down her window, "Aren't we supposed to get your stuff today?" she asked.

I nodded. I stood with my back to them looking into the distance, contemplating walking. Don't stop or look back, just go. But my feet were rooted to the security of my back seat. I wasn't prepared to be a bus-stop dweller yet. I needed to be more desperate. Desperation was a great antidote to fear, as I'd discovered on many occasions.

By the time I left Manchester to come to LA, I thought my drug problem was already serious enough. I thought I could leave the miserable drug addict part behind. I was desperate enough to run. Leave my family and friends, Friday night chippy, my brothers' grave—everything I knew. It hurt to leave, but it hurt more to stay. I was afraid of myself.

Tony scared me, too. When I saw him fighting with Mam, shaking her wrists or slapping her face, the fear that paralyzed me melted away, and I ran to the neighbors' house for help or leapt on Tony's back and hooked my arm around his neck to strangle him.

I'm not quite desperate enough yet. It could be a lot worse. Where would I go? I thought.

"Hop in. Lets go."

I'd forgotten that Gina's belongings included her two precious pets, Roscoe and Dite (short for Aphrodite). I mocked Scott for getting the kittens when he was supposed to be looking for work. They jumped onto my lap in a tumble and softened my mood into a low giggle. They would become the only ones I could eventually trust, apart from my luggage.

When the five of us pulled up to the house, Grandma was sitting on the front porch with Fe and Ali. Feeling distinctly stressed again, I wheezed to Gina to remain in the car. I stumbled out and climbed the grassy slope at the front of the house looking like a heart attack victim. As I approached, the three of them sat stiffly, as if posing for a family portrait that I no longer belonged in.

Ali peered down at me, appearing superior, even with her short and sparrow-like frame.

"Hi, honey, let me look at you," she reached up, touching my face and swinging my head from side to side so she could check all profiles. She was a photographer when she was "resting" from acting. Mid-swing, I could see Grandma smiling at me, obviously with no clue as to what was happening.

"So, how are you?" she continued in a low confidential voice, as if that would trigger me to confess my worst sins and crumble in her arms a remorseful wretch.

"I'm fine, really."

"You look thin. Have you eaten recently?"

"Yeah sure," I responded mechanically. I was even more pissed at her now, it seemed. She was here to take notes on how to play a drug addict in case she gets a role. She had transferred the stereotype of a drug addict on me and wanted to make sure I didn't steal the furniture on my way out. She was never here for Grandma.

"Have ya been to any meetings? I mean how ya confronting this, Flip, ya havta be serious. Ya could die otherwise, d'ya even understand that? I know you're English. Em and Oliver are just the same. Why my brother moved to England, I don't know."

"Yes, we've been to meetings. I'm dealing with it. I go to one on Pico every day. I learned I'm not responsible for my past, but I am for my own future, and I learned that one's not enough but a thousand's too many."

A few days later, I realized the expression is actually "one's too many and a thousands not enough." Ali didn't seem to realize my gaff.

"Okay, well I still think ya oughta consider rehab, I can have y'in there as quick as ya want. I've not told my mom anything. She just thinks you're moving in with friends. But ya need to speak to Fe. Look at her. Ya gotta understand the position she was in, honey. The agency that she works through requires her to report anythin' like this. She didn't wanna do it. It was for your Grandma. Ya know she was right. Go speak to her before ya grab ya things, honey."

Feeling decidedly like I ought to have been higher than weed could ever make me to attempt this visit, I turned to walk away. As I did, she lobbed a curveball that smacked me in my head.

"Your mom's been calling the house, honey. You should call her. She's worried. It's been a week, Flip. She must be frantic."

Hearing Mam's name was like being dragged by the scruff of my neck back to earth. Venice was its own universe where I fit because no matter who you are and where you came from— in Venice you belonged.

Now, I could hear her voice, and I imagined her hauling me home when I was young sending me to my room after she'd slapped my legs. The sting seemed real. I had to call her. I couldn't escape that. What was I supposed to say? How was I supposed to defend myself? Dare I mention their names?

Ali shooed me off, forcing me to do things I don't want again, but I knew it was almost impossible to contradict her.

"I love you, honey." Grandma whispered as I bent down to kiss her. I turned to Fe, who was huddled over on an unsteady stool staring at the concrete below her.

"Fe." I waited for her to look at me, but she didn't, "I know you only wanted to help me, I'm not mad." I lied, knowing Ali was watching me.

I patted her shoulder as I went into the house to go to my room. It was dark, since the dresser had been pushed against the window so it couldn't be opened from the inside or out. I assumed that was to keep the likes of me out. My suitcase was already laid out ready to be filled. I didn't have much. I'd already traded my stereo for rocks. I decided to leave all my going-out clothes at the house, figuring they didn't really come under the essentials column. Instead, I opted to take letters from my friends, photos, and basic items of clothing such as shorts, T-shirt, jeans, sweaters. I looked around my room one last time and noticed the bed had been changed and anything that represented me, like mess, had been tidied away, eliminating traces of my existence. I wished I could tidy my memories away so clean and neat.

I couldn't resist lying on the crease-free bed, even just to feel a mattress underneath me for a minute. I thought of all the nights I'd drifted to sleep listening to the voices of Grandma and Mort.

"Honey, I love you very much. Think positive, honey, always think positive. I hope you live to one hundred and twenty," Mort would say.

"Thanks, honey. Know I love you, too, more than anything." I'd hear Grandma. It was like living in an old black and white movie. I wished I could eject and put it back in its sleeve and pack it in my case. I wondered what it would be called. Something like *It's a Wonderful Life,* or simply The Folks Back Home, or better still De Polks Back Home, the way Fe would say it, that always made me laugh. I leapt up, filled with bitterness that she'd done this to me. Pissed at her and pissed at Scott. Why couldn't she just have spoken to me about it instead of speaking to the agency that placed her in the house and having me *removed.* Not only that, but she'd had Gina drop her off at the agency the day she went snaking behind my back. *Fuckin' bitch!* I thought.

Before I left, I grabbed my pipe from the back of my drawer. It was clear, since I'd smoked up any hint of resin.

I made my way down the dark hallway, dragging my suitcase, being watched by painted faces of Grandma's past, most of whom I thought must be dead now. I felt like I was walking the plank for dishonoring the household. I picked up my mail and went back out to the porch.

"Are you leaving, honey?"

"Yes, Grandma, but I'll be back to visit, don't worry."
I turned to Fe. "I can visit, right?"

She nodded. Still she was huddled over as if it was me who had just had her thrown out of her house, and Ali was on the phone about a part in a movie.

Mort had appeared and was sitting with his arms folded across his belly. I didn't know what he knew but he knew something. He'd not suffered a stroke yet, like Grandma, to affect his memory.

I kissed Grandma and hugged her hard. I'd miss seeing her everyday. With her red hair and red lipstick, twinkling eyes and sense of humor, sometimes I preferred to be with her than with anyone my own age. If only she could drink and smoke we'd have ourselves a party.

Faint screaming bristled between the chirping melody of the birds, like static in a radio. When I realized it was Scott and Gina starting a lovers tiff, I left quickly after having reassured Ali that they were perfectly sane, my suitcase falling from side to side in my rush. I didn't look around because I didn't want to be reminded of what I'd lost. Instead, I looked ahead at the fighting couple in the middle of the street—apparently what I'd gained.

CHAPTER EIGHT

THE CAR BULGED WITH OUR BELONGINGS AND HUFFED ALONG THE ROAD LIKE AN OUT-OF-SHAPE MULE. Scott and Gina had tempered down from a war to bickering. We stopped at a park on Ocean Park Avenue and emptied out the back. There was no way we could live like this. Then again, I never thought a car would ever be where I lived in the first place.

We had a pile each that we had to sort through and decide whether it was a basic necessity or not. Then we neatly folded everything back up and rearranged our piles into the back of the car. Even with our belongings in order, it still wouldn't be possible to fold the seat down to stretch out and be able to sleep. But the back seat had to be better than either of the front seats. Families walked past us, mothers steered the kids away from us. I couldn't imagine why.

Across the playing field under a white gazebo, kids ran playing tag at a birthday party. Green and red streamers hung down, tempting mischievous hands to tug at them. Delicious smells drifted in the wind, awakening a hunger I had forgotten could exist. My tummy rumbled in retaliation. I looked on, jealous of what the children had and what I'd lost. I could remember the days I ran carefree under the blanket of my family. How safe I felt and how invincible I was. Those days were long gone. It was odd that drugs had given me similar security and a sensation of super powers.

At the end, I was left crushing a fag between my fingers and clutching a letter from my attorney. I tore it open. It was thicker than the slim envelopes my checks arrived in. I needed money urgently. I stopped and thought about the last hit of crack. I regretted spending the money. Why did I spend that much? Every last dime. Every time.

I flicked through bundles of stapled papers, searching for my cash, nothing. I stopped and read the paperwork, my eyes growing wider than the oncoming moon.

"What the fuck!" I shouted.

"What?" They asked.

"Me mam and me attorney 'ave cancelled me money. Me mam 'as guardianship of me." I stopped and looked up. "Dun't she know I'm twenty fucking eight?"

"Whadda ya mean she cancelled your money?" Gina asked.

"How can she do this? *How?*" I turned and kicked a pile of belongings, releasing some frustration. "What I mean is I've gotta 'ave a drug test every week so I can get me money. What the fuckin' fuck?"

"That's insane," Gina said.

There was no time to waste since we were already living on pennies. It had become habit to scan the pavement or sand when we walked. I called my attorney and set an appointment. I stopped at that. I still had to call Mam, but now I was mad as well as scared. I'd never said a swear word in front of her, only under my breath, but I could tell by my jangling nerves that courtesy would be in jeopardy if I called her at this time.

I decided to wait until the next day and instead we went job hunting. The instant it was mentioned, Scott was visibly shaking, like my dad did when he stopped drinking. That only happened once, and Mam took the opportunity to serve him with divorce papers while he was conscious. He never stopped drinking again.

Scott had been threatening to get a job since he told Gina he dug her. And a place to live. There was always a reason that he didn't have one, though—an "accident" would happen or he had wrong directions. I was off the hook because of my disability checks, but they had to get work if we wanted to find a place to live. I was going to maintain the household while they were gone. A housewife was the last thing I wanted to be, but for a few hours freedom a day, it was a worthwhile trade.

Scott tried Ralphs, a supermarket, but they drug tested. Across the car park was a California Pizza Kitchen, CPK, since Americans were so fond of acronyms. I'd first noticed this when I worked at the public relations agency and people were too busy to say complete sentences. LOL became "laugh out loud," but Mam had used it to say "lots of love," so for a month I thought I was really loved by the people in the office.

CPK gave Scott a job as a host because of his lack of fingers he told us. *Lying scumbag,* I thought. It wasn't enough money to live, but his tips bought us bread and peanut butter. After a few days, they both landed jobs on Wilshire just a block apart—Gina as an assistant manager at HoneyBear Ham and Scott as a shop assistant at a costume store called Ursula's.

Scott's job meant, come Halloween, we would have great costumes. Gina's job meant we would have at least some of our daily bread, since she was allowed to bring us big, door-wedge sandwiches everyday. But over the course of years of amphetamine abuse, my stomach had shrunk to the size of a pea and my appetite was satisfied with a few deep breaths.

We were broke until I could get my money from my attorney and until Scott and Gina got paid. I searched my purse for lost treasure but only found Hannay's number. I shuddered and tore it into tiny pieces. I wanted to put as much time and space between me and that memory—that life—as possible. I wished I could sprint through time.

Still not desperate enough to delve through the bins, we searched the footwells of the car and between the seats for dropped coppers. The money we found went to buying Gina two thirty-nine cent burgers from Maccy D's. All I could think of was ground up cow bollocks and eyeballs.

"Eric from Rock 'n' Rollers owes me about sixty dollars."

"Call him, lets go," Gina said.

We headed out on the freeway towards Pomona. This was a new adventure to me, but my camera had been exchanged for crack weeks earlier.

I collected the money, but not without his trademark monologue about his ex-girlfriend.

"She's nuts. She follows me to work, flirts with me my whole shift in her transparent tank top and short skirt, then some other dude comes and picks her up..."

Blah, blah, Eric, was all I could think. Didn't he actually get that I really did live in a car when I called him for the money? From the corner of my eye, I noticed Gina's face scrunched into an expression of torture and used it as a cue to leave. She was having a bipolar meltdown, which was now common—or at least noticeable—without the guise of drugs.

"Eric! Eric!" He stopped blabbing. "Gotta go, mate. Soz. Need to see a man about a dog, if you know what I mean." He clearly didn't.

Scott floored it to the end of the road and abruptly slammed the brakes at the stop sign. I was pitched forward and nutted the back of Gina's headrest so she went slamming forward.

"What are you doing?" Gina cried. "This is my car and our fucking home. Are you crazy, babe? Babe, are you crazy?" He looked at her and then turned back to me, "Can you please ask someone in the store over there," he said and pointed to a deteriorated shop that flashed the "l" and the "q" in the word liquor. It looked like the other letters had bullet holes in them. This turned out to be the only time Scott and I would cement together, when it came to handling Gina's progressive psychoticness. I almost prayed to have the paranoia back and now I was sandwiched between living with my hate for Scott and stress of Gina.

I ran quickly in and out of the store, clutching the money Joe had given me loosely in my fist. I got back in the car and Scott took off. Gina continued to wail, unable to accept that we lived in a car.

"My mom...my mom," she cried, "has all these fuckin' houses, my grandmother's loaded, and I live in a fuckin' car..." It was the most annoying and torturous display of self-pity I had witnessed. She didn't see how lucky we were to be living in a car. We could live in a roach-and-rodent-infested bush, or a doorway, or a bus stop. At least we had heat and shelter and pets. We were like the royalty of bums. Besides which, her and Scott had a perfectly good commune to live in. She left because she couldn't control her temper, and he bailed because he couldn't pay his rent.

"Damn it," Scott said and banged the steering wheel. "The police are followin' us."

Behind us, the lights flashed and siren wailed, similar to Gina's wail, and Scott steered the car to the side of the road. None of the seatbelts in the back worked. I pulled it across my lap and held it there so the policeman wouldn't realize. Gina caged her madness into a whimper.

The policeman asked Scott to stand outside the car. He had to climb over Gina's lap in the passenger seat since the driver's door was locked shut due to some electrical fault. All I could do was watch traffic whizz by and count the money in my hand over and over until I got bored.

"Shall I see what's 'appenin'? They seem to 'ave taken a really bloody long time."

"Yeah check it out," she managed.

I slid out of the car. The cop was talking on his radio, and Scott appeared to be behind bars in the back of the cop car. When the door slammed, the cop spun around on his heels and drew his gun.

"Take your hands out your pockets," he shouted.

I too spun around to see who the cop was pointing at. This couldn't be real, I thought. I tried to get an accurate reading of where the gun was pointing. Was he planning on taking me out or just maiming?

"Put your hands above your head now!"

This time his words shot through me as if they had been fired from the barrel of his gun.

"Move slow towards the car and place your hands on the hood.

"Do it.

"Move."

Hood was one of those words I needed a second to translate. I was scared of getting the wrong part of the car and being shot. Just like when I walked into my exams at school after studying for weeks and my mind went suddenly blank like a cloud that has covered the sun.

Hood, bonnet. Hood bonnet. Seems like they are the same. You wear them both on your head. It has to be the bonnet. Okay, I'm going for the bonnet. Please don't shoot me...

Life and death flashed before me the same as they had done the night of the fire. The uncertainty and fear of my next breath being my last, crushing everything around me. Cars screeching to a halt or revving away were silent, voices tingling the air faded out. All I could focus on was the tip of the gun following my every move. And God. This was a good time to find renewed faith, if only temporary.

The gun didn't go off. It didn't need to go off to have an effect. The fear had maimed me. I sat on the curb in the criminal squat, arms and legs stretched out and crossing over each other. Gina was made to get out of the car, too. The cop reached for his radio, but I thought he was going for his gun and flinched, then Gina, then the cop. It happened in a nanosecond, a surge of nerves that shot through us. He called for backup for the two female Caucasian suspects. I wondered what we were suspected of? Then he started asking questions.

"How long have you known this fella?"

"A few months," I responded. I looked at Scott with his arms strapped to a bar on the ceiling of the car. He looked so pitiful I almost felt bad for him. Almost.

"Why did you lie to me, son?" the officer asked Scott.

Yeah why did you lie about that you moron? I thought.

"You need a Californian license to drive if you're a resident. S'pose to change it within fourteen days of arrival, son." He turned to me and Gina. "Which one of you ladies is with this loser?"

"Hey," Scott protested.

The cop spun on his heels again, and I had to wonder if that was a trick they learned in training academy. This time, he pulled his baton. I knew cops could be bent, and I secretly hoped this one would sock Scott in the face—even if it were unfair, since he posed no threat cuffed. Bent cops don't think about fair, they just pop you—it was on the news all the time and in movies.

The pavement was starting to grind on my pelvic bone and my posture became floppy until I remembered the hunched old ladies on Salford Market walking past Mam's stall. The only thing they could see any more was rubbish in the streets mixed in with rotten vegetables thrown into the gutters. In the rain, they could follow the reflections of the orange street lamps that led their trail. Snow caused confusion, a blank canvas, no sign of previous paths. No, that couldn't be me, and I shuffled on my bum and tightened my torso to sit straight.

The woman cop showed up, but tdidn't find anything on me or Gina and just a tiny bit of weed and the bale of hay cutting penknife on Scott. Apparently Pomona was a rife-with-heroin area, and the cops had seen me with the money and put two and two together to get nine hundred. We were told to never return to Pomona or we'd be arrested. I didn't want to go back. Gina and I had joked about how we'd be dead if we got into heroin. We'd OD or get a nasty disease, but we would be dead.

Scott floored the car back to LA. Now we had sixty dollars but with that we had to buy weed, petrol, and food. Gina called Brendan, our weed dealer, and asked him to front us an eighth and grabbed a loaf of bread and peanut butter for dinner. Of course, we had to make sure Roscoe and Dite got fed, too, another dollar on pet food. We had become those bums that had no money and spent what little there was on pet food.

In our house, the pets always came last if we even remembered them. The responsibility of walking a dog every single day, maybe even a few times, was too much. Mam would only allow us self-supporting pets such as gerbils and cats and the local RSPCA had been warned not to release any animals to us. Even on the approach, the dogs would start howling as if fear and neglect could be smelled.

We invested some of the money into crates of water and loaded them into the back of the car.

"Lets sell water on the beach. We could clean up," I'd suggested. It was a stroke of brilliance. We split up and I headed down the beach yelling, "Water, water..."

Most of the time when I was stopped and thought I'd made a sale it was only to ask me to repeat what I was saying. "Water," it turned out, was one of the most difficult English-to-English translations. Me with my elongated "a" compared to the American cropped "a." Then in the American version the "t" was pronounced like a "d," I noticed Americans did this a lot. The name Katy was butchered to sound like K.D.

"Whaddare you selling?" I was asked.

"War-ter."

"War-tuh? War-tuh? Whaddisit?"

"The source of all life," I'd respond.

That was met with a confused, "Huh?"

"War-ter, I'm selling war-ter," and I picked a bottle out of my rucksack. A confused frown would soften into a laugh when they realized what I'd been saying all along.

"Oh, you mean wad-er?" They laughed and I laughed with them only because I wanted to make the sale.

"No. I really mean war-ter," I'd manage to choke out between laughs.

Mam had sent me to years and years worth of elocution lessons. The kids at school picked on me for pronouncing t's and sounding a little (very little) like the Queen.

Two hours, three pints of sweat, and numerous blisters later, I arrived at the racquetball courts. I shouted, "War-ter, war-ter." And the words multiplied in echoes and bounced out of control. It was a finale that earned me five dollars, the only five dollars I'd earned in two hours. After that I scurried back to the car banging the remaining bottles against my calves and dehydrated by a sudden flush of heat. As I walked I heard whispers in the wind "War-tuh, war-tuh."

My work here is done, I thought. I reached in my pocket to feel for the money. Gone.

After a meeting, we spent the night sleeping on Ashland, another favorite sleeping location besides Stoner Ave. The next morning, Gina didn't have to be at work until late and Scott didn't start work until the afternoon so we had a lie in. Before Scott went

111

to work, we dropped him off at Santa Monica College (SMC) to have a shower in the changing rooms. This was Gina's idea and something we could get away with since she had an ID if we were stopped.

When Scott was in work, we went back to SMC. We drove into the spiral car park and up a few levels before we found a parking space. It reminded me of the car parks we went into to smoke crack, and I drew a sharp breath in as if I were hitting a crack pipe, but I was trying to diffuse my nerves and the sudden craving that had slithered into my mind.

It was a Friday and happened to be the thirteenth on a dreary October day. I opened the door and stepped out. Behind us pulled up a golf-car-looking vehicle with "security" written on the side. A man of large proportions perched half of each of his butt cheeks on the seat while the other halves flopped over each side. Next, a police car rolled up, and I could see two faces peering from behind the reflections.

"Gina, I think something is up," I said.

Gina had one foot in the driver's seat and the other in the passenger seat like a sprinter about to take off from the blocks. She peeked her head around the door, and I could see her body/face tighten into a knot. I was still traumatized from staring down the barrel of a gun the previous day. I was paralyzed to my spot.

"We've had reports that there was a smell of marijuana coming from this vehicle," said one of the cops. "Can you both please give me your IDs?"

The only ID I had was my passport. The same chewed and torn passport that had rendered me a lecture from Border Patrol in Mexico because it lacked a visa. My legal status as well as the crime we were being accused of swung heavy and somber in front of me like pendulums of doom. I was sure they knew I was a crack addict and certain they could tell I'd prostituted my body and now I'd be kicked out of the country, too. He looked at our IDs and threw them on the bonnet—the hood, as I'd never forget again. The security guard screeched off at five mph in his golf cart. Now it was just us and the cops, again, and I couldn't believe this was happening, again.

"What's your business here?" Cop 1 asked.

"I'm a student here, this is my friend. I'm on the way to the library," Gina said.

"We're going to have to search your vee-hicle. Do you have anything you want to declare?" Cop 2 asked.

I didn't look at Gina even though it was my first instinct to turn and grab her arms and shake her, *What's in there? What the fuck kind of trouble are we in now? Am I going to get deported over some bleedin' weed?* I didn't feel her glare on me, so I figured she must be running her own internal monologue. And we were both trying to play it cool.

"You can't do that! You've got no proof," Gina's coolness melted into a fiery, temperamental volcanic lava.

"This is school property, Ma'am. We have to investigate allegations of drug use," Cop 1 said.

Cop 2 walked by us and peeked into the passenger door. Cop 1 followed him. Gina nudged my arm and started mouthing words at me. I looked over my shoulder to see if either of them were looking before focusing on the shapes her mouth was making. It was something about the pipe, but I didn't quite get it. I shook my head so she understood my confusion. She tapped on her handbag and that led me to believe that that was where the pipe was stashed.

"What's going on in this car? Do you guys live here or something?" A second later, Roscoe and Dite leaped on Cop 2, and he jumped back.

"Leave the cats alone," Gina screamed and grabbed Cop 1's arm.

He turned and tried to grab her. I could only see this out of the corner of my eye, as I still seemed to be paralyzed to my spot and was too scared to turn all the way around. A ninety-degree angle seemed a compromise. Gina flew past me and the cops after her. The door was left wide open so Roscoe and Dite could escape. This was when I had to dare to move, to save the cats. When I returned to my spot, Gina and the cops were playing cat and mouse around a car. They both descended on her, but she slipped out of their grasps like a wet bar of soap.

They finally cornered her by pinning her to the passenger window of an ancient Toyota Corolla. Gina was screaming and crying, and the cops were shouting at her to calm down. I wasn't sure whether Gina was putting all of this on, but it was an Oscar-worthy performance if she was. So I joined in her manic episode.

"You're manhandling her! Get off her. She's not taken her meds...I mean it, I'll report you both for manhandling her!" It dawned on me that being in America such an allegation might work. I looked across at my passport and a thought crossed my mind to snatch it back while the drama was playing out. But the jingle of handcuffs and the jangle of bullets in the barrel of a gun rattled the thought from my head.

"She's not taken her meds, I tell you. Get off her, you are manhandling."

At that moment, Gina was led from behind the car in cuffs and another police car rolled up. I knew we had a chance when a woman stepped out, and I saw her rank as Captain. Gina was placed in the back of the cop car, her handbag still hanging from her shoulder. I glanced at her and then at the approaching Captain.

"Your officers were manhandling my friend, and she's not taken her meds yet. She's bipolar and they pinned her to that car," I pointed.

She looked at Gina and back at me. "What are her meds for and where are they?"

"She's bipolar. They're in her handbag. But, look, she probably wouldn't have been so barmy had she not 'ave been chased and then manhandled." Captain looked at me confused, *I shouldn't 'ave used "barmy,"* I thought. "I mean, nuts, erm no not nuts...manic. She was manic." I corrected myself, even though either nuts or barmy were appropriate.

Gina whimpered like the rumble of a volcano before its explosion. I was starting to recognize it.

"I need to get your meds out of your purse," the Captain said to Gina through a half open window.

"No! No!" Gina screamed. "Don't touch me. Don't come near me." She seemed obviously traumatized by what had happened. I was sincerely impressed at her instincts on how to play her character. I wondered whether she was a schizo.

"Can I get them out for her?" I asked.

"Yes. Yes, do it," the Captain said.

The moment I slipped the pills into her mouth she calmed down. It was almost too obvious, and I panicked we would be found out. I hopped from foot to foot like I did as a child when I was bursting for the loo. The officers searched the car and found nothing. The pipe was still safely tucked in Gina's purse and they were too scared to go for that.

"Since we found nothing, we are going to take your keys for a couple of hours to allow you to calm down," the Captain said to Gina. "But given the seriousness of the allegation, I must remind you that marijuana is illegal and it is punishable even more so on school property. Do you have anything to say?"

"Thank you," I mumbled.

"Can we take the cats?" Gina asked.

I spent the last of our money on a phone card to call Mam and then we begged for money outside Starbucks with Roscoe tied to a piece of string and Dite attached to a belt. It was cheaper to buy refill coffees so we found old cups smashed between the seats in the car and under the seats.

I drank my coffee and smoked some weed before calling Mam. *I should be higher than this,* I thought.

"Hi Mam, its me." I didn't have to say who. I was her only daughter.

"How are yer, love?"

"Okay. Off to the beach."

"I can't believe this is who you turned out to be. I mean it seemed like Charlie was the one off the rails with all his pot. But you, I had hopes for you. And now this. At least we knew where we were at with Charlie."

"Mam, you don't understand. You don't think my brothers aren't addicts too? You think booze is okay?"

"Well it's certainly not crack, love. Where are you living? Are you still with that Gina and her boyfriend?"

"Yeah, we're fine. We go to meetings. It's all good. But, Mam, I don't see how you can cut all my money off. I got a letter off Heather, and I have to go pee in a cup. Don't you realize I'm twenty-eight?" I tried to stay calm, but I could feel myself boiling.

"Luvey, you need to come home. You need to be with your mother. Did you know that your brothers were going to come and find you? I told them not to because they'd never find you out there."

"No, Mam! I'm not coming home. There's no help there. Do you even know why I did this? Do you know it was because I never got over my brothers' death, Mam? I'm not coming home, and I want you to call Heather and get me my money back. This is bullshit." I never swore in front of my mam usually, but this seemed like a special occasion.

"I can't help you with your brothers. You need to file it. And we need to make sure you're not doing anything. You need to come home to your mother."

I was now shaking with rage. Not even after I'd been killing myself could she talk to me? She couldn't even try to understand? Where was my mother when I needed her?

"No! Mam, I'm not coming home. You can't help me there. You don't understand. I'm not coming home and my brothers'll never find me." I slammed down the phone.

❖

We picked up Scott after work and went to a meeting. I was still wound up from Mam, clutching my sides, trying not to explode. Every time I heard the word *relapse*, there was a clanging in my head. I should have listened.

The night before Mike and Sammy died, me and our Mike had an argument. He chased me around the house with a dart, and I made him cry when I threw Sammy's tricycle at him.

116

After Mam got home, I left in a huff at Mike. When I got home, he was in bed sleeping and I could hear his snores. All my brothers snored, even Sammy had cute baby snores. I stood on the stairs that led to my bedroom and thought about waking him and saying sorry. But I changed my mind, *He'll paint me a picture at school, and I'll buy him sweets and we'll make up. For now he'll stew,* I thought. *I mean, it's not like we're gonna have a fire or something.*

If only I'd've known. If only hindsight wasn't so hind. If only.

That night, we agreed to spend a portion of Scott's pay on recreational coke. Not a hard narcotic to us anymore, we agreed. A bubble-gum drug. I gave Ron a call, and he was exactly where I'd left off. Scott was making a concoction in the front on some foil. Then he lit the underside of the foil and smoked a plume of smoke. We all took turns. I didn't really question it until images of Scott and flashes of conversation with Em crossed my mind.

Crack is bicarbonate of soda and water mixed together.

"What have you done?" I screamed at Scott.

Chapter Nine

For the next few days, I planted myself by the ocean. Lapping waves and a bubbling surf, my favorite melody. Sitting on the sand and looking out, it seemed infinite. Beyond the horizon, there was more water, infinite water.

Everything else I'd experienced had ended and the gut-wrenching anxiety of "The End" haunted me. The ocean only seemed to have a beginning, and I could breathe again. Maybe it was because I'm a Scorpio, a water sign. Astrology was my replacement for God. A new kind of faith that I could read about everyday if I wanted. But those types of horoscopes seemed unrealistic to me. I used to save the *Manchester Evening News* and read my horoscope from the previous day to see if it had come true. But I didn't see how anyone could be *that* precise and it apply to everyone.

My love for water could also have been because Mam took us to the beach all summer when we were at the caravan. Sammy wasn't born then. It was so long ago that Mam and Dad were still man and wife, sort of. Dad came careening down the pedestrian path to the beach drunk in the car one sunny afternoon. Mam was so humiliated that she banned him from further excursions. Nevertheless, memories, like gusty grains of sand, blew around me and I was protected in a shield of serenity.

On Sundays, I'd discovered the drum circle—a massive gathering of people who danced and clanged and banged. I would hear the low rumble of music and think it was an angry wave, but then vibrations thundered under the sand and synchronized with the current of my body.

Tink, tink, tink.

Boom, de boom boom.

The contagious beat mixed with the applauding waves picked my spirit up and tangoed on the sand. I was swept away from my misery, jiggled out of my thoughts, and for an instant only that one happy, carefree moment existed.

I'd left the back of the car in a tip and it wasn't easy to differentiate between the smell of the cat litter or the sweaty, fermenting clothes. Scott and Gina were getting impatient that their housewife was having a mid-life crisis. Returning from work to find me missing and nothing washed or tidied. They would have to wear their work clothes for the second day running. *What kind of sodding bums are they?* I thought.

On top of that, when I did return Scott wanted me to leave again because he was sexually frustrated.

"Can't you take a walk or something?" he said.

"Mate," I said, but not whatsoever meaning the term "mate"—especially because Americans took that to mean lover. "It's bloody freezing outside, and its dark and you want me to just wander around like a moron just so you can shag your bird? No way. Yer in-fuckin'-sane, mate." Again, not meant as mate.

"I thought you were English. Isn't this summer for you? Can't you just go for half an hour?"

Gina sat in silence. I imagined she wasn't even conscious for any of this. It was like when she smoked crack and she became a shell. I didn't realize she didn't even need the crack to do that. Either way, she didn't seem to have an opinion.

"I'm not wandering around the dark, cold streets so you can gerrit on with 'er. You should've thought about that while you were busy getting stoned and sleepin' 'til noon. It in't my fault you can't 'ave a shag."

And the drama continued. And every day I thought about Mam's offer to buy me a ticket home.

The conversation I'd had with her echoed in my mind: *File it.* What did that mean, exactly? I'd tried to forget they existed since I was fourteen. I hid photos of them and continued my life as normally as possible. School, dinner, laundry. But at the end of the day, left to my own devices, when I came home and I was faced with the wreckage that really existed, my heart broke all over again. In my house, the British stiff upper lip wasn't just stiff, it was supposed to be made of steel. But mine was made of corrugated cardboard and had become flimsy with secret, salty tears. My friends had told me: *Try puttin' yer face on, mate, you'll feel much better.* But makeup never made me feel better like it did them. It seemed an odd thing to do to boost my spirits.

All I could think about was when I was four with whooping cough. Those days, we still lived on Gilda Crescent, just around the corner from Victoria Crescent. Every time I turned my head, I was sick and Mam would run behind me with a rag and a bucket of hot water. She wasn't full-time at the market at this point, because Dad hadn't drunk his ink business into the ground. In between puking, I sat on Mam's knee, cradled in her arms, rocking on her knee, safe. The exact way I'd held myself after the first time I smoked crack. I wished I could feel that again.

I passed the first drug test, apart from weed, which takes a month to flush out. After a month, I planned to come up with an excuse. A relapse didn't seem to matter so long as it wasn't crack. I was terrified our relapse from just a few nights earlier was going to show up—a creeping line on a container of pee revealing my secret. Gina and Scott didn't even flinch. It's the reason addicts smoke crack or meth, inject heroin, or become boozers if they're on probation—because they take the least time to clean out.

I was reveling in the success. The first anything I'd passed since GCEs. A-levels I'd flopped twice. I'd scraped through my degree and spiraled into drug addiction—so this was an achievement. It was an odd feeling. It was a feeling. Like a shooting star racing through my heart. A flutter of my pulse, a flush of heat and a flare of light. It was over in the blink of an eye. But something captured me in that moment. A flash of hope, like a photo, was printed into my mind. A rush of energy charged my body, like a tiny line of coke, but without the grotty depressing after-feeling. I wondered if I could string a thousand of those moments together. How happy that would make me.

My attorney's office had wood paneled walls and a dark carpet, like a dungeon. I scanned the room for signs of natural light. Her desk was piled high with organized sets of paperwork. I sat at a long, dark wood table with three chairs down each side and one at either end. It looked like a table the Vikings would have a hearty feast around. But I didn't know the etiquette for where I was supposed to sit. Which chair was appropriate?

It was like the time Mam took us to a fancy restaurant when we were on holiday at the caravan. It was so posh that there were four or five knives and forks per plate, topped off with two spoons. It was anyone's guess what I was supposed to do with all this silverware.

At first, I thought I'd be sharing the plate with a few different people. A plate shortage seemed possible. But when no one joined me and all the others seemed to have their own spaces, I realized it couldn't be that. Maybe they expected us to steal them the way people would from Salford and on Mam's market do with anything not nailed down. Or drunk people who steal ashtrays and pint glasses, especially students.

I put the silverware back from being tucked in my knee-high woolly boots when I realized that not even our Charlie was thinking about nicking it. I got hungry working it all out and just used a spoon and my fingers. Across the table, Chris was teaching three-year old Mike how to wipe his mouth with the tablecloth. Now which chair shall I sit in?

This was only the second time I'd met Heather. She was a recommendation from Gina's mam. But given Gina's mam was drunk most of the time, and I was enjoying copious amounts of legal heroin, legally injected into my vein every legal four hours at the time of agreeing to retain her as my attorney, I couldn't be sure I'd made the best choice. That was when Mam could have helped me. Not now, leaving me with nothing to live on.

She appeared, taller than I remembered, behind a chimney stack of papers. She was as thin, too, and I remembered Gina telling me about how she'd had her stomach stapled so she could lose all this weight. I thought how nice it would be if someone could just come and slice a piece of me off and staple me back up as a different person. Cut out all the once-wonderful memories that have tightened into knots of pain overtime. Happy thoughts that have turned violent, every flash of memory tightening the noose around my neck. Choking my remaining happiness.

But I wasn't sure I really wanted it all to go away. If that happened, it would be like my brothers never existed, they would be lobotomized from my life. And instead of having at least what I have now, my sun-bleached memories, I would have nothing at all.

"Are you okay?" Heather asked, staring at me as if I was a specimen that wasn't quite human.

"Yeah, yeah, doin' great," I told her.

"When was the last time you smoked crack?"

"Blinkin' 'eck. Lemme think, erm, couple a nights before you called me at 'ome." *Unless you count the "do-it-yourself" version the other night,* I thought.

"Good. You know your mom was worried sick."

My jaw clenched. My anger at mam was draining me, like a car with its headlights left on. I was about to be stranded in a muddy, dark field filled with cow dung.

"Yeah. I spoke to 'er the day before last, so I think she feels better now."

"Excellent news. And now I can tell her I saw you and you seem perfectly fine. I just need you to take the test. If you've not done it before Jerry will explain."

I cashed the check immediately. I sat on the bus reading *On the Road* and empathizing with Jack's character Sal. Wishing that my adventures were a bit more zany instead of so desperate. All these situations were being forced on me, it seemed. In my heart I knew it was only because of what I'd done. But I'd only done what i'd done because what happened happened. Now I slept in a car with two lunatics—either that or I was the lunatic—and two sweet but smelly cats. What a mess.

I went home to the car in the car park behind HoneyBear Ham. Gina left it open so I climbed in the backseat and lay out smoking a joint. Roscoe and Dite jumped on my stomach from between two bags of laundry, and that reminded me I needed to play housewife and get the laundry done while they were at work. The kittens fell off me and tried clawing their way back up, digging their nails into my skin. For some reason, this tickled and then Roscoe swung himself around and up, his long grey hairs tickling my nostrils and neck. The buzz I felt earlier tingled through my veins. *Laughter,* I thought. *Laughter is the tonic for a sick soul.* I dreamt on that glimmer of hope like a feather pillow for the next few hours.

By the time I woke up, it was too late to do laundry. Gina would be off work soon, and me and Scott still had to go shopping for Gina's birthday dinner at the park. I took off to Ralphs on foot with an empty rucksack. This was the first time I'd been to the supermarket in months.

Fe did the shopping at Grandma's, but I didn't eat anyway. Living in the car, Scott was the one who did the shopping. Me and Gina would wait outside the entrance with the engine running and Scott would come running out, his arms hugging his waist. Gina leaned over and opened the door and he jumped straight into the seat, screeching away before it was even half closed. On one occasion a chubby security guard who moved like a slug, came out after him yelling, *Stop! Thief! Stop! Thief!* A few heads turned but no one was interested in us petty thieves.

Waves of sweet smells came out of the sliding doors like sugarcoated bonbons that melt in your mouth. The aromas were familiar, their names on the tip of my tongue, but I wasn't quite sure. Bread or cookies? Whatever it was had awakened my dormant stomach and the air even tasted sweet. Inside, I stood still blinded by the lights, stunned by the air conditioning and a rainbow of shiny fruit. People bustled around me, snatching things off shelves and throwing them in baskets and trolleys without looking. I imagined them taking it home and cooking and eating it, instead of chewing and savoring.

Gina was at the car when I got back. I saw her look of surprise as I walked up with groceries. I smiled and dug into my pocket for the rest of the roll of twenties. It felt good in my hand, solid and secure. The rough, embellished pattern let me know this is more than a receipt.

"Happy Birthday!" I shouted.

She smiled. She actually smiled.

Then I pulled out the money and she lit up.

We decorated an area in a park—streamers in the trees, foil place settings, homemade cards, and a radio for music. For dessert, I'd already called Brendan to arrange a pickup. The party was fun. It renewed my faith that you didn't need to have an actual place to live to survive in this town. For once, we didn't gripe and groan at each other. The cold, cramped night ahead was in the future, if only a few hours, and we lived the moment for what it was. Roscoe and Dite scampered around the picnic table legs and scrapped with our shoelaces. Scott took the helm at the barbecue and people's heads turned from all the way across the park wondering where the rich, dripping aromas were coming from, looking up to see if it was falling from the trees. We were the proud owners of that smell from the meat that we'd cooked and paid for with the proceeds of my broken wrist and nearly clean drug test.

After the festivities, soon after sunset at six, we set out to meet Brendan so we could pay him off and buy more weed. We decided to roll a blunt, which was lavish because it used at least a gram of our stash, but we were celebrating, after all. Lincoln Boulevard was crammed as usual. We wanted to get the weed, pick up some booze and find ourselves a nice space to park by the beach, so Gina sped down the curb lane. We jolted to a stop at the lights and moments before we nearly crashed. I couldn't take the suspense—my heart seemed to be rolling up and down my insides like a yoyo. I turned to focus on the kittens. Dite hung from my arm, and Roscoe tried to trap her swishing tail. I laughed when they scratched and clawed because their tiny paws were only strong enough to tickle. Soon enough, they would be grown and able to draw blood. I wanted to appreciate the kitten years.

"*Watchout!*" Scott shouted.

I spun around. Bang. I flew to the other side of the car. Before my head splattered like a fly on a car windshield, I grabbed the side of Gina's seat. The impact flung me into the other side of the seat, crunching my ribs and shoulder. I fell to the floor, tipping the cat litter that sprayed into the air with the impact. The car was screeching at what felt like incredible speed, sideways. One wheel, then two collapsed and we spun around, powerless. I couldn't tell whether I was injured. I didn't care. Was I going to live? Would the car explode? Bang. We hit something else and the car came to a violent halt.

There was no smoke. No fire. No more danger. And the pain. The pain became real. I clutched my right arm, held it tight and roared through the grill of my teeth. I knew this pain from when I was eighteen.

Me and Mam got into a fight because I'd loaned my friend, Caroline, my new (but really fifteen-year-old), orange Morris Ital to drive to her boyfriend's house, even though she had no license. One of Mam's mates spotted Caroline driving and happened to talk to Mam that night at keep-fit class and mentioned what she saw.

Mam came home with a mission after that. All her moves were deliberate. I heard her car pull in the driveway. The outside light detected the heat in her fierceness and clicked on before she got out of the car. I heard the door open and slam and then her heavy, blunt footsteps clomped upstairs shaking me in my skin. *One of us is in forrit,* I thought. But there was only the three of us living at home at that point. Rick had left to

125

live with his girlfriend. I listened to where she was going. I was still in my Greggs uniform, just back from work.

I was distracted by fear and lost count of how many flights she had climbed until the last second when the footsteps boomed. The door flung open, and it was my turn to tackle her. Most days there was some tackling involved and usually Charlie got kicked out, like he was that night—over at Martin's house, probably smoking weed. I just wandered the streets wishing I could move out. And after I got my car back, I did. That was my first experience of living in a car.

Some days I wondered if Mam had regretted I'd lived. Would she have preferred my brothers to have lived? It struck me as a peculiar question. One you wouldn't really think you'd ever have to ask yourself, same as you'd never expect your kids to die before you did. But what it really came down to was Mam was angry she was left alive. Why did she have to live through this?

We battled. She accused. I denied. On the stairs, we sparred back and forth, up and down, using our quick wit and tongues as weaponry. Mam was slick with her sarcasm, but as I got older I could give her a run for her money.

"It's a killing machine, you bloody idiot. What do you think you're doing giving your keys to that girl? Driving is a privilege, Philippa," she blazed.

I slowly backed my way out of the house, keys clutched in my hand with every intention of getting out of there. It was raining, and I didn't have any shoes on. I stomped out into the rain barefooted and ran for my car. Mam chased me and tried to grab my keys. Instead, she grabbed my wrist and I struggled to escape. I yanked and she yanked. Screaming at each other in the middle of the street. Curtains twitched and passersby stopped and then moved on. Chance presented itself and I bolted out of her clutches. My hand shook as I put the keys in my car door. The rain was dripping from my lashes, blurring my vision. I heard the click and jumped in. Pushed the blobber down and reached over the passenger seat to lock the door. Her face appeared like a dripping watercolor through the window. I screamed and then screamed again as I felt a wrenching pain and realized my arm was stuck in a *Turn right Clyde* position from Clint Eastwood's movie. I panicked and walked to my friend's house, where I was then transported to the hospital with a dislocated shoulder.

My car was confiscated for months.

I leapt out of the car. "My shoulder, aaagh, I dislocated my fucking shoulder." Ten years later, exactly.

I staggered and swayed to the pavement, where a crowd had gathered and parted to let me fall to the ground and breathe the pain in and out. Scott and Gina appeared, Gina in tears, but neither of them visibly injured. From my view on the pavement, I could see a smaller car sticking out of the side of our home, Gina's car.

I tried to stand, but people told me to sit. Gina and Scott were talking to the cops. I tried to breathe. My arm hurt, my chest wheezed, and my breathing was shallow. I felt a mask cover my face and a whoosh of air.

I woke up with bright lights shining in my face and thought I was dead. *Is that God coming to greet me? Will I see my brothers? Hold on...am I going to hell?* I stirred between consciousness and oblivion.

"What's your social security number?" a human being I finally recognized as a nurse asked me. I blurted out some numbers and laughed. I knew I didn't want to give her my real number, or I would be stuck with a huge bill. But I was really enjoying the painkillers. "So, erm, your social security number is the same as your phone number?"

I sat up and looked at each of the six of her I saw and said a determined yes to each one of them. Believing everything I told her, too. The doctors came in and tied two blankets around me at the top and bottom of my torso. Gina looked worried, but I paid no attention to her. Each doctor held the ends of the blanket on either side of me. I looked up at Gina and laughed. "Where the fuck are we gonner live, mate?"

The doctors pulled the blankets in opposite directions with a mean yank. My body twisted, my face contorted into previously unknown expressions of mankind. Before the pop, I could hear the slurping sound of my bone being sucked back into its socket.

I slumped back down into the gurney. I couldn't lift a muscle. "Where we gonner live, Gina?" I slurred and passed out.

CHAPTER TEN

THE CAR CRASH WAS ONE OF THOSE BLESSINGS IN DISGUISE THAT MY GRAN, MAM'S MAM, ALWAYS HARKED ON ABOUT THAT I'D YET TO WITNESS. Gina and Scott had been approached by an ambulance chaser on the scene of the accident. He was one of those blokes who sues the other driver and took fifty or sixty percent of the settlement. Dodgy bloke. But it definitely inspired us to find a lawyer and sue the bastard who drove his car into our home.

In the meantime, we moved in with one of Gina's mates, Pamela, and her boyfriend, Taylor, way away from the beach, out in a place called San Fernando Valley. Locals called it The Valley. Pamela called Taylor "Boo." At first, I thought it was a poor attempt to scare him, but when I mentioned it to Gina and she set me straight. Taylor was not black but African American and I learned at Rock 'n' Rollers it's not acceptable to get that wrong.

There's a fresh set of jargon to learn with African Americans. Taylor would say things like *Holler later, hommie.* Or *Meet me at my crib, fo' sho' in an hour.* I needed a translator at first, same as most people do with me, but after a few days I was *chillin' in a dude's crib* and smokin' blunts with Boo and Pamela—Pam.

The first few days were fun. We boiled in the hot tub, and I allowed an underwater jet to massage my back and stomach. But if it got too close to my ribs, a white flash of pain shot through me. The accident had blown up my ribs, too, somehow. I'm not sure if they were broken or bruised but when I smoked weed and if I coughed, I doubled over as if I was trying to prevent my ribs falling out of my chest. It didn't make me give up, though. We ate, we drank, we smoked bong-loads, and we slept. I could see how the car accident was a blessing in disguise. But normal life, for us, had to resume.

Pam and Taylor's gaff (as us northerners called it) was miles and miles away from HoneyBear Ham and Ursula's. Thirty minutes in the car but two hours by bus. We got up early the first morning so we could find the bus stop. Catching the bus was my only means of transport after I broke my wrist so the bus system was a cinch to me. Lying in my hospital bed, I'd had to try to find somebody that could move a car with a gear stick. By the time I was released, I had five tickets tucked under the windshield wiper like a losing poker hand. Automatics are the rage in LA and not one of the twenty people I called knew what I was talking about. For one thing, Americans call a gear stick a "stick shift" so no one could fathom what I meant.

Gina had only ever caught a bus for fun when she was wagging school after the limo had dropped her and her mates off. We were on our second bus and had been traveling an hour and a half by the time she lost it. Warbling screams stabbed at the eardrums of innocent travelers. At first, she didn't say anything legible—and I was scared this was what it looked like when a human soul internally combusted.

"This is what being on the bus means?" The jumbled sounds she was making at last settled into a sentence. "Oh God, there's men on top of the Federal Building."

I looked in the direction she was pointing. I don't know why I looked. If it were true, they had to be painters or there wouldn't be any buses casually driving by. She was obviously crazy. But she was all I had at this point.

"They're gonna get us! *Duck! Everyone duck!*"

I answered Scott's mortified glare with a smug smile. *Wanna shag 'er now, fuck wit? Ha ha,* I thought. Using only our eyes as communication, we decided to get off the bus at the next stop. That seemed an eternity away, especially with the Federal Building under fire. I had to wonder if we would even make it.

From the bus, we hopped straight into a cab to make the last mile. I was furious anyone could be that spoiled. At the same time, I was thankful Mam hadn't raised me to be unable to catch the bus. Even a limo can break down, then what are you supposed to do? What if the driver got hammered?

But Gina had gone from being chauffeured in a limo and prancing around the countryside on a thoroughbred horse to a simple SUV after her parents' business collapsed. An SUV with leather seats but no driver was like being piss poor to her, even after visiting the slums of Mexico and walking on a daily basis past the homeless on the boardwalk holding signs that read "Work 4 Marijuana," "Homeless Vet Seeking Work for Beer." At least we weren't those poor fucks.

At night, a hoard of umbrella people gathered under the arches by Big Daddy's and La La Land. They arranged the umbrellas to shield the gusts from the ocean, which at night could be especially chilly. I walked past their cozy setup wishing I could dive into the little community and witness the mysteries of their existence. What did they do? Play cards, drink, smoke, write to their mams? I wondered if they had a better deal than me. Was it one of those clans that I could just join? Or was it one of those where you have to sleep your way to the top?

In any case, as appealing as they sometimes appeared to be, we had a place to stay and soon enough an insurance payout so we would be able to buy a new home. At least at this point we could look for an interior design to suit our needs. For me, it would be the length of the backseat and how much the seatbelt clickers could be tucked away so they didn't dig into my craggy hipbones. Gina and Scott would be noticing the gradient in the recline of the seats and the distance the center console put between them. If we were really lucky, we might even find something with a niche for the cat litter tray.

The moment we got to HoneyBear Ham, Jose the manager told Gina to take the rest of the day off. That would cost us a day's pay, three door-wedge sandwiches and me personally another few chunks of my precious and rapidly depleting sanity. Following that, Scott announced that he, too, would take the day off so we didn't have to wait around until six to go home. So thoughtful. It was at that point a moment of clarity—something else I'd heard about at the meetings—struck me like a thunderbolt, as if God himself was sending me a message written in His blood. Nothing bolder. Nothing clearer.

I realized I was a pawn in their game of survival. With me around, they would take days off and be happy to rely on my disability checks. I thought about all the nights we got high together. Where did the money come from? I pulled the most money in and blew the most money out. Scott thought I owed him in some pseudo way because of his missing fingers. The fact I got money to do nothing because I broke my wrist irked him like freshly filed nails scraping a blackboard.

"I don't see how they give *you* that money for *that* injury. Look at my fingers."

"I can't, mate, you 'aven't got none. Ever heard of Vinegar Vera?"

He looked at me as if *I* was the nutter. I wondered if the real story behind his fingers was darker than what he had let on and there was a Texas Vinegar Vera lurking in his past. "Well, I'm sorry you don't think my injury is serious enough. But my check 'as saved our arses many times. And you weren't complainin' when it paid for your drugs. I don't owe you nought. Time to get a job."

Gina was a great actress. She could be playing me like she did the police, the po-po, as Taylor and Pam called them. Scott was just lazy. All his excuses to not work, his attitude, empty efforts, they all reminded me of the way our Charlie used to be before he decided to go back to school when he was twenty-two or something. I don't know what he took me for. It was time to get out. But where? But how? But with what? So many "But's" to add to my "Just In Case."

Gina recovered from her "meltdown," but it took a few days. She spoke to her therapist, Sarah, the smart lady who had no idea she usually attended her visits straight after a crack run.

Sarah said she would arrange for Gina's medications to be evaluated by her shrink. *'Bout time,* I thought.

After that, we got a call from Gina's mam that she had some money from the insurance for Gina to get a car. She quickly got over her bus phobia, packed her handbag with her cigarettes and phone, and we started on the trek to her mam's house. It was all the way in Hollywood, up by the sign that had been an obsession to me as a tourist. I spent hours getting as close to the sign as possible, driving up windy roads that reminded me of country roads at home, trying to find the direct path. Considering such a path didn't exist, it was like hoping to stumble on a pot of gold at the end of the rainbow.

I soon found out I couldn't walk right up to it and touch it like it seemed in the movies. I'd imagined myself somehow being able to sunbathe in the curve of the "O" or sip martinis out of the "Y." At forty-feet tall, the "Y" was just the right size martini glass for me. But that when I was doing coke. The crack had got me off the booze and the coke and that's when the tourist interest faded, and I hopped on a different kind of bus.

From Hollywood and Gower, we had to walk. Keep heading north, keep going up, and we would reach the top at some point. Gina walked and puffed, walked and puffed. One drag of a cig would have left me choking for breath.

Her mam answered the door and staggered away, leaving the dogs yapping at our ankles. They were small Yorkshire Terriers that nipped and screeched, but were easily disposed of with a quick whip of the ankle. Gina sent three furballs across the hardwood floor, leaving a nice sparkle in their wake.

Gina's mam's name was Grace. She hardly emulated any type of grace of God, not that me and God had been friends recently, but I was pretty certain he doesn't stagger around drunk and brag about how many drugs he's taken and how many men he's slept with.

We followed her mam into the lounge and sat on the large L-shaped sofa. This wasn't the first time I'd met her. When my accent was still a novelty and Gina still semi-lived with her, we scored some weed for her and dropped it off. I couldn't believe her mam smoked weed or even knew about it. I didn't think any parents knew.

With the latest antics, though, my novelty had worn off. She had no idea about Gina smoking crack. She only knew about me. I was the bad influence. We were lucky that she was already drunk. She finished one martini and shook herself another before sitting down, using Grey Goose vodka, just as Gina said she would. Then she launched into tales of taking acid and ecstasy in New York while staying with her parents. *That explains a lot!* I thought. I'd wondered why Gina wouldn't move back to a gorgeous house with high ceilings, probably a pool (I'd not seen the back), light, telly, food, heating, cooling, a fridge. But after spending half an hour with her mam, it was easy to see why she might prefer the car.

I laughed at her.

Mam was clueless about drugs. *I wish your brother would get his act together and stop smoking that cocaine,* she had said to me once. *Cocaine?* I thought. *Our Charlie only smokes weed, he's not a crack'ead.* When I realized that she'd got crack and weed confused, I knew I could go home in any old state and Mam would probably be clueless. So I started dropping ecstasy.

At last, Grace got down to business. Her skirt sashayed as she walked to the mail slot. Her footsteps resonated around the room, and I thought with the addition of a cowbell we could have ourselves a drum circle. She returned slurping her drink so no more spilled on the floor, licking the drips up the side of the glass like kids do with ice cream cones. I imagined after we left she would be on all fours licking the floor clean. Alcohol could make people behave in similar ways to crack, I noticed.

"Here's your check, honey," Grace said and passed the envelope to Gina.

We had no idea how much she was going to get. But this was the change out of all the horses and homes she had had over the years. After this, there would be no more. I studied Gina's face. The familiar wrinkles in her nose, the change in her breathing from long to short bunny breaths. Her eyes were covered as usual. I didn't know if I could recognize expression in her eyes since I never saw them anyway.

I studied her other facial nuances before looking at her eyes. Her thin lips disappeared behind a smile. Her wrinkled forehead smoothed out, lines of stress dissolving. It was a new reflection of her, like a sunset or a sunrise, either one—both are radiant.

We bolted out of the door, not giving Grace a chance to fumble after us in one of her infamous blackouts. The escape was all uphill, but with six thousand dollars burning like rocket fuel in her back pocket, Gina negotiated the hill with athletic performance, smoking the whole time.

First me, then Scott took off after her, reaching for her braids to cling to for fear of losing her, but not quite managing to catch them.

I'd earned fugitive status with the banks where I'd had accounts. One way or another—consciously, subconsciously, and unconsciously—I'd ripped them off. Placed empty deposit envelopes in cash machines, run up unauthorized overdrafts until I could withdraw no more, same as any self-respecting drug addict. The other two had as much hope as me of having a bank account. A check-cashing place was the only way to get the six grand.

A place opposite Santa Monica College that we rarely dared to drive by any more, offered to cash it for us for a couple of hundred dollars. Gina pulled her sob story out of her handbag along with the check. I was no longer stunned by her performances. I realized they were all in her daily routine. I felt sick about losing that much of the money. I wanted her to cling to every cent after we'd been so desperate.

We signed up at Westside Rentals and when Gina and Scott finally went back to work, I scoured lists of properties that we could maybe afford. Not based on a precise calculation of income versus overheads, but a decision based on what seemed like a good figure. Was it an odd or even number? Did it make any of us draw in a sharp breath of anxiety, like the edge of a knife sliding up and down my throat? These were the real considerations, we thought, of potential new renters.

We were also supposed to pass a credit test. I was getting fed up with these tests I kept having to pass. In America, they had this system of earning points based on paying bills on time. Beyond being drug addicts and incapable of organizing a piss-up in a brewery, I grew up with Mam's filing system. Piles and piles of paperwork around the house. One was utility bills, then there were her suppliers for the nets. Mam had to file her own taxes every year. That was when everything in the house went "dark" like a theatre. All activities ceased, chippy night, chinky night, Sunday outings to museums. Every so often, we heard the ruffle of papers and the scurry of feet, and we knew Mam was alive and stressing. Once every so often, like a geyser, a stream of papers shot into the air. This was our sign to leg it upstairs and stay out of the way.

I'd also inherited Mam's legs, Dad's gut—I felt doomed.

The large, airy, brimming with sunshine apartment that I'd imagined, hoped for, wasn't going to transpire. Besides the credit reports, anyone we spoke to wanted a hefty deposit but we needed money to replace the car, too. I thought about showing my latest drug test to the landlords, with a "Look buddy, I may not have any cash but I got a mainly clean drug test." Then I could show the person the line that meant I was only positive for weed. *That has to count for something,* I thought. But it didn't.

In one of her more manic moments, we took off to car dealerships at Van Nuys on the bus, determined not to leave without driving home. Chintzy music thrummed between my ears from an ad I just saw on the telly followed by some bloke in a huge cowboy hat promising a ninety-nine-dollar-a-month payment plan. I knew it was a con, anything like that is. It was a petrifying feeling to know it's the likes of Gina—the untreated manic depressives and bipolars—who are swayed with this ad. They're behind the wheel with untreated madness. The thought had never occurred to me as a crack fiend. Gina blubbered the whole way. Scott sat next to her, arm clamped around her shoulder, as usual, helping her through the traumatic act of sitting on a bus. Gina and Scott signed up for a Jeep, as big and as petrol-guzzling as the Explorer. They'd already forgotten how many times we'd had to scrape our bags and pockets, or hope my credit card would work just for a few liters of petrol. Still, I wasn't about to stick around. I was alert for opportunity. The backseat was a bit firmer than the Explorer's but I thought that would be better for my back. Gina and Scott didn't even consider their front-seat status because they just wanted a place to live but Just In Case, I made sure I appropriately tested my possible future home.

We drove off the lot, onto the freeway. It was a huge relief—maybe Gina wouldn't keep having manic meltdowns now. And so long as my name wasn't on the paperwork, it wasn't my problem. Right after that, we drove to West LA and met Timothy. He had a nice big one-storey house that he shared with two friends. When he opened the front door, laughter and music spilled out before he had a chance to speak, and I knew this is where we would live. He led us down the side of the house, the pathway shadowed under tree branches and crunchy from the fallen leaves. The end of the pathway opened onto a backyard, where there was a pool instead of grass. Romantic notions of summer days with margaritas on the rocks jumped with excitement in my mind. Then he showed us the room, or one-car garage as they are more commonly known. I thought it was smart on Timothy's part to buffer the drudgery of the room with the pool.

We collected our belongings from Taylor and Pam's crib and hung around for a hot tub and blunt for old time's sake, before setting off to our new palace. That night, we crashed asleep the moment we got home. Sleeping on the floor but under a roof, where I could get up in the night to use the loo or look in the fridge. It was weird and exciting. Different from being at Pam and Taylor's because this was home. Over there, we were visitors crashing on the sofa. The bathroom was so small that I had to put one foot in and one foot out of the shower cubicle to close the door—a cute quirk that eventually turned into an agonizing, torturous burden.

But it wasn't as comfortable or as warm as the car. At least a car seat has some sponginess, whereas the garage had a solid concrete floor and there was no underlay to divide the cheap carpet from the concrete. I woke up in the middle of the night and got back in the car where I knew I would be warm and comfy. The next night, I slept on a pile of clothes which wasn't so bad, apart from buttons on jeans and jackets jabbing my ribs.

The first day Gina and Scott had off together, we drove to SwedenWorld. I was thrilled to find that this SwedenWorld sold the same ginger thins and hot dogs as the ones at home. SwedenWorld was my brothers' and my favorite place to go, above any of the museums or pubs that Sunday afternoon traditionally meant. SwedenWorld and antiques fairs, where at least we could let our imaginations run riot with all the stuff we found. Mike loved to dress up in superhero outfits, charging at us with one hand out as if he were flying through the air. Either that or he would find something and make up a new character—his and my favorite was Rainbow Ranger.

At an antiques fair, he found some old flying goggles and a silver piece of rainbow reflective material that he made into a cape. Rainbow Ranger was a goody. Most of his characters were goodies and his friend, Little Rick, was the baddy. Unless they joined forces to both be goodies who fought me, Charlie or Chris—the baddies—but without knowledge that we were the baddies and we thought we were just being attacked.

At SwedenWorld, I loved the displays that represented different rooms. It was like walking through a huge mansion. Browsing there, I started to feel happy desires that existed in a dream instead of some cracked-out desperation. By the time I'd walked around, I had a seven-bedroom-five-master-bedroom-eight-bathroom-three-lounge-five-kitchen house—not to mention a vast array of accessories to furnish each one.

Beyond that, I pictured myself walking on the sand with two children, one of each. Whose were they? Mine, I hoped. A house where I could see, or at least hear, the ocean. Waking up in each of those bedrooms with the sun bleating gently in my face. Then I would walk downstairs into any of my five kitchens to grab a coffee before picking fruit and reading some fantastic book before I really started my day, writing. I yearned for the peace I found in the visions of those rooms, a life I'd not yet tasted but was starting to drool for.

We bought kitchen utensils to cook our own food and cups and plates, a futon for a sofa and somewhere to sleep for Gina and Scott. The plan was to get an interim solution for me until we saw how everything fit. There was a shelf for the telly built into the wall but we still bought a bookshelf that we could throw junk and mail and food on—even underwear, although the thought of any of Scott's boxers landing in my pigeonhole sent shivers down my spine, so knickers became another item I kept in my Just In Case rucksack.

The best part of the trip was that the checkout girl missed the shelving unit and the expensive shower curtain Gina absolutely had to have, and the fanciest duvet, feathers and everything. So we bought that for free. When we realized what had happened, we legged it and Gina took control of the escape before anyone at SwedenWorld figured anything out.

I was getting tired of stealing, too. Scott had no guilt or conscience—he would happily steal his way through life. I didn't consider that I had stolen from the banks, I thought of that as a loan, they could afford it, I'd pay them back later. They'd make sure of that. Although it had crossed my mind to steal from Grandma, I couldn't and I didn't. Instead, I stole from myself, cashed in wads of my soul for crack. But who could count the real cost of the drugs? What was the exchange rate? How much had Hannay's hundred dollars cost me in soul-currency?

I'd robbed myself blind.

The futon was the first and only thing built that day—just so we could sit in the place where we lived and watch the telly that picked up a cable signal from Timothy's. We smoked weed, drank beer, and cooked dinner in our kitchen that had an oven—and now utensils. An actual oven. Who could believe it? And now we had an address, too, where we could have pizza delivered. We kept having to pick it up because none of the pizza joints we spoke to would deliver to "between a ninety-seven, red coupé Acura with seventy-eight thousand on the clock and a Toyota Tundra, grey, maybe silver, with a flat tire on Stoner Avenue."

For the first time in a long time, I felt like I had defeated the odds, accomplished something. Passed something more than a pee test. I could give an address to Mam, and I could imagine the lines on her face dissolving like Gina's. Mam had good teeth, too—she was always flossing and visiting the dentist, and I could picture her smile even though it had been a long time since I'd seen it. The real smile, that is, the one with depth and feeling. Since my brothers died, it was more like an eclipse that happened every few months.

"I'm ready for bed," Gina finally yawned.

"Me too," Scott said. "Babe, get up and let me pull out the futon."

We both stood. "I guess I'll make a bed here out of blankets."

"Yeah. Don't worry, Flip, we'll get a bed or something so you can be comfy. Then maybe we could hang some sheets so you don't have to listen to us," she paused. "Well, you know."

"No! Gina, what do you mean?"

"Well, we live here now."

"Yeah we live here now," Scott piped in.

"Yeah but I'm still not a fucking teenager. And I already lived in dorms. I'm over it. You can pick a night and I'll leave."

"That's not very romantic," Gina said.

"But it is with me behind the cotton sheet? Having an audience is romance to you? Pick a night, it's the only way."

"No. We wanna do it when we wanna do it," Scott finished the argument.

I decided there and then this was a losing battle.

"Give me the keys," I said.

"Why? Where are you going," Gina asked.

"I don't wanna stay in here I'd rather stay in the car."

All the hope I'd felt—the excitement—disappeared. I traipsed out with my rucksack and the keys and made myself comfy like those first days in The Cage—Adam and Dr Drew, the emotional waifs and me—one big, happy family.

CHAPTER ELEVEN

LIFE CAME BACK TO ME IN BURSTS. Swells of jasmine tingled my nose, orchestras of sound—the tweeting birds was my favorite—same as Grandma, the wind pushing me and me pushing back, scalding water drumming on my skin (unlike the lukewarm version at Santa Monica College). Life-candy, and they tasted so sweet—the things that kept me putting one foot in front of the other until I decided on my next move.

I was still sleeping in the car, which I now realized was another blessing in disguise. The car seat was narrower than the one in the Explorer. But for that moment of time, at night, all night, this was my space. I could let as many thoughts float out of me as I wished and watch them suspended in the air in a halo of my cold breath. Each was like an epiphany, transforming me.

Minutes and seconds had at one point churned through my days. Every increment of time dragging. In the garage, time passed easily in blocks. I woke up early, about five—the time I would normally be getting home. I slid out of the car, half paralyzed, and shook the rigor mortis out of my joints. For the first two hours of my day, I hobbled until the stiffness of lying on one side most of the night was paced out of my knees. This had only been a serious problem since staying in the Jeep because of the depth of the vehicle's seat. Switching sides was usually a major logistical ordeal, so I stayed in one place.

I walked half a block to Bundy, and when I got to Santa Monica I crossed the road to get Starbucks, which was good at the time. I was proud to be able to pay for a coffee without rummaging through the rubbish for a cup so I could claim a refill. My pockets jangled with change like my dad's used to. When I was a baby, that sound filled me with fear because it made me think he was rattling apart organ by organ. Now it made me feel like a part of society.

Jose, Gina's boss, had added me to the list of his illegal workers and gave me a job at Thanksgiving, and said I could expect more work at Christmas. All I had to do was give out samples at the door and welcome people. I liked chatting to everyone—this is when Mam shone through me. I remembered her on the market when I could just peek above the stall but was still hidden by the rolls of nets. Phil Collins' "You Can't Hurry Love" blasted on radios all around in static-y, stereo-y unison, and when the chorus played, voices from all over market swelled to the tune. Even those who hated the song hummed under their breaths. I could see their cheeks sucking in and out, silently, but obviously.

Mam would hum and gossip, exchange her nets for cash. Even though I couldn't see, I knew when Vinegar Vera was approaching because Mam would cup my head, her fingers squeezing my crown until I started to get a headache, so I stamped on her thick boots hoping to get her attention. After Vera left, Mam would hold me by my shoulders checking my limbs and counting fingers and toes.

❖

I took my coffee back to bed and smoked a joint and listened to morning radio, which I didn't enjoy as much as *Loveline.* Sometimes Gina would come out to the car early after an argument with Scott and disturb my peaceful entry into the day. Those days, she would top and tail with me on the back seat and even that space became unsacred.

After they left for work and before I started any laundry, I wrapped myself in a blanket and watched the morning chat shows. I missed *Supermarket Sweep* and even Dale Winton and *Trisha,* but not Trisha. Me and Emily watched Dale before she had her class at university, shouting prices of groceries at the telly. Then we'd argue about whether he was gay or not—he seemed to know too much about the price of beans to me. But I liked to make toast with slices of butter and steaming tea to try and feel that moment again. Sometimes it worked.

Jerry Springer seemed too false, so *Jenny Jones* seemed like a good compromise. A healthy dose of pregnant teenagers, drug addicts, failed relationships, and prostitutes, I at least knew all of this was real. Right after Jenny finished, I jumped up and folded whatever I could and threw in a load of laundry. With everything so close at hand, I was getting lazy and complacent in my new surroundings. Gina and Scott might decide to come home for lunch, and, in that case, I had to make the place look unlived in, showroom status—just so they wouldn't moan at me about doing nothing.

Christmas was a few weeks away and Thanksgiving had just passed. My birthday, which is the week before Thanksgiving, had been a drug-less event. I was annoyed that my birth hadn't warranted a couple of wraps of coke cooked into a fresh batch of crack, not even any of wraps to snort. What made Gina and Scott so special? Instead, we went horseback riding. *Fucking horseback riding,* I thought. I went to bed that night with a few of bottles of Cisco—liquid crack—and woke the next day certain I was dying. Gina and Scott had a rude awakening with the sound of my retching. There was no time to hop in the shower cubicle so I could close the door, I rammed my head into the toilet bowl and made myself comfortable. After that, I was off the liquid crack, too.

Gina's mental stability was as reliable as a bus timetable. Dr. Manzard, the shrink, had added this, reduced that—and it had only succeeded in making her fall asleep at eight at night, give or take an hour. I didn't want to sit with Scott, so I would walk around the neighborhood or sit at the beach absorbing the vibrations. The chatter of the wind, the earth's belly rising and falling when it breathes, letting out the day and welcoming the night. Everywhere I looked, there was a tiny miracle happening that I'd not noticed the first time around.

Gina burst through the door one afternoon when I was engrossed in my afternoon session of chat shows. *Montel, Tyra* and, of course, *Oprah. Maury* and all his "guess who the father is," is a drag. The secret was about to be revealed, and I missed it—and she'd just been home for lunch anyway. Gina barreled in—I knew it was her, even though her mouth was open so wide I could only really see her tonsils. *Here we go again,* I thought.

She plummeted to the floor and lay on her back screaming and crying. She'd either not seen me or had chosen not to acknowledge me. I thought the time on the bus was bad, but I wondered if this was it. *Gina is finally insane. This is what happens when you smoke crack for any longer than I did,* I thought. I stood slowly so as not to startle the human equivalent of a mad dog. I hovered over her and she was on her back. I called her name, but she didn't respond. She wouldn't stop crying. I tapped her with the toe of my shoe, almost expecting her to turn around and bite my ankle. But she cried even louder.

I found her handbag dumped by the front door and rummaged through it to find her phone. I scrolled down to Sarah's number and dialed. While I was waiting for her to answer I noticed my heart was pounding. I clutched the phone and squeezed my other hand into a fist. I didn't even realize I couldn't hear Sarah when she answered. It was only when I heard a tiny voice that was too gentle to have come from Gina that I thought it must at least be her voicemail.

"Hold on!" I shouted. "Let me get away from the noise."

I stepped out of the front door but, feeling the cold, went straight into the laundry room three feet from the front door. I closed the door and switched on the dryer for warmth. Now I had some insulation from the world. *Why hadn't I come here before,* I thought.

"Hello?" I said. "Sorry, I had to get out of the room. There was too much noise."

"Hello, Philippa?"

She knows me, I thought. *What has Gina said?*

"Yeah, yeah. That's me," I said. Now all I could think was how was I supposed to make Gina seem crazy when she'd probably made me seem off my rocker, too. "I have an emergency. Gina is lying on the floor crying uncontrollably. She won't respond to anything I say. I don't know what to do."

"Philippa, you must get her to Cedars Sinai." Her voice was gravelly and soft, and I knew I was talking to someone older, someone with some years behind her words, so I listened. "Tell them she's suicidal, and they will admit her for a full evaluation. They'll focus on her meds and see if they need to be changed."

"But tell them she's suicidal? Won't that go on her report or something?"

"Huh? What? No, it's just a technique to make sure she's admitted. This is the only thing we can do now, and Dr Manzard has agreed."

I peeked back in the room where she hadn't stopped crying and looked more pathetic than ever on the floor. I realized this could be real, this time it wasn't one of those acts. I hung up with Sarah and rang Scott.

❖

I'd not been to Cedars Sinai Emergency since I'd broken my wrist, and even then I didn't have a chance to stop and check it out. They drove me straight through on a gurney and loaded me up on drugs. But someone who is suicidal has to wait the same as someone with a common cold. The lady next to us sniffled while Gina clawed at the skin on her wrists. If she were really serious, wouldn't she have done it by now? But since she was only metaphorically on a ledge and not actually, they treated her with as much urgency as if she had a boil on her foot.

I don't remember much about the intake process. The only image that comes to mind is when I turned around when Scott and I left the mental ward, a subliminal response from watching too many Lifetime movies with Grandma and on my own. There was a small porthole window that Gina peeked through. Her face was so contorted it seemed her head must be made of papier-mâché. It was worth waiting a few hours to palm her off onto someone else for a week. A whole week, I breathed. At least they could sedate her. If I had a tranquilizer gun maybe I wouldn't care so much, either.

Scott drove us home, the music booming, releasing the obligation for conversation. At home, he sat on the futon leaning forward with his head in his hands. Gina would be in the mental ward for a week, but they could bump up her incarceration another week if she didn't show improvement.

I switched on the telly to keep the silence filled and to distract me from the discomfort of being alone with Scott. He was a loose cannon, flying into rages without any obvious trigger. I was alert to his energy. It was as if Tony's ghost were prompting him what to do, living on through Scott. Our Chris had sent me two shot glasses and a mini bottle of tequila that had a hallucinogenic worm floating around. I used the shot glasses but was contemplating the worm. Can I drink a worm? Do I have to chew it? What happens if I do accidentally? Scott had taken a frying pan and smashed them all in the sink.

All my nerves stood at attention. I could feel the adrenalin rushing through my body. *Just let him try anything. Just one thing, and he won't know what hit him.*

"What d'you do that for yer wanker? My brother sent me that, not like I can replace it. How'd you feel if I smashed yer last brain cell in?"

He turned and looked at me, but didn't say a word. Didn't need to. For the rest of the time Gina was in the mental ward I prepared myself. I carried a weapon everywhere—usually a metal pole, but if I lost that I'd use a vegetable knife. I wasn't looking to kill, just escape alive and maybe maim a bit. I took my weapon of choice to bed, in the shower, everywhere I went in case he jumped out of a bush.

I remembered Tony's first attack vividly, like I remember the fire. I was mad that day because my jeans didn't fit properly, and they somehow were tighter.

"Nellie..."

"Nellie..."

"Nellie the elephant..."

My brothers—Chris, Charlie, and Mike at the time, but Sammy was about to make an appearance—all started going on about my weight, again.

Mam was upstairs sorting laundry—at this point, she was eight months pregnant and hardly able to fit behind the market stall.

The lounge door was closed to keep in the heat but it was flung open and a rush of icy air sent chills through me. A plate on a stand that Gran had given Mam from a trip to Rhyl wobbled, and when it fell chips of plaster scattered on the carpet. Tony stood in the doorway, arms spread wide as if expecting us to run and welcome him.

He wore a long, dark brown suede overcoat with a seventies-style collar that I'd never seen him in before. His eyes were disguised behind dark glasses.

"Hi, kids," he said.

None of us answered. The tension was visible.

"Well don't be so fucking rude! Isn't anyone going to say 'hello'? I am the father of your unborn brother or sister, after all."

We sat in silence. Still. I followed him with my eyes as he paced the room, his jacket flowing behind him like the evil weirdo out of a comic book.

His breathing was heavy and deep, his breath was thick with alcohol, whatever kind I didn't know—I knew he drank lager and whisky. He rambled under his breath, spitting. Charlie was lying on the floor, hands propping his head, sucking his thumb. When Tony's shin brushed his face, he flinched. Mike ducked under the tail of his cloak and for a second disappeared. Tony stopped at the armchair where Chris sat and removed his glasses. I could see the color had drained from Tony's eyes and instead of blue they were a cold grey, as if they had changed season from summer to winter. He gritted his teeth, and I could see his jawbone flexing under his skin.

"You're the eldest. Are you not gonna make your brothers and sister say 'ello?" he said and leaned toward Chris, who seemed to freeze. I held my breath, too.

"You're drunk Tony. Leave us alone."

Faster than I could blink, Tony's hand slapped Chris's cheek. The sound rippled in the silence like a belly flop. Chris clutched the side of his face, and I could see the remote control shaking in his hand and his Adam's apple bungee up and down his throat. I knew he was fighting tears. The remote dropped from his hand, and he grabbed his jacket and left.

"It'll be the same for all of you if you don't show more respect," Tony slurred.

"What a nob," I muttered. He came stomping towards me and before I could move or duck, I felt my cheek stinging from the back of his hand. His finger whipped my nose and tears pricked my eyes. My nose felt like it was dripping and when I wiped it with my hand, not the way Mam taught me, blood smeared across my fist.

Charlie ran out of the room, and Tony bolted after him. He ran for the stairs but Tony grabbed his collar and yanked him back.

"Mam! Mam! Tony hit Flip. Mam!"

Tony covered Charlie's mouth with his hand, but it was too late because Mam had heard and she came thundering down the stairs.

"Get away from my children. Get your rotten hands off them."

She turned to the three of us huddled in the doorway wondering what had caused all this. "Go in the lounge and close the door."

We knew *that* tone, and it was the one not to ignore. If any of us disobeyed her while she was using *that* tone and she didn't have Tony with his hands around her throat, you could be sure she'd slap our legs with her hairbrush. One time she broke it right on Charlie's head.

They argued back and forth behind the closed door.

"I've told you not to come home like this. You know what you get like—"

"Shut the fuck up. This is all your fuckin' fault anyway—"

It was ugly. The ugliest day of my life to that point. Frightening. The most frightening day of my life to that point. But it was just the start of those types of days.

The piano was outside the lounge door. The lid was being slammed up and down, rusty notes bleeding out from years of happy abuse. What was happening?

"Kids! Kids? Run. Get help," Mam's voice boomed through the door, and we knew it was serious. Charlie turned the knob and slightly opened the door. There was Mam backed against the piano in her red plaid dress. The size of her pregnancy made things awkward, but it certainly didn't stop him from having a lumberjack grip on her throat, the throat that was allowing his baby to breathe.

I tried to cover Mike's eyes but he brushed my hand out of his face. We fell away from the door and let it shut behind us.

I scanned the room for a way out. The windows in the lounge had locks, since we were such a hi-tech family with all the mod cons. It was when we moved to Victoria Crescent that we got a color telly, and we were the second to last house on our street to get a video player.

Outside the door there was silence, which was more worrying than Mam's screams. Charlie pulled open the door again, and they were gone. There was a trail of destruction for us to follow, a tipped-up table, decapitated ornaments, crooked pictures on the walls. We saw the fight had moved into the kitchen. Mam had put the dinner table between her and him, and they were chasing around it. I legged it out of the front door and across the street to the neighbors' house to ask them for the first time, of many, to call the police.

Gina called from a payphone begging for fags. Hysterical, she was. We walked in, and she ran up to us in a hospital type gown. She had bite marks down her arm—deep red and purple gouges. She looked as if she'd caught some horrendous flesh-eating disease. In fact, that was my first thought, maybe a cute attempt to delude myself from her psychotic reality.

150

They all wore the gowns, the patients. I was too afraid to check whether they wore underwear. I asked Gina, and she nodded towards the few who she'd noticed consistently dressed commando. We sat outside smoking in a courtyard, which was supposed to be welcoming, I gathered, but was actually full of bird crap and creaky, off-balance chairs. But better that than the smell of rotting minds and the antiseptic used to clean up the ghosts of rotted minds that lingered inside.

"I lost my job," she started.

"What?" I shouted, a blurb on a tannoy reminded me where I was, and my anger slid back down my throat and formed a toxic pool in my stomach instead.

"Yeah that's why I lost it a bit, I suppose."

"What 'appened there then?" I asked pointing to her arm.

"Oh this," she seemed surprised. "Well, I needed a smoke. You understand, right?" That wide, white grin flashed at me. Now it reminded me of an evil clown grin instead of an amazing Hollywood smile.

"What happened with your job?" I was afraid of the answer.

"This woman was being a bitch. Asking me to weigh all this ham and turkey. Fuck her, nothing I did made her happy."

"So you 'anded in yer notice?"

"Hell no! I threw all the ham and turkey at her. Then I grabbed hams out of the fridges behind the register and threw them at her and anyone else who came in."

I could imagine the whole scene playing out. Gina yanking the hams, wrapped in gold, out of the huge display cases, and throwing them—huge gold nuggets—across the counter. Hitting tables and chairs like pinballs and collapsing under the weight, wood splinters flying everywhere.

I tried to disguise my shock, propped my dropping jaw between my thumb and finger. But my eyes were so readable.

"You tell me you wouldn't have done the same?" she asked.

"I'd, erm, like to think not. So you don't have a job now?" I didn't wait for that answer. "We have rent due soon, I don't know how were gonna make it."

"Sweetie, we got your money, and you'll be working again soon. Jose doesn't blame you."

I felt the toxic pool in my stomach spread through my bloodstream and intoxicate me with anxiety and anger. Scott, so devoted, told Gina he was taking the whole week off work to make sure he could see her both visiting hours. There were only two opportunities a day to visit an hour at a time. Once in the afternoon and then the evening. I didn't want either of them.

I knew without any doubt I had to get out and as soon as possible.

CHAPTER TWELVE

❖

ON THE THIRD DAY OF GINA'S INCARCERATION, I TOOK
OFF TO SEE GRANDMA AND FE SINCE I WAS SO CLOSE. I
missed them, their comfort, the security of home.

Grandma sat on the front porch dozing and Fe's silhouette
appeared behind the screen as I reached the top of the grassy
slope. A faint aroma of one of Fe's dishes floated out when she
swung open the door. I could almost chew it, taste it, but the
name remained on the tip of my tongue.

"Bloody Dude!" she shouted and Grandma's eyes sparked
awake.

"Hi sweetheart," Grandma opened her arms and I fell into
them. This was where I needed to be. I felt safe. My fears
floated away on the passing breeze, and I didn't feel as if I
were pinned down and squirming.

"Honey, are you still doing drugs?" Grandma asked.

I could only smile. Of all the things she didn't remember,
that was the one thing she did.

"No, Grandma, I'm not. I gave it up. I go to meetings for drug
addicts now," which was a lie because we'd not been there since
we'd found warmth in our own home—we didn't need it now.

"Dude! You look chunky, dude," Fe laughed. That same
old, cackling, machine-gun laugh that was contagious. I did
grab my waist to feel the flab, but I couldn't help laughing with
her. "You eat a lot? You hungry? I make dinner already."

She led me towards the kitchen, shuffling quickly in her
slippers. I walked slowly, feeling the creaks and croaks of the
hardwood floor. Breathing the dusty air. Betty the cleaner
obviously still came. The lounge, which Grandma called the
den, was dark and airless. I sometimes thought it must be the
same way on the inside of a coffin.

The dining room was a stark contrast—windows open, air
gushing in, a strip of blue sky framed in the window above the

white trellis fence. On the table was a bunch of flowers in a vase surrounded with notepads with a Hello Kitty print, an army of pink nail polish and crisps and sweets that Fe munched on throughout the day.

It seemed so familiar and yet so strange. I had been here before, but it was in a different lifetime. In a sense, it *was* a different lifetime, because this was the longest—three weeks—that I had not had some type of amphetamine racing through my bloodstream in ten years or thereabouts. It was like déjà vu, a common feeling for me while I was getting back to normal. My normal, that is.

The aroma from the kitchen was so strong now my taste buds were drooling, but all I could think of was the weight I'd gained. I thought back to the days in the car and how I'd slumped around thinking. Just thinking. I was angry at myself for being so lazy. Why hadn't I written something? Exercised?

Now look at me.

Fe called me from the kitchen, interrupting more thinking. By now, the suspense of what she was cooking had snowballed into unbearable excitement.

I looked around as I had when me and Emily had first touched down in LA. Eyes starting at the ceiling and working down the walls, the sink, chipped tiles on the countertop, the ancient microwave that flickered on the inside like a dying neon sign in a dying neighborhood. For Grandma, it was memories of a life past but that she didn't want to move on from. When she was married with kids. Their heights penciled into the paintwork in several rooms. Ali had been the same height since the age of ten. It led me to believe that while her height and body had kept girlish qualities her head and personality had instead expanded in monstrous sizes.

I could understand why Grandma wanted to cling to her past. In the basement of Mam's house in England (not the one that burned down, a house that her mam gave her), I had a collection of memories that included T-shirts that belonged to Mike and Sammy. When I went home, I took them out and tried to remember them wearing them. The folds in the fabric when they wore them and the heat of their bodies.

The kitchen was the hub of any household I'd belonged to. It was no different here. When my eyes finally rested on the stovetop, the answer to the riddle of the smell was there in thick veins of pure pig belly fat. My stomach lurched and my rose-tinted memories evaporated.

"Wanna stay por dinner, ehm Bloody Dude, eh?" Fe said, her whole face smiling. She took so much pleasure in preparing what she considered to be fine meals, and many of them were, but this particular meal I considered to be life-threatening. Even so, it was difficult to turn down the love she had kneaded into every mouthful. I would find some way to sit at the dinner table and pretend to eat it.

"Sure, I'd love to!"

At least I wouldn't have to go straight back to the car. I needed to get home early enough to get the keys and that was it. I had four more days to survive without Gina, unless they decided to keep her, and when she did come home I had an undetermined amount of time to survive with her. Sometimes I felt I could make more progress by standing in one place and beating my head on a brick wall. That would at least save time.

"You still live wid Gina and her honey? What his name?"

"Yup," I sighed.

"What's up, dude? You don't like it? You stopped taking drogs?"

"We've not taken anything. Just weed, we smoke weed. I still sleep in the car cos I don't want to listen to them doing it—"

Fe burst into a fit of laughter. Her favorite topic.

"Dey have de sex wid you der, dude?"

"No! That's why I stay in the car. I don't wanna listen. But Gina went nuts, you know—crazy, and got locked up in Cedars so now I'm left with psycho, violent Scott."

"Dude, you need to leave. Quick! Why didn't you call de rehab place Ali tell you to? They crazy I tell you!" She left the kitchen and while she was gone I went through the laundry room to my old bathroom and room.

I stopped at the mirror, lifted my shirt, and twisted from side to side, inspecting the source of my chunkiness. I stood to the side and breathed in and out, in and out, inflating my belly as much as possible to see how big it got. I looked pregnant. I exhaled and shifted my shoulders back, holding in my breath, and looked okay.

If I shed my physical weight, I thought all the other weights would shift too. The weight on my heart and my soul would lighten, and I might be able to breathe again.

I gave up manipulating my breath to look fat and thin and peered into my eyes instead—getting close to the mirror to see what I looked like, while breathing in spurts so as not to fog the mirror. My eyes had flecks of brown and green color instead of black discs. Fine lines had appeared around my eyes, and I wasn't even thirty yet.

Fe returned to the kitchen clutching a piece of paper.

"Bloody Dude, I have de nomber. Give dem a call now."

I hesitated. But what was the point? I couldn't come back to Grandma's and living with Gina, and Scott was becoming hazardous.

"Acton Rehabilitation Center, Dave speaking, how may I help?"

"Er, hello?" I didn't have any idea what to say.

"This is Dave. How can I help? Why don't you start with your name?"

"Flip, erm, Philippa."

"Okay Flip. Nice speakin' with ya. You know someone here or you need a bed?"

I was glad he seemed to be able to read my mind.

"I need to check myself in."

It was bizarre hearing those words leave my mouth. I couldn't possibly need rehab, just the bed. I didn't have a skinhead, or use needles. People don't go to rehab for coke. Then I thought about the actress from EastEnders with a hole in her nose from too much snorting.

"Okay, let me see...There will be a free bed in four weeks. Shall I pencil your name in?"

"Four weeks?" It seemed like an eternity. "Okay, yeah. But write it in Biro, I mean pen, use a pen, Dave. How long is it?"

"Ninety days."

"Ninety days? What about the movie where it's twenty-eight?"

"Just like you say, sweetheart, a movie. The twenty-eight-day program costs money, two and a half grand. If you got that, you can do it. Shall I still use pen?"

"What about visits and getting out?"

"After sixty days—"

"Sixty days!?"

"Yeees, after sixty days, you get a thirty-hour pass off the compound, and you can have two weekend visits."

I was silent. That seemed like an eternity, too. As if I would be agreeing to a trip to the Bermuda Triangle. But what else could I do?

"Are there phones? Can my mam send me letters?"

"Suuure, you can use the phones from six a.m. until ten p.m. And mail is Monday through Friday. But we don't provide stamps, so you gotta get someone to send them."

I quickly calculated the time differences between LA and France, LA and England, and LA and Australia, on both coasts, for all the people I hoped to keep in touch with. I was getting frustrated, and Dave was calm and chirpy, his happiness grating my nerves.

"Okay, yeah, write it in pen, Dave. I'll be there."

I put the phone back in the cradle and stood alone in a room with people. What was I doing? Why don't I just go home? Be with Mam, be with my brothers. Something in my gut told me to stay, and this time I decided to go with my instincts. What good would come from going home? How could they help me? *I 'ave to help myself*, I thought. But I felt as if I were leaving them the way I'd left my other brothers. Turned my back on all of them. Why did I deserve to be saved, again?

I sucked in a deep breath, and that somehow stopped me from shattering into a million pieces. I sometimes imagined my body disintegrating into molecules, and I would evaporate into the air unnoticed.

Breathe.

I turned and smiled.

"Done."

Grandma had come in from the porch and was sniffing around the stove.

"What did you do, honey?"

"I'm going to rehab, Grandma."

"Oh, honey. What is that? A play or something?"

Fe laughed, then said, "It's so she won't do drogs any more?"

"Honey, you were taking drugs? Why would you do that to yourself?"

"Grandma I told you that. That's why I can't live here now." I could see sadness in her eyes, maybe because of her once-razor memory that had become blunt with the years—or maybe for what I'd done to myself. In that moment, she looked so frail and tiny. I hugged her as tight as I thought possible without hurting her.

"Let's sit down and 'ave dinner," I said, taking her hand as if nothing had changed.

❖

Four days later, Gina came home. She said she felt better, but somehow I didn't believe her. I wasn't sure what or whom to believe anymore, but Gina and Scott weren't high on my list. I had to try and stay with them until my date at rehab came up. I didn't know where else I could go.

Scott went back to work when Gina came home, but Christmas was a few days away, then New Year, then rent. There was no way we would make the rent. If we ended up back in the car, it would be for a few weeks only—for me. Even though the rules and thought of rehab scared me, it was also like a secret weapon, a position of strength they knew nothing about.

My household chores became sloppy or ignored. Scott moaned he had no clothes, the dishes piled up, the cat litter stank, and I could not care less. Even though I looked a bit chunky, according to Fe, I had pushed some of the boulders out of the way of my path. I felt airy, as if I could run a million miles and not run out of breath. Throughout Christmas and New Year, this is how I looked at them, as two boulders I had somehow heaved out of the way.

January second was rent day. Timothy had been away on New Year's Day, so that was a day of reprieve. Today, I would have to try to avoid him. My check was a few days away, Gina had nothing, Scott had only worked six hours in two weeks.

"Don't worry, don't worry," Gina kept saying.

Now I wasn't worried. I had a plan.

Gina still hadn't found a job since the HoneyBear Ham saga and hung around at home most of the time trying to define herself. Dissecting years of childhood, her relationships with violent sobbing followed by loud, rumbling belly laughs. But she was okay, she reassured me.

I told her I was going to Ralphs to buy dinner. It was an excuse to leave, but I decided to go anyway. From the pedestrian crossing at Bundy and Wilshire, across six lanes of traffic, I could see a white plastic bag flapping around in a muddy puddle. I thought I spotted my second favorite shade of green, money. My first favorite was weed.

I looked at the other people who were waiting to cross, wondering if any of them had spotted it, too. There was an old couple, I was safe there, and an older Mexican lady pushing a pram that I knew I could outrun. The people across the street were the problem, if one had noticed the bag, there was no possible way I could beat them to it.

The light changed. Before the walk signal appeared, I shot off the curb. I kept my focus on the bag. No one walking towards us had seen it, and I knew I had a chance. My heart started racing, and my feet followed. I felt as if I'd been running for miles but in reality was stepping into the fourth lane—over halfway there. I stooped and grabbed it, bundled it up and coddled it under my hoodie. I didn't dare turn around—afraid I'd feel the weight of a heavy hand on my shoulder at any minute.

I walked quickly to the car park behind Literatti Café and pulled out the bag. I gasped when I looked inside. The dollar bill I'd seen was part of a whole family, second cousins included. I pulled it out and counted. There was a magical hundred and twenty-three dollars in ones and fives, waitress money—I knew that from my days at Rock 'n' Rollers.

Inside me, there was a shift in emotion. Sudden and slight but deep, as if the plates on the earth's surface were rearranging. A new landscape was forming—a strange sensation that something somewhere was looking after me, so big that it existed in the air. Unexplainable.

I left the money in the plastic bag, bought dinner and went home. I was excited, inspired, and there was no way I was telling anyone about my find. Now I had two secret weapons. I was safe.

At home, Gina was whooping for joy. *Fuckin' 'ell, she knows about the money*, I thought.

"Why you so bleedin' 'appy?" I asked.

"I got a call from my counselor on the psych ward. There's a group therapy session tonight for people with bipolar at UCLA. Wanna come?"

"I don't really 'ave a choice, do I? Unless I wanna stay 'ome with Scott."

So much for containing my anger. Yet again I was left with a choice without choice. *Three weeks and I'm out of 'ere. Maybe two weeks and six days. Stay calm. Don't hit her,* I told myself. I was so close it wasn't worth the fight and the uncertainty of where I'd live for the next few weeks.

Only people with bipolar were allowed to sit in the meeting and they could somehow tell I wasn't one of them. I was glad of the excuse to leave. I had to think. It was chilly outside, but my blood was boiling with compressed anger. I paced up and

160

down in front of phone box thinking of answers, not knowing anymore if I could contain my anger for all those weeks.

I stopped, struck with an answer as I had been all day. Mysterious doorways opening, paths appearing as if from nowhere. It was such a mystical day, and I stuck with my hunches. Mike and Sammy were looking out for me from somewhere, I felt. It wasn't really a mystery. I dug in my pockets for my phone card and walked back to the phone.

"Hello?"

I felt my body breathe in relief when Paul answered. There was a possibility he wouldn't if he didn't recognize the number.

"Hi, it's me."

I knew my accent would give me away. *Can you not change that gawdawful accent*, he said to me when we used to work together. He was my boss, at one point, when I worked in public relations before Rock 'n' Rollers. *When you stop being gay, I'll stop being a northerner,* I retaliated. Soon after that, when I questioned my own sexuality, whenever we spoke he always asked, *Are you gay or straight this week?* We hit it off from the start, and years after we left the job Paul shifted his role from protector in the office to protector in the outside world. He walked me through unwanted pregnancy, unwanted sexuality, unwanted visa issues.

"Honey! How are you? Gay or straight?"

"Good. Good. An' I'm not sure. How are you?"

"That's it after all this time? Last time we spoke you'd just broken your wrist. You thought you might have a crush on that Gina girl. What's happening now?"

"Paul, I'm in trouble."

"So what's new? Tell me."

I spoke quickly, scared that Gina would walk up on me at any minute. I kept my eye on the area I thought she would walk out of. It was black apart from unknown noises and voices that shed light on the darkness.

"Pack your stuff and come over tonight. I have a spare room you can use until you go to rehab."

"Tonight? They'd kill me. They're both a little nuts, Paul. I think I should move my belongings slowly so they don't notice. I'm afraid of what will happen otherwise."

"I think you need to get the hell outta there, sweetie. But just let me know what you want to do, my door's open."

All the signs were screaming at me to get out. The money, rehab, a place to go before rehab. My mind was racing. How would I do it? How would they respond? How would I respond to their response?

"Hey," Gina said.

I jumped back to the present. She blabbed on and on about the meeting, which to me sounded like a huge fan whirring in my ear. I was still trying to make sense of my jumble of thoughts, find some order out of the chaos. I was mostly scared of them killing me. I wasn't sure whether that was my overactive imagination or a real risk. I decided tomorrow I would leave. I would tell them I'm staying at a friend's and take my most precious belongings. I would come back for the rest of my stuff, tell them I'm heading out for a pint of milk and never return. *That's my safest bet,* I thought.

I remember my dad doing that all the time when me and my brothers were young. He came back every few weeks until after the divorce. Then he never came back.

Gina and Scott were lying on the futon watching telly, and I was sitting on an armchair we'd found on the street and had dusted off for the house. I pictured the number of mites and bugs climbing through my clothes to suck my blood through my skin. I shivered and itched. I was looking at the closet doors trying to imagine what belongings I had behind each. Where should I start?

"I'm going to bed," Gina said.

I looked at the time: eight p.m.

"Awww! Are yer kiddin' me mate? I 'ave to sit outside all night now, or sit and watch you sleep? No way. It's fuckin' ridiculous."

I paused. For a second. "Look, I've been offered somewhere to stay. I wasn't gonna go, but I can't live like this." I picked up the car keys from the table and headed for the door.

"You can't leave," Gina demanded. She was now standing, and so was Scott.

"Am goin'. That's it."

"Put those keys down! Where are you taking the keys?"

"Am getting my stuff out the car, chill out. I'm not nickin' your precious vee-hicle." I pronounced the "h" in vehicle, the way they did it in America that always made me laugh.

As I walked down the side of the garage, their voices slipped through the cracks in the drafty windows, sounding like two hissing snakes.

I checked the car for any stray belongings and checked my rucksack for the essentials, mainly the money that was still wrapped in the plastic bag I'd found it in, mud and all. When I went back to return the keys and get my weed, I was thinking about bus routes and timetables. I should call Paul the moment I leave. Maybe walk a bit in case they follow me. Try to lose them.

Later, I cursed myself for being so distracted. Before taking one step through the front door, Gina gripped the freshly knitted bones on my right wrist. I was too weak to wriggle free. As my foot landed, Scott pushed behind me and locked the only way in and out of the room.

I was tragically aware that this could end in death. My mind flashed back to the night of the fire. Dropping to my knees and praying for an answer from God. There was no time for that now, so I had to rely on my wits.

Out of the three of us, I had the most sanity—but that wasn't saying too much. I'd seen movies with scenes just like this one, and they never ended well. Never.

I broke away from Gina's hold and stepped into the room. The bag of weed was on the table, I scanned for anything else, but had all the essentials in my rucksack. In the closets above my head were my photos and letters. There was no way I could get those now. I would just have to hope. At this point I was hoping for my life.

"You can't go now, Philippa," Gina said. She'd moved into the room, too, and was on the opposite side of the table. If I leapt on her now, I could gain leverage and height from the table. But Scott would leap on me and beat me to a bloody pulp. I wasn't in the mood for that.

Instead, we eyed each other across the table. But my peripheral vision was alert to dark shadows approaching, evil enemies trying to trick me.

"You can't keep me 'ere. Why d'you think I wanna stay? So I can support the two of yer and sleep in a car. No. No way, mate."

"Y'owe us money, you spent all ya money on weed. It's your turn to pay the rent."

"You've got to be kidding. You're more nuts than the doctors think."

"Don't talk to her like that," Scott said and started walking towards me.

I walked to him, but with the intention of legging it through the front door. He tried to grab me, but I pushed his arms to the side. I got to the door and wriggled with the lock. My hands were shaking, my breath quivering. I was yanked away from the door by the scruff of my neck. Scott came up and stood in front of me. I didn't know where Gina was.

I tried to force past him, but he grabbed me by my throat and held me at arm's length. I swung my fists, but I couldn't reach. His expression slithered into a smile.

Fuck you! I thought.

I didn't want to kick in case he tripped me up by grabbing my leg. I struggled to loosen his grip on my throat. He squeezed. I choked. We spun around. I beat his arms with my fists and suddenly hit his elbow so it bent the wrong way. Crack! He yelped and let go.

I fell. Back and back and back. *Crash.*

My left shoulder and arm, hip and knee dangled outside the

glass-paneled door. The frost nipped at my skin. For a second, there was silence. Peace. You wouldn't think this was happening.

"You did this! You did this!" Gina screamed. There she was. The lunatic.

My rucksack, I thought. I saw it just behind them. I wriggled my limbs out of the doorframe, jagged, shark's-teeth-shaped glass dragging across my jacket, etching my skin. Wood splintered off, small spears stabbing through my jeans. If I was bleeding or wounded, I didn't feel it. I plowed forward, head first, ripping past them.

I thought I'd made it. Just as I was reaching for my rucksack, Scott came behind me and put my head in a chokehold. My eyes bulged, and I noticed he was barefoot. I lifted my leg and slammed my heel down on top of his foot. His arm went limp around my neck, and I held onto it and threw him over my shoulder—a well-practiced judo move.

Scott lay on the floor. Gina's screams were as loud and disturbing as a gunshot. Until now, I'd not heard her and wondered if she'd been like that this whole time. I stamped my foot on Scott's stomach, grabbed the weed, barged past Gina, knocking her onto the sofa, and slung my rucksack on my shoulder.

I ran. I didn't look back, just ran. I listened for footsteps following me, for screeching tires pulling out.

I stopped at 7-ELEVEN—for the longest time I thought the name of the shop represented its hours of operation. I finally dared to look behind me. I saw no one. The adrenalin that had been fueling my courage drained from me, and I started to shake as if having withdrawals. I went inside and bought a phone card and called Mam. An older man, his decade indeterminable, lay groaning next to the phone boxes asking for change.

"Mam. Can you 'ear me?"

"Yes, love. What's wrong? You sound upset."

I was never so thankful to hear Mam's voice.

"Go to Paul's or get a room. Promise me you'll find somewhere safe?" she said after I told her about the fight.

"I will, Mam. I will."

"I'm just glad you're away from those drug-crazed lunatics," she said.

I called Paul, but he wasn't home. Fe didn't answer, either.

I headed up Bundy back towards Ralphs. I'd seen a motel up that way. I checked in.

I sat on the bed with the lights on, rucksack by my side, staring at the door.

Petrified.

CHAPTER THIRTEEN

A WOMAN DIED.

It happened at the first meeting I attended at Acton Rehabilitation Center, five hours after my arrival onto the compound—five hours after I'd been stripped of my mouthwash because of the alcohol in it, five hours after I became a patient and a number and my horizons were blocked in by a fishnet fence.

Dusty red mountains heaved out of the surrounding landscape, the rushing howl of coyotes whipping through the air. Log cabins surrounded by trees.

Those first idyllic moments were just that, an idyllic vision. It turned out the log cabins were for men only and the mountains were a tease. They dangled in the scenery, but we could never get there, not until the ninety days were up. Even an escape didn't warrant hiding in a mountain. Anyone could walk out at any time and the train station was a few miles away.

I was hustled into a waiting room, clinical and small. It got chilly quickly because the door opened and closed to a cast of patients. Most of them stopped and said, *Welcome. My name is...do you have a cigarette?* Or more commonly, *Do you got a smoke?* The short wait cost me nearly a whole pack of fags. That was three or four days' worth of rations. I'd only bought one carton, the most patients are allowed to have, and thought that would last me forty days and nights but without giving any away. *Damn it!* I thought. I was hardly one to say "no," otherwise I probably wouldn't have ended up in rehab. This could cost me dearly. Problem being that I'd not told anyone I smoked cigarettes, and I didn't know who I could ask to send me any.

The whole time I was busy saying hello and handing all my fags out, a woman sat across from me whimpering. She was held in the arms of a much larger woman who was quite possibly her girlfriend.

It was an hour before Sheryl called me into the room in the back where I'd seen the hysterical woman go before me. I picked up from the goodbyes that the larger woman was her sister and she was hysterical because she had to leave her kids. Her name was Ashley and she had to do this thing or she would die. Her sister kept repeating those words to her. I thought it was a wee bit dramatic and not very friendly or hopeful. I'd not thought of the addiction as killing me. *I* was killing me. The addiction seemed a fun ride to pursue death in.

And it was.

The coke, the booze, the ecstasy, the raves. How could death be more fun? I felt guilty that that would be the way I would die when I couldn't imagine, couldn't bear to imagine, the terrors of my brothers' deaths.

Crack changed everything.

Crack showed me life by putting me on the brink of death.

But I felt like a failure and a coward, as I had after Mike and Sammy died. *If I couldn't save them, then I should have died with them,* I'd thought. Here I was again, cheating Death that was rightfully mine.

Sheryl asked me when was the last time I had used. I thought for a minute. There had been no crack for a couple of months. The ham bakers at HoneyBear Ham scored some coke for us at a get-together they had in the kitchen after the shop had closed. It didn't rank anywhere near the quality I used to buy from Ron, that Scott eventually rocked up into crack. I understood the expression "bubblegum drug," which is the feeling of snorting cocaine after having dabbled in crack. Whereas coke used to lift me to the horizons of the universe, now it was as fun as a flavorless stick of Juicy Fruit. But it was better than nothing.

I finished the bag of weed I'd risked my life running back into the room for on the night I'd left Scott and Gina. I missed weed the most—it was a veil between the daily absurdities of life and insanities of my mind. I didn't want to call Gina's dealer in case he tipped her off where and when we planned to meet. The painkillers I was given for my wrist helped lull me into sleep, especially when I doubled the recommended dose.

Then I thought about the slug of morphine, legal heroin, a kind doctor had injected into my vein just days earlier. Paul offered me work in his office as well as a place to stay. Before work, I woke up early to walk and buy a coffee. I kept my focus on the pavement in consideration of any crack smokers who would probably have intense paranoia. Even though I knew my presence alone would make them feel as if an army were about to descend on them. But I couldn't be certain I wouldn't jump in to ask for a hit, either.

On my last day of work before rehab, I was stretching up to a shelf when my arm dislocated from my shoulder. The doctor in emergency asked me if I wanted ibuprofen or morphine to dull the pain of the shoulder relocation. Since I'd learned morphine was legal heroin, I took that option.

I knew I'd made the right decision when I wobbled out onto the streets of LA with kaleidoscope vision and jelly limbs. The old familiar sensation of a beating, disorienting sun blinding my way. Where will I end up? I giggled to myself and breathed deeply at the clutch of Vicodin I had for later. I couldn't believe my luck. I'd not been this relaxed for years, not since I'd adopted the boulder-sized problem of Gina on crack. Just for fun, I stopped to call her.

"Hello?" she said, putting on her depressed voice, probably because she didn't recognize the number I'd called from, and might need to pretend she was broke or busy. I'd seen this act live. The pressure of answering the call creased her forehead.

"Gina! My fuckin' shoulder just fell out! This is not a joke. I'm in a lot of pain and 'ad to go to the 'ospital. This is all cos of that fuckin' accident," I growled at her.

She er, ered down the phone. I hung up because I knew the raucous laugh that was about to blurt from my gut would tip her off that I got good drugs, even though what I said was essentially true.

It didn't seem the type of detail that would help my admittance into Acton, so I tucked that memory behind my smile.

The day after that, me, Fe and Grandma hung out on the end of Santa Monica Pier, all of us eating chips and salsa. Fe ordered us margaritas on the rocks to quench our salty thirst. I didn't think this would matter to Sheryl, but the more I went into detail, the more her head shook.

"Honey, that gonna stay between you and me," she said. "And, of course, the good Lord."

I didn't understand the big deal, and I was angry that she'd brought God into it but didn't allow it to show. Little did I know most people drove into Acton smoking crack pipes and injecting heroin laced with coke or speed. I was forced to lie my way into a program based on honesty, and that suited me just fine.

"Okay, honey, I just gotta check through your belongings, then you can go see your room."

She made it sound so exciting, "my room." *A penthouse suite or even the garage minus Gina and Scott*, I thought. I was so desperate I would have taken a tent or a kennel as options. At that moment, Ashley walked past me looking much chirpier, and I could only imagine she was excited about her room, too.

Sheryl gave me a feeling of warmth. Not the same warmth as morphine in an IV drip, a comfort warmth. Her white hair against her brown face gave me a perception of wisdom or that she at least knew a thing or two. Her accent was Southern, I think, and I thought any minute she would whip out a plate of rice and chicken to feed me. All the counselors had been addicts or drunks themselves, but I couldn't imagine Sheryl in any of the states I had ended up in.

"This is all good, honey. But make sure you don't give out none of them cigarettes," she said as she pulled out the carton. "Oh, they'll ask ya ai'ight. They'll be throwin' themselves atcha feet." She paused to look at me before routing some more, "Nail clippers aren't allowed honey. I have to keep them here 'til ya leave us again."

❖

Sirens wailed through the silence and stopped outside the dorm where the dead woman was found collapsed. Natural causes—probably accelerated by years of drug abuse and drinking—was the cause of death.

At least she'd died sober.

Thank God she had a chance to find sobriety, were the whispers I heard in the meeting. My first thought was pity. *Poor sod wasn't even drunk or high. Didn't even get to be wasted one last time. When I die, I don't want to feel it, just hit me with a bus or summat.*

"Excuse me. Excuse me," a voice interrupted me talking to myself.

I looked up and smiled through my fear.

"Hi, my name's Roland," he said and extended his arm.

"Flip," I reached for his hand.

"Welcome, Flip. You obviously new, and you in the best place. What was your drug of choice?"

"Crack."

"Crack! You?"

"Yeah. Why not?" *Am I not good enough to be a crack addict?* I thought.

"No reason, honey. You don't look like the typical crackhead, that's all. Anyway, I'm gonna have to ask you to move. You see, there's gender-designated seating in this meeting. I need you to sit over there."

I looked to where he was pointing at the gaggle of women clad in county-issued denim jackets, one row twisting around to speak to the row behind. Ashley wasn't in this meeting, and I wondered which anonymous group she belonged to. Next to me was a black woman dressed in an outfit nice enough for a royal wedding. A peach dress suit and a matching hat with veil. She was fully accessorized with gloves, handbag and shoes. A splendid outfit for a not-so-splendid location.

Confused, I looked at the women across the room and then back at the potential royal wedding guest. When she turned her head, the harsh fluorescents revealed a whisper of a five o'clock shadow, and all her feminine features were lost in a flinch of the light.

Embarrassed, I stood, blurted out something unintelligible, and tried to wipe the flesh-burning glow from my face before crossing the room to find a seat. I couldn't find one and started to panic— eyes boring through me from every direction. My head felt like a furnace. A hand shot up, and I wobbled towards it.

"Hi, honey. I'm Jody," she said.

"Flip," I said.

"What dorm are you in?

"Erm, L, yeah, I'm in L dorm."

"Rad, me too! What cube are you in? Why haven't I seen you?"

"A cube? I just got here today."

"Rad! I'm in F cube at the other end of the dorm. You'll have to stop by. But I gotta tell you, honey, I've been to Betty Ford, and this place is a dump."

My body temperature had cooled to its regular chilliness, and I could focus on Jody. She was wiry and long. Her limbs would dangle unless she had them wrapped around herself. Like me, Jody wore her own clothes. A white tracksuit and white trainers and a matching smile. She had the Hollywood teeth they should warn tourists about when they are being fingerprinted on the way through customs at LAX. Or that should be printed in books next to "never look directly at the sun." I knew I would have remembered if I'd seen her.

Sheryl called on the phone for someone to come and get the newcomer. Apart from the fag hunters and Sheryl, the only other person I'd met was a redheaded bloke with blood-vessel-blown cheeks.

"Did you ever go to one of them free heroin clinics in Amsterdam?" he asked me when he got whiff of my accent. Before I could answer, he continued, "When I get outta here, that's where am goin'."

172

"Great. That's great, mate," I said backing off. He didn't seem like a drug addict, a boozer maybe. He definitely needed to be in rehab and, apart from being homeless, I didn't see how me and him needed to be in the same place.

That wasn't the person Sheryl had called to take me into "my room," thankfully. Instead a young girl—*too young for 'ere*, I thought, *few more good years of gettin' fucked up*—with a skinhead and a Cheshire cat grin, bounded in the office wearing jeans and a wife-beater.

"Hi, my name's Jen," she said and took my hand and shook it and then replaced it by my side. Sheryl gave me some sheets and a blanket, and Jen carried my bag to a grey wheelbarrow.

"Bye, Flip. Drop by if I can help ya ad'all."

I turned and looked at Sheryl, feeling as if we'd developed a bond while she was rummaging through my bag, and waved. I walked out of the door and twenty feet across the road into L dorm. A concrete ramp led the way in and at the top of the concrete plateau a group of women huddled together smoking. There were a couple of chairs and a tin can with butts in it. I stopped for a second and noticed Sheryl's desk was barely visible—but visible—from the smoking gallery. I was distracted by the wolf whistles that followed me and Jen through the doorway.

"Where'd ya get that one, Jen?" a voice shouted and was followed by a chorus of laughter. *They must know,* I thought. *I must have "queer" stamped on my forehead or summat.*

I flushed with heat and cursed myself for making fun, even if only to myself, of the redheaded, blood-vessel-blown cheeks bloke because I knew I must be as startling as he was right now.

Jen showed me to "my room," and I understood the meaning of LA3 that appeared on all my paperwork. L dorm, A cube, and bed number three. It was horrific. "My room" wasn't "my room" for a number of reasons. The room wasn't a room at all—it was named a cube because the walls didn't touch the ceilings and the doorway had no door. There were also three other people in the room.

Two of them jumped up when Jen pushed in the wheelbarrow. The cube was about eighteen feet by twelve feet, and it seemed as if my meager belongings took up most of the space. There were four white lockers against the back wall. Sheryl told me one would be empty for me to use but to make sure I locked it—otherwise I might find my cigarettes missing and drugs or banned items planted on me. *Liars, cheats, and thieves,* she'd whispered to me—which I thought couldn't possibly true, was almost mean. But as I sized up my surroundings, it seemed as if she could be right, and I wanted to run and jump into her arms.

Donna stepped forward first.

"Hiya, I'm Donna. Need help with anything?"

"Hi," I whispered. I felt as if I was in jail and this was all a setup. They would be nice then beat the shit out of me and take the cigarettes. I wished my arm wasn't as messed up as it was in case I needed to throw a punch or two. The one girl who hadn't stood up was rocking from side to side on the bed across from me. She hummed notes and clutched at the headphones and every so often her fists would punch the air. I thought she was the nutcase they were going to use as a distraction. Turned out, Wanda was weird, plain and simple.

The other girl was Marlene—and while Donna talked I could feel her eyes rolling up and down, sizing me up.

"This is Marlene," Donna said, introducing her. She grunted something at me, and I whispered, "Hi," to whatever she'd said. The situation had all the awkwardness of a first date.

I made up my bed and then Donna remade it for me the way it was supposed to be, hospital corners and tucked in all the way around. It would take me extra time at night to kick the scratchy blanket off so I didn't feel as if I were strapped down in a mental ward. The purpose of the tight beds was to reduce the temptation for a patient to jump into bed during the day when that was, strictly, strictly banned unless you had a letter from the dispensary, clearance from your counselor, and asked for forgiveness from God. Many had been kicked out for lesser crimes.

After Donna helped me with my bed, I followed her outside to smoke.

"I'm a nurse," Donna told me. "I failed a drug test, and they made me come to rehab. I went to one in Brazil already, but I gotta tell you it was weird. Diversion therapy. You had to pretend you were a bird or a tree. I'm not all that jazzed to be here either."

As she talked, I watched people walk by in groups or alone. One bloke was picking fag butts out of the bushes, and I made a mental note just in case I ran out. But there had to be a black market somewhere among these drunks and junkies, I knew that much. There's always an underground circuit of breaking the rules, which I preferred to view as overcoming petty bureaucracy that could only serve to agitate its victims.

"I checked myself in here but most people are from jail," she said. My ears pricked up, and I started listening again.

"Jail?" I asked.

"Yeah. If you can get a transfer from jail to rehab then it's half the sentence. But you gotta pay a lot for those attorneys. I paid for one for my son once. Wiped out my whole bank account, and I had to steal food off the other nurses for a month. Good job. I was snorting meth," she laughed. I thought about Sheryl's warning, *Liars, cheats, and thieves.*

I relaxed for a minute, my muscles submitting to the laughter, and I felt floaty. Another good moment, like I'd had on the beach months ago, the same happiness. I think it was happiness. Like the voices and touch of my brothers, happiness—real happiness—seemed like a distant memory.

A gruff voice barked orders from inside the dorm.

"That's Kel," Donna said. "She's the dorm Mom. We'd best go in. She sounds pissed."

Donna led the way. We passed our cube and then two more cubes, which I assumed were B and C. No one was in them, but I could hear the rumble of an approaching crowd that had gathered in the communal area of the dorm. There was also a distinct odor that my vibrant imagination told me were the remains of "missing" dorm members. I was never so excited to discover a foul-smelling bathroom around the corner. It reeked so much it made me gag.

"You'll get used to that," Donna laughed. "They don't allow bleach in this place 'cos if you drink any liquor and follow it with a bleach chaser a piss test will come up clean. And they pee test if ya blink too much in this place. There's been six girls kicked out since I arrived." Donna had been there fourteen days.

"Fuck, this place probably has enough bacteria to cause a nuclear explosion!"

I was particular about germs since I'd stopped taking class-A substances. It was peculiar the extremes I went to and the standards I accepted as a drug abuser and the moment it stopped I became incredibly fussy. I'd long decided I would have to be able to belt out a chorus of "Jingle Bells" on my ribs before I would resort to eating food out of a bin.

I became itchy suddenly. The physical itch lasted the full ninety-days, partly due to the industrial-strength laundry detergent. The mental itch of addiction—I found out—was constant and can't be scratched without using drugs or alcohol. It was frustrating. I thought of our Chris after he broke his leg and it was cast in a heavy plaster of Paris shell. Mam was in a daze trying to find her knitting needles that Chris nicked for his itches. When the knitting needle didn't reach he ran in circles like a rabid dog trying to get its tail. I used to get angry that he was blocking the telly, but now I felt his torture.

Still, I wasn't buried under concrete, and when I looked at the mangled, pitted and scarred faces surrounding me I knew that was entirely possible.

"Everyone sit down and shurrup! I'm on the rag an' am not in the fuckin' mood."

Donna squatted on the carpet.

"What's the rag?" I whispered.

"She has her period," Donna laughed.

I'd not expected that as the explanation, and I thought it must be jail slang.

"I'm Kelly, Kel, and I'm the dorm Mom. Put your hand up if you're new."

Kelly was a well-built, tall woman with piercing eyes. When she spoke, I noticed her missing canines. Her two front teeth crossed over each other, too.

I raised my hand.

"What's your name, hon?"

"Flip."

"Welcome, Flip."

Kelly smiled her gappy smile, her eyes crinkled, and her decades of drug abuse were written all over her face.

"Hey, where ya from?"

When I turned to see where the voice came from, the crowd behind me was like a blanket of black with white polka dot faces, and that sums up the ratio of African-American and Hispanics versus white patients.

My eyes searched for the voice, and it was one of the polka dots—a thin-faced woman with a portly, mushy body. She wore a red baseball cap and flicked her top set of teeth in and out of her mouth with her tongue. Every time she swallowed her teeth, she reminded me of a frog catching a fly.

"England," I said. "Manchester. Two 'undred and twelve miles north of the Queen."

My accent was out. I would have to explain myself all over again. In LA, I would always be an accent. The girl who asked me the question was named Liz, LC4.

Most of the girls in the dorm were from jail, Liz included. At first, I recognized them by their teeth. That way, I was able to associate teeth with names and faces. Liz looked at me as if I were from another planet, and that was the way I felt, too.

Kel ran through the dorm rules. She read quickly, probably bored from all the times she'd heard and read them. I was bored from listening to them once—they sounded like a repeat from what I'd just read checking in: Be up at this time, make the bed, lights out at 10:30. There were so many rules that at this point I was afraid to move in case I was kicked out. Where would I live then?

"Okay girls, that's their version of the rules. I have my own ideas," Kel said.

My ears pricked up, and I waited for word of a secret tunnel to get us out at night or something. There was a bar down the road that looked like a saloon and people who hung out there wore cowboy hats. Real-life cowboy hats. Kel had advice of how to break the rules.

"Lie on top of the bed, not under the blankets. Security Sid won't bother us after 10:30 if the music is at a reasonable level—if you gotta laugh, cover ya mouth."

None of this information was going to make this feel less like jail, but at least I knew there was an underground system, which also meant cigarettes would probably be available.

After the meeting, we filed out—everyone still talking about the dead woman. Jody was sucked into a clique of girls, and I ran to the phone box. I'd made a mental map of each one I'd seen on the compound. They were all full, with queues at each one. I couldn't believe it. I just wanted to call someone, ask if he or she really thought this was the best place for me, since people seemed to be dying.

I slumped into the cube.

"Hey. How was ya meeting?" Donna asked.

"Did you hear about the dead woman?"

"Oh yeah. Sad, real sad."

"I wanted to call 'ome or someone, but I can't get on a phone, either."

"They call those the relapse boxes. Probably half those people are calling their dealers or druggie friends and arranging to get loaded. They'll leave in the night or get kicked out anyways."

A tannoy sounded outside. A list of names was read and summoned to the Recovery House.

"See," Donna said. "They all probably got busted for something."

The lights went off, and I unwrapped my bed like a Christmas gift and hopped in. I tried to keep my eyes open, one at least, in case, just in case. Giggles and gossip, pattering feet, burping and farting were the sounds of the night, coyotes howling the chorus at the moon. I was lulled into a deep, sober sleep.

CHAPTER FOURTEEN

THE COUNSELORS CALLED US PATIENTS. They rammed it down our throats at every opportunity, as if to remind us how low we had sunk. If we continued, the other two institutions we were likely to belong to were jail and a mental ward. I shivered at the thought. I couldn't imagine anything worse than this place.

The antidote was a spiritual awakening, which, I gathered, was similar to an epiphany. I didn't understand what it meant exactly but many of the patients chased it with the same vigor as they had chased a high. I decided the excessive fuss could be explained by the culture of excess in LA—a small soda at the cinema resembled a bucket, fast food was the cheapest in town, and meals could be made super-duper large for a measly thirty-cents. In Manchester, it was the sarcasm that was excessive—it seemed as if the rain was spiked with sarcasm and people's sentences were saturated with it.

Mam was the Queen of sarcasm, it was her "verbal machete." But, in the end, I could meet her head-on, and it became a duel of venomous wit. But she owned the house, earned the money, fed us, and I would have to retreat when I remembered she was always the winner and could trump me any time with any of those cards. I would storm off with a farewell, *"I wish I'd never been born!"*

I always stopped to see if I heard a *Me too!* before returning to my escape plot—Exit Mam. I stayed with friends and with my gran. But I realized I craved solitude and decided to sleep in my car, driving around with the heater blasting before finding a secure place in the car park of Hope Hospital, where, for some reason, I felt safe. No tension existed, no ghosts, no jarring memories, that once passed, clung to me and I felt like I was climbing through a sticky web. My car was the oasis and it was mine.

❖

Donna and I strolled the periphery of the compound supposedly everyday, but in reality it was three times a week, then not at all when she started taking Benadryl. She was so lazy that she wouldn't even get up to go to the meetings where doughnuts were served. Instead, she asked me to nab them for her.

Our walks were the only time I got to be with her without Marlene, who was probably in a lithium-coma. Apart from forcing me to get my CD player back from Psycho and asking me to hand her a towel as she stood naked in the shower cubicle the second day I knew her, she made me feel safe.

On the way around, we passed Luis, who I knew from the kitchen as the bloke who served me porridge for breakfast and slop the other meals. From behind the counter, he seemed tall and hulkish, but in person he was small and stocky, like a Hispanic munchkin from *The Wizard of Oz*. That is, a closely shaved head and a long mustache twisted into a fine point at the end and a modest five feet tall. I almost didn't recognize him until he spoke.

"S'up, ladies? Eetheraya wanna break the ten-second rule?" He spoke like Taylor, who we lived with after the car accident, so his vernacular wasn't completely foreign to me.

Donna looked at me, and I returned her stare, sparking us both to crack up into laughter, squeezing in breaths when possible.

"Gotta a fancy crib somewhere, 'ave yer, Luis?"

Just when the intensity of the moment was losing its momentum, my comment fueled it all over again. Luis laughed, too, now.

"So is that yes or no then?"

By the time I recovered, my gut ached. But for the next few days the ache regurgitated the memory and I laughed a little more.

Luis told us he'd had a spiritual awakening which for some reason slowly extinguished the mood. I couldn't believe a munchkin gangster like Luis would believe in God.

"Just carry a gun," I told him.

He smiled at me, "You ai'ight, Flip." That was a tough one to translate since his accent had the Hispanic twist.

Then I remembered a few occasions when I'd been sat in Starbucks and had seen groups of men reading from the same book about divorce or diet, something spiritual.

It was strange at first. That kind of behavior wouldn't fly in Manchester. The lads I knew, and didn't know, huddled over their lager, ogling at the day's topless page-three girl. *Just 'ave a few beers and smoke a few spliffs* was what a Manchester lad might say to the divorced, dieting, or even dying. *An' a copy of* Penthouse *is always 'andy, ha ha, 'andy! Get it?* It was an obvious joke, corny. Annoying when it disrupts a good conversation and yet deeply comforting as a memory.

Luis did believe in God, and he prayed. It seemed impossible. I made a mental note to watch him in the next co-ed meeting. I occasionally saw him at the Hill House early in the morning where a handful of people gathered to strike off a meeting for the day on the cards we had to have signed.

"Go-awn Luis, what was it?" Donna asked.

"I was with the hommies, ya know, shootin' shit and tawkin' bullets." There was a delay between him speaking and my ability to translate, as if he were being interviewed on telly in New York. "I was transferred here from jail, like a lotta folk. This was supposed to be the fast track to the outs. There's people out there waitin' on my product. Man, they fiends! But they my people, they my folks, you hear me?" We both nodded. I was amused to find out "folks" in gangster speech were the people you respected, not an elderly couple like Grandma and Mort.

"I've been sellin' to the fiends since my dad taught me how to weigh grams and count money at five." I wondered how small he'd been at that age. "I didn't know I was one of 'em, or my dad. Man, dude! I'm an addict. But thank God I know." He looked up at the sky and then us, hands held together as if in prayer. "And thank God I have an answer. Some people aren't as lucky."

"Luis! Move away from the ladies," Sweet Sheryl's voice boomed through the tannoy, and Luis scarpered as I imagined he did at the bank jobs he'd pulled off.

"Have a blessed day, ladieees," he shouted back.

"Holler at yer 'ommies!" I replied, getting back into the swing of Taylor's dialect. "Is this a cult?" I asked Donna.

"Gawd, where's mine?" she shouted up to Heaven, as if a spiritual awakening would be dropped to the earth the way the stork drops babies down chimneys. "What did you just say?"

"A cult. I asked if this place is some kind of cult. In which case, isn't that just switching to a different worship from an evil maniac before bathing in each other's blood because we were part of a group suicide."

Donna laughed. "That's some imagination you got there, Flip. But no, I think there's a jail cult and they tend to get into the Bible. Prob'ly a way to get out the cell. We have one here on a Monday night, you should come. Free coffee and pastries, but don't eat the poppy seeds."

"So we read the Bible to get out of our cells, too? I'll think about it."

By the time I noticed where we were, it was the end of the walk.

"I just don't get it! If I don't get an awakening before I leave this place, I'm asking for a refund."

Luis had set her off, and he wouldn't be the last.

Whata lotta rot! I thought.

I'd been waiting for time to heal. I imagined one day, after a certain amount of time, a puff of smoke would appear before me and I would be magically cured. The pain orbiting the memories, gone. Aching love becomes love. Guilt evaporating, polluting the air but no longer poisoning my body and mind. It hadn't happened.

The first day was one of hard-learned lessons.

I woke up early. It was still dark and the level of noise seemed unnatural compared to the quiet solitude of the car.

Chattering echoed through the hallways, and people were showering. Angry *Shhhh's* followed, but I couldn't see how anyone could sleep above the perpetual snoring. I was already restless, worrying about my exit plan before my head was off the pillow.

My options were limited, since my work visa was no longer valid, my right arm was still feeble, and the lawsuit against Rock 'n' Rollers meant I couldn't lift a finger to earn a penny. My whole sleep had been disturbed, and I couldn't be certain whether it was the noise or lack of controlled substances. I was yet to be convinced that I could take nothing.

I lifted my head to peek over the top of the blankets and was struck by a severe pain in my neck. I gently returned my head to the pillow and massaged my neck. Sensing my face was cold, I put my hand on my cheek, then forehead. It felt frozen and half numb. I realized it was from the cold air spilling into the room through the window. It was colder than the car. I buried my head under the pillow that had been a fortress all night to my cigarettes.

When a spark of sensation returned to my face, I slipped on a jacket over my tracky bottoms and trainers. My bladder was screaming at me, and I yelled silently back. Did it not realize where we were? Going to the loo could result in death or maiming in this place. Maybe even a Cuban necktie, a quaint method of torture—which I learned about from one of the girls—where the attacker slits the victim's throat and pulls the tongue through to hang like a tie. But I couldn't ignore my bladder forever.

Some girls I didn't recognize were wrapped in towels, fixing their hair, rubbing moisturizer into their skin.

"If ya thinkin' of takin' a shower, ain't no hot water. Ya gotta be up early for that," one of them said to me. I'd seen the time on a clock in the communal area, and it was half past five.

"Gonna be two or three now 'fore there's any more."

"Cheers," I mumbled. I was trying not to breathe, as the smell was pungent and left a weird aftertaste in my mouth. My stomach gnarled worse than my worst hangover, and I thought I was going to throw up. The next day, I got up and had a shower at five—the one and only time that ever happened, at that time. The rest of my stay, I didn't care how I smelled—I would just blend into the revolting smell of the dorm or Donna's feet.

Outside on the concrete patio, a couple of women were smoking. One of them was Marlene, and I contemplated running back to bed.

"Morning," I said, pulling out my fags. An early morning fog had settled, and it was hard to see anyone. I didn't know who else was there and not even their teeth could save me now. "Where's everyone goin'?" I nodded towards snapshots of figures that were visible where the fog had thinned, but it was mainly too dense.

A picture popped up in my head that startled me. I was fourteen, the house was on fire, and I opened my door to see if I should go downstairs and outside to escape. The smoke was a swirling black wall. When I stuck my head out I couldn't see in either direction, but the sounds were what I thought of as "The Orchestra of Death." Wood creaking and snapping, explosions of glass and the angry, screaming rush of the flames. I retreated and shut my door. *That's when I should've gone. I could've run down and saved our Mike. I hate myself, I really hate myself.* It was overwhelming. I realized it was a flashback that I'd read about in the book *Grief and Addiction*, part of the PTSD and the reason I didn't want to be conscious, I imagined. *This sober crap had better work*, I thought.

"Dining hall. They goin' a get kawfee."

It wasn't Marlene, she was from Alabama and whoever this was had an eastern twang. But I was certain I would understand the word coffee in every language, in every accent in the world.

"Where's it at?" I asked.

"I'll take you. I'm going there now."

A figure appeared in front of me the way ink blots through paper. She looked burly but as she passed through the fog I realized it was the bulk of her clothing.

"Hi, I'm Amanda," she said.

She reminded me of Mam when she came home from the market. The headlights of her car sliced through the lounge as she pulled into the driveway. All our activities ceased, even our Charlie who could usually be found sleeping somewhere, unplugged his thumb from his mouth. We all lined up like it was a military operation, automatically, in pecking order ready to pass the contents of the car down the line and into the house.

Mam's unkempt, wavy hair got out of the car before she did, and she followed in her chaotic mass of clothes—skiing salopettes, long johns, and a heavy jacket and gloves. The market could be brutally cold—sleet, rain, and snow—and all the worse for being in the north. All the traders suffered, victims to the elements.

Our Chris held the most distinguished position at the base of the steps, ready to scramble into the house and back out again. This required stamina and strength, two qualities only the eldest can possess, he told us. There'd be rolls of nets, a bundle of yardsticks, Mam's wicker basket filled with essential tea supplies.

Afterwards, we congregated in the kitchen and Mam stripped her layers off, losing half her size in clothes and looking human again.

When we reached the dining hall, Amanda shed her layers and was a tiny little person. Her head was so small that her eyes and mouth didn't seem to fit. Amanda was a crackhead, too, and I reacted to that news with the same shock that people responded to me. I couldn't imagine this skinny white girl hanging around the same dodgy neighborhoods as I had.

"My neighbor sold it to me and my sister," she said. "It was too easy to walk across the street and get it."

I didn't ask where she got her money. We stood in the coffee queue. At the end of the line were stacks of clear plastic cups, plastic spoons, sugar, and milk. There was no soothing music to accompany the delicious smells or bright smiling staff to fill up the half and half. There wasn't even any half and half. The cups were like thimbles, just enough for a couple of swigs. I could imagine me and our Charlie talking about mugs of tea.

"That's not a mug, that's a thimble," Charlie would say to Mam if she gave him the small mug. I'd nod along to his complaints, maybe even pat him on the back. He'd drink it fast, his face burning red as the hot liquid heated him up from the inside out. Then he would turn and pour himself another brew out of the old tin teapot covered with its fluffy tea cosy that Mam had knitted. He would think these little cups were an insult, and I would have to agree with him.

We joined a table of people, mainly men, and I was concerned this was a breach of the rules. They looked up and smiled, a skinny balding white man, Dave, the same Dave who had answered the phone when I called to get a bed. I'd imagined him to look completely different, his voice was too deep for his body. It belonged to a man of much larger proportions. Mission Milo wore a tight wrap on his head. It looked like a black pair of stockings that could conveniently be pulled over his face in the event of a spontaneous robbery. I soon realized it was cultural. The young men sagged their jeans, which meant they would wear their trousers so they could show off their boxer shorts. I didn't understand that at all.

"'Ere, mate!" I shouted. "Yer about to lose yer trousers!"

After a few weeks, I was overjoyed to watch one of the women go around pulling all the blokes' trousers up. She dared to do what I only imagined doing.

Then there was Henry, a geeky-looking man who looked as if he might be big enough for Dave's voice. Gold-rimmed glasses and a thin, neat mustache above his lip, as faint as if he'd drawn it on himself the way women do their eyebrows sometimes.

On the table was a radio and Mission Milo nodded and rocked back and forth on his chair legs, "That's right, that's right," he said. Henry was taking notes. We sat down and I realized we were listening to a sermon.

Ya gotta find faith! Without it, there's nothing...

The coffee had yet to give me any spark, and I missed the sermon to refill the thimble several more times to no effect. *Brown fucking water, that's all this is.* At this point, I'd not found one thing I liked about Acton rehab. The sermon ended as I gave up on catching a buzz off the coffee.

"Hello, young lady," Mission Milo said offering his hand. "You were just listening to God's station."

I didn't mention my fight with God and how I had no faith whatsoever anymore and never would have.

"We here every morning at five praying and listening to God's word. You welcome to join us."

I kept my mouth shut and politely listened the way Mam had taught me. They got into a conversation about faith.

"It's about God's will not self-will," Mission Milo said.

"That's right!" Henry shouted. Him and Mission Milo were both African American, Henry the darker of the two—the blackest black man I'd ever seen, and it made his eyes shine. "Self-will run riot, that why we here," Henry said, nodding at his own statement and the others did, too. I wondered if they were being polite or if they really meant it.

Fuck God, I thought. But I listened to their stories. Mission Milo had been the target of drive-by shootings, Henry robbed people using cash machines and pimped his girlfriend, Dave turned houses over and wheeled his shopping cart full of goodies to his dealers, Amanda and her sister stole from their parents and visitors, occasionally throwing themselves at the mercy of the dealer and offering themselves. I was horrified— they seemed like such decent people. They didn't seem burdened by guilt or shame—in fact, they were astonishingly casual about the details of their stories. It made no sense. I was taking my transaction with Hannay to the grave. And I was relieved we had ripped off our dealers, not Grandma or other innocents.

"It's 6:30. We'd best start clearing up," Dave said. He was the quietest of the group, apart from me.

"Hey, Flip, if you wanna stay and help, you get to eat breakfast first," Mission Milo said.

"No worries, mate, yeah." I had no idea what I was helping with but I'd not eaten for nearly a day and skipping the line to eat breakfast before the other two hundred and eighty patients seemed like a good idea. It was simple, just ten minutes' work when we all pitched in. The tables were wiped, chairs unstacked and arranged around the tables and trays filled with plastic spoons and knives and metal forks.

We finished right before seven—breakfast time—and lined up to collect our trays which were plastic with sections to dump the food on. Outside, I heard a rabble of people that sounded like a riot, and I felt safe to be in this band of robbers, pimps, and house burglars who were shot at.

Breakfast was SOS, which is institution talk for Shit On a Shingle—potatoes sliced and doused in a white sauce and sprinkled with a mystery meat that had a dubious rubbery texture. I tried it once, but it continued to show up on the same day and meal every week. I ended up exchanging it for porridge or eggs with whoever walked by, or to stay in favor. It was barely identifiable as food but I ate it anyway. It was gross. Mam's burned dinners were more edible.

The rabble had been let in and the volume level increased to the point I couldn't hear the conversation next to me. Clattering trays drowned Mission Milo out, who shouted between people slopping the food and patients with no choice but to eat it. Total chaos. Men and women sat together, one of the only times to get away with it. Some played footsy under the table and others held hands, eyes scanning for the counselors, who were on the lookout for canoodlers.

The dining hall was dingy and grimy, too. The paint and windows were frosted with dirt, the doorframes crumbling, and a beaten floor. I watched other patients flood in, and there was still a sizeable queue outside. The collective population of drug addicts, mental patients, boozers, and jailbirds had me on edge. It didn't take more than a dropped syllable to instigate loons. I learned that with Gina. I tipped her into manic episodes with a comment or look. A blazing argument might ensue and we got full feeding off each other's negativity.

"My mom is such a bitch! She left me with nothing and my sister has *Everything! Fuck her!* You have no idea how bad I feel."

"Yeah, 'cos my life has been a breeze. Actually, a breeze while walking through a park on a hot summer day."

"If you say one more sarcastic comment, I'm gonna, gonna scream." As if she wasn't already. I despised these one-upping contests, but wringing out the last of her sanity was one of the only pleasures of living with her and Scott—revenge for me sleeping in the car and putting up with them.

I saw a familiar red baseball cap bobbing through the crowd and before I could remember who it was, Liz was in my face spitting her teeth in and out on the end of her tongue.

She leaned in and shouted, "Alright, mate!"

I'd taught her this when I was teaching her "real English" while smoking on the balcony. This along with wanker, div, tosser, prick—all the swear words. But when she said it, her teeth flew out too much and hit me in the cheek and slid down to land in a slice of porridge. Liz was rolling on the floor laughing and now drooling without her teeth in. The commotion sent counselors flying in from every direction. I stood raising my hands as if under arrest, looking at the mayhem surrounding me, wanting to join Liz in her hysterics, but afraid to in case I got shot at dawn or flogged, whatever the rule was.

The sensation rose in my body, and I remembered the last time I'd felt like this, in the car after I'd picked up my money from the attorney and Roscoe and Dite jumped on me. It had forced a smile on my face along with a shy giggle. I could see Liz would be my comic relief.

"'Ere, Liz. Liz," I said tapping her with my foot. "Excuse me waiter, there's dentures in my oatmeal," I said in a squeaky voice and then switched to a deeper sound. "Ma'am, could please keep your voice down, everyone will want some."

This set everyone within earshot into hysterics. Butterflies of laughter fluttered into the air. An infectious moment.

That week, Amanda held my hand while I was figuring who knocked about with who. She was coffee chick at the cocaine recovery meeting I attended in the evening. Her duties were to collect the coffee urn from the dining hall and roll it over to the meeting in a cart. She shared the same cube as Jody, who'd decided to change my name to Penelope. She had the other two girls in the room ironing her immaculate tracksuit and probably knickers too. I wondered if she was the head honcho like Bea Smith in *Prisoner Cell Block H* who was nicknamed Queen Bea.

By the end of the week, I was fetching Jody stuff from the dining hall on my way back from breakfast. She bought me with small tins of Starbucks double shot espresso that I added to the brown water they tried to con us with in the dining hall.

"Penelope! Thanks so much. That's rad, baby. Let's have lunch together today. We can order out, on me."

"Well, erm..."

"No buts, be here at twelve."

Amanda shot me a look, and I shrugged back at her.

"She can't be that bad?" I asked Amanda later.

"She can and she is. You'll see. Just don't get dragged down."

Every Friday, there was a graduation ceremony for those who had completed ninety days. There was excitement in the air, a taste of freedom. For some, the freedom was going back out and doing the same old thing, but for the rest it was the freedom of new life and potential.

Families drove from miles away to see their loved ones graduate from addicts to recovering addicts. They brought junk food and cigarettes, reminders of the riches that lay waiting for us on the outside. Graduation never lost its buzz.

For us in A cube, it was also laundry day. Since I was last in the cube, I didn't race to use the machine. I thought I would allow Psycho Wanda and Marlene to go ahead. We each had one bag of county-issued laundry powder for one load once a week. But it left the clothes itchy and unbearable. Some girls had Tide, the American equivalent of Bold, that they'd purchased while out on their day passes—and told anyone who dared ask for any, "No, you can't have a cupful, fuck off! Everyone's been taking it anyways." Psycho (I'd since dropped the Wanda part) dared. She came scurrying back to the cube with an expression as if she'd seen a ghost, eyes so wide her eyeballs might roll out. She hopped on the bed, put on headphones and started rocking.

She was using my CD player and headphones. Donna looked at me, "You gotta get those back off her. She won't leave you any batteries but that's annoying, I can't think."

"If you leave it to me to do, I'll beat her. Then you and I'll keep yer damn batteries. Your choice," Marlene said.

Staring at the ceiling the whole time and then closing her eyes again. I wondered if this was the part where I got stabbed with a pair of well-hidden nail clippers manipulated into a weapon. I was rooted to my spot, so rooted with fear I doubted whether I'd move even if the eye of a tornado passed through our cube. Everything around me would be shredded and ripped apart.

"OK I, erm," I took a deep breath. "I'll ask."

Donna patted my shoulder and said, "Don't look so worried."

I did my laundry during the graduation ceremony. The whole compound was packed into the dining hall, leaving stragglers and guests with standing room only. L Dorm sat together as did Z Dorm and Blair House, which is where Ashley was placed because she put the funds upfront she really did have a room, a cube to herself. But she also had the ghost of a dead woman, and I wouldn't trade with her at this point.

The ceremony was a huge affair. I didn't know it, but as a

newcomer I had to stand up in front of these people and say my name and get a newcomer chip. My head felt like a hot tomato.

"Flip, addict," I said. From the audience came cheers of "Flip," "Welcome" and "L Dorm." The attention was killing me. I ran back to my seat in a special section for newcomers and waited for the heat to evaporate from my head. I was relieved to have a seat next to Ashley, who seemed even brighter than the last time I'd seen her at orientation.

For a week me, Ashley, and all the other newcomers were introduced to counselors and given a tour of the compound and lectured about the rules at every possible opportunity.

We sat together at the nutrition and addiction class rolling our eyes. The counselor, Karen, was a normy. That meant she'd had no addictions and was not susceptible since addiction is a genetic *disease*. I'd never heard it called a disease before. Being a normy also left Karen a coldhearted, unsympathetic bitch, *or desperately in need of a shag!* I thought.

"You are patients in a rehabilitation facility! I suggest you learn before you leave or are kicked out! Sugar is an addiction, too. It alters the brain chemistry in the same way morphine, heroin, and alcohol do. Beware of what you eat," she warned us.

I was stunned by this news. Clearly Ashley was, too. I'd been sneaking out of class since I was seven years old under the false excuse of needing the loo but stopping at the school stock room to dip my finger in the sugar jar, which was my real reason to leave class. Before that, I stole sweets from the pick 'n mix at Woolworths. Sugar was my childhood battle. I made the chilling connection that I'd probably had addiction issues all my life and an addict was who I was.

This thought unraveled further, spiraling down and down uncontrollably. There were times when I'd liked Chris's girlfriends when I was young. I'd thought it was normal to feel this way. Chris's girlfriends were incredibly pretty, and I convinced myself they were role models and that my issue with men was due to the negative male role models, like Dad and Tony, in my life. But given this evidence, I was probably really gay. I couldn't even bring myself to think, let alone say, the "L" word. It turned out most of the girls in my dorm had been molested and abandoned by their fathers and they still liked men, "strictly dickly" was the expression. It was down to me to like who I was.

A cold sweat shivered across my skin, and Ashley reached over and patted my hand. I looked at her and smiled, trying to shove these thoughts out of my consciousness. I leaned over to her and whispered, "Doesn't seem like Karen managed to avoid the sugar, does it?" We cracked up laughing, and I managed to deflect my horror at myself.

Karen shot us a look, "This disease *is* progressive. If you don't learn to manage it in here, starting with diet, one thing will lead to another. A drink, more drinks, drugs, shooting drugs, and probably death."

She never took her eyes off us.

The people leaving also had a special section, and I wished I were sitting there. It seemed just a couple of steps away and yet it was really much further—time-wise: ninety-days, which wasn't much for a lifetime of trauma I'd been told. Weight-wise, it was forty pounds. They had a special diet of four thousand calories per day because everyone went in there skinny and sucked up. Some people's skinny was a hundred and eighty pounds, about thirteen stone. I was eight stone, and there was no way I would allow myself to gain another three.

But there was more to it than that—the spiritual awakening, the growth and clarity that made these people beam, their smiles and auras. It seemed they'd stepped into a new existence and the people that fell behind them in time were just starting to bloom, too. Amanda, Dave, Henry all had a quality I couldn't quite figure out. They magnetized me, as did the energy in the room.

Most of the ceremony, I thought about the laundry. I needed to put it in the dryer. I hoped no one was waiting, getting mad, spiking my clothes with spider eggs or itching powder. I was momentarily distracted with cheers for L Dorm, and I would vaguely recognize the speaker.

"Hi. Clarice, alcoholic addict and very grateful to have started my recovery here at Acton. I wanna thank the girls in L Dorm."

Behind me, the rowdy group jumped up, Liz's red baseball cap flying in the air, and an out of tune and mistimed by each "L Dorm!"

"I came in here with nothin' but a police record. I was beat down, beat up, too," she said and paused to laugh. "But I'm leavin' with hope and love. I have a direction today. But most of all, I gotta God."

"Truly!" people shouted from the audience.

Clarice continued with how she had changed and what her future held. A group of people all carrying similar messages of hope followed.

"'Fore I got here," Tommy said, "I was fulla shame. My daddy abused me, and my mama was too scared to stop him. He drank and when I was seven he forced whisky down my throat and when I woke up, I knew I'd been abused different. Sexual. I couldn't tell no one. After that, every time I knew my daddy was gonna be home, I drank the whisky 'fore he got me. Then he got angry for his whisky!" Tommy slapped the podium with his hand and laughed. My heart had already sunk for the poor bastard. His cheery demeanor startled me. How could he smile?

"Thanks to my time here at Acton and my faith in a Higher Power, which for me is the stars and the moon, I can look myself in the face now. When I shave, I can use the mirror without wanting to drag the blade across my jugular. I never thought this could happen and I want to thank you all and the moon and the stars." Another smile and a round of applause. Tommy had just knocked my socks off. His courage, his acceptance, his smile. This became my favorite part of the week so far, a real life American-Feel-Good-Factor. *Maybe there is a point to this after all,* I thought.

The final speaker was more of a blur. Attention in the room had scattered and the conversations around me steered my attention from the speaker. When I did listen, he talked about his first high. "Eight minutes it lasted. Since then, I've been chasing those same eight minutes over and over..."

I remembered the first time I did coke and thought my teeth had fallen out because my mouth was numb. The first ecstasy tablet that had me speaking Irish for six hours. The firsts are always the best, but you don't know it at the time. I was the same as the bloke at the podium, chasing, sometimes sprinting, but never arriving like the first time.

Before the end of the ceremony, the crowd had started to thin, but newcomers had to stay until we were told to file out. After we stood up, I made a break from the line and ran for the laundry. There didn't appear to be anything wrong.

"You gotta get your CD player back from Wanda. She's drivin' us freakin' nuts!" Donna said. She'd snuck up behind me in the laundry room.

When I went back to the cube, Psycho was draining my batteries and singing but no one else was around. She didn't see or hear me in the doorway as she was snooping in Marlene's locker. I jumped back behind the wall. I screwed my clothes up into a ball and walked back towards the communal area where Kel was sitting with Nancy and Lucinda. When I first met Nancy, she thought I was called "Joe Boxer" because that was the name on my socks. She was a friendly giant.

"What's up, Flip? You look like you've seen a ghost," Kel said.

"Oh," I said and looked around behind me. "Nothing. S'okay. I thought I dropped a sock, that's all. Shitty to have a missing sock in this place, I don't have much else."

They looked puzzled. *Maybe it's me accent,* I thought.

I crept back down the hallway and peeked into the cube. Psycho was lying down rocking to the music. I walked in, threw the ball of laundry in my locker, bolted the padlock, and ran.

I ducked into the library, where I knew I would find someone I could hide behind, another sanction where the Ten-

Second Rule was broken religiously. Couples sat at tables in the back room with open Big Books groping each other. I recognized a girl from my class about recovery literature but she had some bloke stuck to her face so I didn't go over.

In the corner, Amanda, Dave, Henry, and Mission Milo sat around a table with Big Books open, but they were actually discussing the contents. Alcoholism and drug addiction as symptoms of something else in your life. I'd heard this briefly mentioned in meetings. It was pretty obvious to me what it was a symptom of in my life. Tony—his violence and burning the house down—my brothers' deaths, my dad—where did he go? From the books I'd read, I realized that these were possible reasons for my addiction problem. Mission Milo asked how I ended up at Acton. Like the girls in my dorm, when I told him about living in the car he thought I said cart.

"You lived in a cart? What, like a shopping cart?"

"Car, Milo." I felt an idiot calling him Mission Milo. I'd not figured his mission out yet, and I was sure the answer would be long and detailed, something I had no patience for. "C-A-R."

I told them about how my dad was an alcoholic and he was eventually kicked out. "After that, Mam had a few more boyfriends. One of them really proper, nice. But, 'course that's the one she ditches. Then she had this boyfriend Tony. He was a violent drunk. My dad was never violent, that was the difference. Most people thought he was pretty funny," I said and paused, feeling the weight of the memory. My lungs felt as if they'd turned into concrete and I was choking for each breath. At the table, everyone's expressions were nonchalant. They'd heard this type of story before, and it was common among addicts and drunks. I was feeling the pressure of not having a tragic life like theirs, just a tragic story. I hoped the fire somehow qualified me to live among them for a couple of months.

"Anyway, he came 'ome drunk one night. It was back in the day when no one thought anything of smoking inside. Tony was smoking and fell asleep. When he woke up, the front room was on fire and he ran upstairs to tell my mam to get out of the 'ouse. Their bedroom was above the front room and flames were coming up through the floor. Mam never made any bones about jumpin' in a situation like that. She used to scream at the telly when *Towering Inferno* was on, "Jump, jump!" That's just what she did. But she broke her back because it was about a twenty foot jump."

I stopped to take a deep breath. I'd not told this story out loud in years. It came back to me in flashes or in long roaming stories in my mind. I would become distracted and it was easy for me to step out into traffic, and once I poured half a pint of lager on myself thinking I had the glass to my mouth.

"Go on," Amanda reminded me.

"All right, erm, well, I woke up for a glass of water. It's all I wanted. I suppose my throat was dry from the smoke. It was weird, but the moment I woke up I knew the house was on fire. Before I even switched on the light I could feel how thick the air was. Thick and black. I mean, I couldn't see my hand in front of my face. I switched the light on and of course I was right. I opened my bedroom door and more smoke rushed into my room so I slammed it shut. And then the window wouldn't open either! I mean talk about luck, right?"

"Did you get it open?"

"I'm standing 'ere aren't I? Believe me, the smoke was so toxic I'd be dead if I didn't get the window open. But just enough so I could squeeze my head through sideways, like this," and I turned my head to show them. "The two youngest died of smoke inhalation. One was eight and four days old, our Mike. I'd had a fight with him before he died, and we never made up. I threw one of his toys at him and went out with my friends. But listen to this. I came back later that night and walked past his bedroom to bed. I stopped on the stairs listening to him snoring and thought 'Shall I make up with him? Nah, let 'im sweat 'til tomorrow, and I'll buy him some sweets and he'll paint me a picture. Not like there's going to be a fire or something.' It was like a premonition. A fucking premonition!" I squeezed my head between my hands like a vise grip, hoping I could crush that memory and the rest.

"I wished I'd listened to myself. Then there was Sammy, the baby, twenty-two months old. His body was found with Tony's. Tony was Sammy's dad, not mine or my other brothers."

I paused. I could transfer myself into every moment. The burning wood, smashing glass, and roaring flames. I could picture it all, almost touch it. *This is what I don't want to feel*, I thought. *This is what I've been hiding from.* Pricked memories that bled until I was tortured.

"I was so scared I got on my knees and started praying. What should I do? Should I get my brothers? Stay in my room? In the middle of the prayer, the lightbulb shattered above my head and I screamed. I also didn't move from my room. In my head, that was a sign.

"A fireman came to my window and got me out. I climbed down the ladders. There was no way I could've jumped and lived, that would've been forty feet onto my mother's freshly laid concrete path. I didn't smash the bloody window 'cos I thought she'd take it out of my pocket money, and I wasn't about to get blood on the floor. That was before I got out of the house, though, and saw what had happened. Flames were coming out of all the windows. And we had a big 'ouse, twenty-one rooms. There wasn't a pane of glass left anywhere.

"The front lawn was piled high with debris, firemen crawling all over the place. My two eldest brothers, Chris and Charlie, were in the back of the ambulance. They made it. At the hospital, they forced hot, sweet tea on me. I hate sugar in tea, and all I wanted was a glass of fucking water. Pretty much, half the family was killed and the other half kept in hospital. I was sent home, erm, to my mam's friend's 'ouse, Aunty Liz. She picked me up, and we drove back to the house. It was awful. It was six in the morning by then. The house was still smoking and creepy-looking without glass in the windows and totally black on the inside. A huge grave.

"Me an' Aunty Liz drove around to a few people to let them know what happened. But it was all over the news anyway. I think that's why I started doing drugs and stuff. Jesus, guilt is stage four soul-cancer."

There was a pause. I was in the past, still. I realized I'd been there a while. I didn't even hear the clutter of people in the room.

"Girlfriend!" Mission Milo started. I jumped back into the present. "Don'tcha see you were *meant* to live? There was a *reason* they died and a *reason* you lived. You could've never've saved 'em."

The others chimed in agreeing with him. "God had other plans for them, and for you too, sister! You are here for a purpose and you gotta figure it out."

What he said was so surreal it made sense. Out of all the books I'd read and the *Loveline* shows I'd listened to, it was the only thing that made any sense. *A surreal answer for a surreal life. Of course!* I thought.

It was as if I'd never escaped from my bedroom. I'd been engulfed in the thick black smoke for years, never able to see my hand in front of my face. Now it was being sucked out as if the window had miraculously opened. *I have a purpose,* I thought. *I just have to realize my purpose.*

I felt a weird sense of excitement, "You know, me and the girl I used to do drugs with, Gina, used to talk about writing a screenplay about our adventures of living in the car, C-A-R, and about 'ow there's usually a reason for people to do drugs. It's not just that they want to stick needles in their arms. Right?"

"Start writing girl," Amanda piped in. "I keep a journal every night that I think someone should turn into a movie."

It seemed a silly idea after that. But I remembered Mam wanted me to be a writer. On my twenty-first birthday, she put a photo of me in the newspaper from when I had a dopey mullet haircut at twelve years old. I was forced to have the haircut if I wanted to go to France that year with school on a water sports holiday. "Ace Reporter" was the tagline. When I didn't make the grades for journalism school, I took the public relations course instead.

The sense of constantly plummeting, of trying to set foot on the earth, slowed down. I felt as if I'd been flatlining and had miraculously been brought back to life and was sitting up with a jolt.

I could remember a similar experience I'd had at eighteen when, from beyond the grave, Shakespeare saved my life. I was miserable enough to have started slashing precariously at my wrists with broken glass. Maybe I'd hit the right vein. I used to go in the house before it was rebuilt and dare to climb the ladders that replaced the staircase to my room, trying not to step on the places where I thought my brothers' bodies had been. Once in my room, I would throw glass objects against the wall and scratch the shards across my veins.

It was the last hour of the college day, and we were studying *The Tempest* in Dr. Snell's English literature class. Prospero was discussing the death of the sailors in the opening scene. Line by line, the meaning was discussed and dissected. I was daydreaming out of the window, wondering why four years had passed and I was still heartbroken my brothers were dead. Dr. Snell's voice faded back into my hearing.

"The meaning, class, is that one is not supposed to get over death. One is only supposed to cope with it. Learn to cope, that is what Prosepero is saying to Miranda."

My ears pricked up. *Learn to cope, don't get over it,* I thought. It made sense.

I wasn't sure what was supposed to happen after people in the family die. We had the funeral. There were hundreds of people and hundreds of flower arrangements. I cried and cried at the tiny coffins, while Chris held my hand and Charlie held his other hand. After that, I expected it to be over and done with. What else could there be?

I don't know if Mission Milo knew he'd just changed my life. I wasn't really sure myself. I was afraid to test whether I could really laugh or be happy. If I stuck my head out from under the heavy boulder, would it get shot off? Would another boulder come and squash my head back down? Dare I breathe? And dare I tell Donna that I was possibly struck with a spiritual awakening?

"Wanda! *Wanda!*" I shouted. She opened her bug eyes and stared into mine. "I need my CD player back. Now. Please."

CHAPTER FIFTEEN

THE SUNDAY NIGHT COCAINE RECOVERY MEETING WAS
HELD IN THE DINING HALL. It was the "chip meeting," where
the patients who had been locked up for thirty, sixty or ninety
days, were awarded a small plastic chip. Newcomers collected
a "welcome" chip to acknowledge the bravery of getting help.
In L Dorm, the chips were used as currency for card games.
The number of days denoted the value of the chip.

The tables from dinnertime were left out and used to pass notes
to friends or for sleeping. At the front of the hall were four tables
filled with doughnuts, pastries, and fruit. People walked away
with pockets filled and arms loaded with goodies, some for now
and some for later after lights out, even though it was strictly
forbidden. Everything was devoured—the sweet tastes
momentarily disguising the sour days of being locked up in rehab.

By the time I was collecting my thirty-day chip, Amanda
had been gone ten days, along with Dave and Henry. I hated
goodbyes. It seemed like another form of death to me. It wasn't
possible to see the person, and they may never come back.

Before Amanda left, she bequeathed me all of her worldly
goods that I could possibly use: an empty glass coffee jar she
had used as a mug but would be considered a weapon and
evidence of smuggled contraband if found by staff plus leftover
coffee granules from a baggy her sister had sent to her wrapped
in a sock, then placed in a package and posted to her at
Acton—all packages were searched, so it was a miracle the
coffee made it to Amanda. Donna's sister had sent her a sock
filled with coffee creamer, but her package was ransacked and
the creamer confiscated.

"Fuckin' assholes!" she ranted as she walked away from the
post room. It turned out to be easier to smuggle *actual* cocaine
disguised in a letter.

Amanda didn't smoke, but her sister gave me the rest of her pack that had about five left. That's a pretty big bonus where I was. It turned out to be a tradition at Acton to pass on belongings as you leave, and it was common to mistake a stranger for a friend because of a jacket or shirt that made it through the ranks.

Mission Milo had become Mission Milo to me. He still had thirty days or more, and I continued to meet him every morning. We listened to the sermon, and he dissected the meaning while I collected the jewels that spilled from his mouth, furiously writing. I was enlightened to new ideas of fate I was powerless over and purpose I could achieve. A repetitive image of standing in my room on the night of the fire in my favorite yellow pajamas and opening the door intruded my thoughts. *It's the moment I should have gone. I could have saved them then,* I thought. My breathing became shallow and my muscles tightened into knots. If anyone touched me at that point, whether it was tapping me on the shoulder or accidentally brushing past me, I jumped up and out of my skin as if in a near-death experience—looking down on myself and thinking what a selfish, horrific human I was, undeserving of the oxygen that filled my lungs. Mission Milo's words arrested the thought and replaced it with the purpose of my life. A purpose I had to fulfill so the tragedy in my life wasn't in vain.

I even attended Monday night Bible study. Two nerdy blokes showed up with a big bag of pastries and bagels. We stuffed ourselves more straight after dinner.

"Don't eat poppy seed," someone said to me.

"Why?" I asked.

"You'll come up positive for opiates if they test you."

The man who warned me was Dane. Dane had been in prison for possession and knew the Bible back to front. Most of the blokes from jail could quote it passage and verse. Armed robbers and drug traffickers turned disciples. It was quite a transformation.

❖

The hall was filled to the brim—chairs ran out and latecomers had to sit on tables around the edges of the room. After thirty days, I already felt transformed. I had a purpose to live and there was a reason my brothers died. I was free from narcotics at last. What else could there be? But I had no idea of my plans after ninety days were up, so I needed the time. At the same meeting, Kel received a ninety-day chip and was preparing to leave.

I was sad about her, too. At night, she had a gang of girls gathered in the communal area. The excitement of breaking the rules had us all giggling, even though many of these women had been accused of crimes I daren't think about, that would make me scared to sit in the dark with them. Linkin Park would play on a CD player at low volume, while counselors and security prowled outside praying for prey. A bloke called Smitty was the object of lustful desire amongst the women. Not for me, since I was still confused and wasn't sure whether it was because of my warped sense of male role models.

We played a game that Kel started with an opening statement.

"This morning, I was shocked to find Smitty in my bed when I woke up..."

She stopped, and we went around the room each adding a sentence or word to the story until it sounded like a trashy porno script. I chickened out and said "and" or "so." I would rather have been in bed. It was a laugh, though.

The chip chick stood at the podium.

"Larisa, addict," she said. "Anyone with twenty-nine days or less who would like to collect a welcome chip, please come and get one."

A trail of people walked against the same tide I had when I'd first arrived at Acton. Every ounce of energy thrown into that walk that came so unnaturally for newcomers who were recently plucked from the obscurity of the gutter—Skid Row, some called it. I didn't envy them. I thought the people with time were jealous of me when I first arrived because I'd recently been high and drunk. I knew now that wasn't the case. They were more frustrated and angry than anyone on the compound: raw pain of reality, raw nerves, and demonic cravings.

I didn't envy those on their way out, either. They were about to embark on life without meals being cooked for them, no meetings just a stone's throw away, and bills and jobs, real responsibilities on top of staying away from getting loaded.

Addiction was a fucked-up place to be and most people never wanted to go back—but ninety-five percent would anyway. When the counselors said that, it became an instinctive reaction to look about the room and clock everyone you thought would fall into that population. News of people leaving and getting high again had started to filter through the dorm. I was devastated when one of those whispers was Clarice. I was certain she'd "got it." She was inspiring, reformed—or so it seemed—but now she was lying in the deep freezer of a morgue after an overdose, her body found in an alley, in a pool of her own vomit.

"Thirty days! Anyone with thirty days who wants a chip, come and get one," Larisa shouted into the microphone.

A few people walked up. Ashley was there, too, even though she was in the group for recovering alcoholics. We had a bond from walking in at the same time, but she had her own clique. Even so, if she had left early I think we would have missed each other like twins do. She was my partner in time, this particular time.

When I passed her on the compound, I would tell her in percentages how far we had come. Time seemed to pass more quickly in percentages, and I had good mental arithmetic skills from helping Mam on the market. Multiplying the cost of a yard by the number of yards bought, converting feet into inches, and then into a sale. I knew plenty of kids who followed in their parents' footsteps. Child TV stars often had a parent in the business, and I was jealous of them. I used my abilities to count my way out of rehab.

At the ninety-day chip announcement, Kel stood up. I'd

never even considered she would not be Dorm Mom anymore. I thought about telling Kel about Psycho stealing from Marlene's closet before she left. The potential brawl the revelation posed seemed not worth it—besides, Marlene had said nothing.

After collecting her chip, Kel walked over and handed it to me. "I challenge you," she said.

I took it. Considered it in the palm of my hand. I was touched she had chosen me. People did this to encourage those behind them in time that they wanted to succeed. I didn't know what I'd done to deserve the recognition, but my insides panged. What was previously a dead zone had a rush of emotion I hadn't realized I was capable of any more.

The chip was a physical reminder of time, like a wrinkle. Kel had a powerful smile, even with missing canines. She didn't need to say anything more than what she had. The chip was a symbol of the energies she was transmitting. It was a reminder of who I could become. I held it in my palm for the whole meeting, hoping I would absorb its powers.

I was relieved Kel had chosen me. Sobriety was becoming a slippery concept even with the restored faith I had gained. The compound was shrinking, the mountains closing in. Familiar homesickness returned that I remembered from every school trip I went on, especially overnight. I called our Charlie.

"Hiya, our kid," he said. His accent, as thick as the butter on my gran's toast, drowned me in memories of home. I felt as if I were sitting next to him. "What's goin' on in la la land?"

"Nothing. Rehab. I'm homesick," I said.

"Awwww, our kid! Don't start cryin'. Why don't yer call Mam if yer gonna start cryin'."

"I'm not," I retaliated, swallowing the bitter lump in my throat. Same as when we were kids. "What yer doin'?"

"I was on a lads' night out last night. Keany, Adam, Bert, you know. We ended up in town [Manchester] pissed out of our 'eads, know what I mean?" He laughed. I did know what he meant, too. That's all anyone did at home.

"Yeah, I know. I'm not s'posed to drink anymore."

"You what?"

"Yeah, no more booze for me, our kid. It's as potent as heroin they tell us in 'ere."

"Well that's a loada bollocks, our kid. What the fuck are those yanks tellin' yer in that place? Fuuuuuuuuuckin' nobs!"

"I dunno! I'm just sayin' what they tell us."

There was a cough, a choke, a splutter, and a louder cough.

"Oh, well no prizes for guessin' what you're smokin'," I said. Of all the drugs I missed most, it was weed. Everywhere I looked, it appeared like a mirage. The heads of palm trees swaying in the sky were like perfect nugs of weed ready to be plucked and smoked, the grass was always marijuana-green. In Acton, I aimed to stay on the redder, dustier side of the compound, where the trees and grass didn't get watered and their death became my salvation. I made a private declaration to score weed the moment I left. I didn't see how it could do that much harm. Smoking weed wouldn't make me progress to crack. I was done with that.

"Ah, you know me, our kid. I woke up with a splittin' 'eadache, and I was just about to take some paracetamol when I realized I 'ad a cold beer in the fridge and a bag of weed. What d'you know, me 'eadache's gone!"

I thought about our Charlie as he spoke. His curly brown hair and the thick lenses of his glasses magnifying his eyes. Those gorgeous muddy-brown eyes. Probably a few days growth on his chin that he used to prop the phone while he rolled a joint. The ache became a throb as I realized how much the family had been destroyed. Obliterated. Why did I have to be a drug addict six thousand miles away? Why didn't I go home and try to keep together the little we had left?

Now I knew too much. I knew Dad's problem, Tony's problem, and mine. Alkies, junkies, all the same—addicts. A problem of genetics. I got mine from my dad—that, along with his gut and curly hair. The hair wasn't a problem as I got older, but I hated being different from my straight-haired junior school friends.

There was no pretending at Acton. We were all expected to face ourselves. There were no peer groups to dive in and out of, to hide behind. All the drugs were gone. This was just me and my shadow. What stung me the most was finding out I was just like my dad and Tony. I started young with sugar. I'd been this way all my life. I thought I had problems because of the cocktail of events in my life, and that led me to cocktails of drinks and drugs. But I was born this way—that's why I could never stop when I wanted to. I drank and used to stop the guilt of not saving my brothers and the pain of their dying. In rehab, we were supposed to confront it all and move on.

Going home and trying to forget and trying to pretend was no longer an option. Just as leaving England didn't solve my cocaine problem, leaving LA wouldn't take away the crack issue or guilt because *I* would still be there. I was the problem. In the meetings, they called this a geographic. Tons of people had tried it—it wasn't even original.

That evening I stood on the concrete balcony smoking with Donna. It was a full moon that lit the faces of those who walked by, and I was able to identify the spitters. At Acton, spitting was as natural as breathing. I tried to remember not to walk on that particular sticky patch of grass.

"Does the spitting not bother you?" I asked her.

"Uuugh! It's disgusting! Who do they think they are? But what are we gonna do, piss them off? They'll pull a gun on us or do a drive-by in one of those electric golf cart whatnots," she laughed and so did I. I hadn't realized she was that funny. "Look at the moon," she said and pointed. "Two more full moons and I'm outta here. I'm jazzed. I hate this fucking place. It's dirty, there's always drama. I just wanna be home with my boys and grandkids in my own bed that I don't own," she told me, and we both cracked up laughing again.

Everybody had to attend mandatory classes and meetings. During the day, too, counselors patrolled the dorms trying to catch waggers. People were caught in bushes, hiding in the gym or under beds and were immediately kicked out. A threesome was caught in one of the phone boxes made of glass—two men and a woman going way beyond the ten-second rule in broad daylight. This made me think that some people had short-circuited essential brain cells that stopped outrageously idiotic behavior. The woman, who was supposed to leave the next day, went back to jail.

"That's the disease," people would say. I still didn't understand what they meant by that. I just thought these people were stupid.

I'd heard stories on top of more stories that told the lives of the people on the compound who were born to be drug runners or addicts. That was their purpose, or so they were raised to believe. Then they became junkies themselves and did anything they had to do to get the money to get high.

"I look around this room, all I see is twenty-dollar, twenty-dollar, and twenty-dollar," Destiny Rose said, pointing at a few men during an evening meeting. I was half relieved she hadn't pointed to me, half mortified at what she was suggesting, as well as mortified that we had this as a bonding point. Not that I would ever lower myself to twenty dollars, but I had slipped into this realm, if only dipping my toe, with the likes of Hannay.

The most frightening realization was that all my ideas of not belonging in Acton—because I'd not been in jail, had an education, hadn't been raised as a runner or a dealer—were all slipping away. Instead, the similarities were forced into my line of vision, seeping into my consciousness. I was lucky to have been found out and kicked out of Grandma's house. Lucky that Mam's caveman knowledge of drugs had made her take all my money unless I passed a drug test, and even if she thought I could be cured at Acton, she probably had a big hand in saving me. Had none of these events happened, I knew it could be me in the morgue with Clarice, back in a crack house like Marlene, looking from the podium at the people in the audience as potential sales. For the first time in my life, I could see my luck and glad it didn't boil down to winning a prize in a raffle. If fate was always going to claim my brothers' lives. then it was my luck to have not ended up like Destiny Rose or Marlene.

Mam's main source of income was selling net curtains on Salford market. My gran had been selling nets on the market since the day after the Queen's inauguration. Mam said she had a day off school to watch her being crowned and the next day was the weekend, so she had to help my gran.

I remembered my first day on the market helping Mam, like it was an heirloom she was passing down. It happened to be on the same day as the Queen's silver jubilee. I was short enough to stand underneath the stall, without cricking my neck, and pass the rolls of net to her.

Her yardstick wafted up and down, as yard by yard, she measured the mountain of pristine white nets—to replace the nicotine stained yellow ones—and gossiped with the customers.

"Ooooh, really?" was her favorite expression. An expression I now use when I'm being indulged in gossip. The mountain of unraveled net would finally disappear and was wrapped in a paper bag ready to be taken home and hung proudly in a window.

❖

The frosting on top of the relief and mortification was the guilt that I'd taken Destiny Rose's only hope from her—the head librarian position. I wasn't even supposed to have a job because of the lawsuit related to my wrist, but one of the counselors, Billy, insisted I take the position under the table, like all illegal immigrants. I'd aced a test they'd given us to see how many brain cells people had left.

"Hey Destiny Rose," I shouted after the meeting. "How about we share responsibilities at the library?" They seemed benign words to someone who saw dollar signs in a room filled with addicts.

Destiny Rose was gone the next day. Whether she left in the night or not, nobody knows. But the horrors of addiction and the lengths people went to just to get a fix were becoming clear. I thought about the yarns me and Gina had told Scott when we were shacked up in motel rooms and were off to score again. The last one was that Grandma had been taken to hospital, I felt rotten bringing her into it. If it ever came true, I knew I wouldn't forgive myself—but I absolutely had to get high.

We ended up in an alley behind the motel after going through what we'd bought and scraping the resin. At the time, it seemed normal. With the clarity of the days I had added together, I was overcome with shock and disgust that this is who I turned out to be. I had a family, an education, hope, and yet crack made me feel better inside.

It was at stag meetings that I really got to know my roommates. I'd been to these before with Gina. It was either all men or all women, supposedly to make people talk with fewer inhibitions. At Acton, we were required to go to five a week, but most of the time people dropped off their cards to be signed and took off. The meeting leader chose someone to speak and then people who wanted to spoke about their experiences, relating them to what the leader had shared. At the third meeting I attended, I heard Marlene speak. I hunched forward and brushed my hair behind my ears.

"Marlene, addict," she started. Her eyes still staring at the floor, her fingers clasped together, and I could see she bit her nails to the bone. "I ain't sure where to start, so I guess I'll tell y'all how I got here. I'm wanted in three states for armed robbery. I wanted so bad to get the hell outta Alabama that I robbed a bunch of people at gunpoint when I was cracked outta my mind," she said, then paused and the serious expression on her face fractured into a faint smile.

We were sitting outside, so I lit a cigarette. I wished I had a pint of Stella, too, which would be a perfect accompaniment to such a story, like salt and vinegar on chips. One without the other somehow didn't work. Or maybe I just wanted to try and forget the fact that the girl I shared a room with was a wanted armed robber.

"When I was a kid I was molested by my daddy and my uncle, they both drug addicts. But my daddy found out about my uncle and shot him to death in the street. Now he in jail and Mamma blames me."

Between my fingers, the cigarette burned and was out before I could take one drag. Tragic life after tragic life, and I couldn't compete. Compared to Marlene, my story of molestation when I was ten was bordering on an overly zealous kiss from an old man.

"I met my man, Julius, out here in LA when I was staying in a crack house. Our eyes met across a room filled with crack smoke," Marlene chuckled, and the others laughed with her. Marlene being funny was rare. This was possibly the only attempt at making light of her situation. "I never met a man who defended my honor, but Julius did. I moved into his room in a house he shared with a bunch of dope fiends. It was easier to find crack than food, and I got worse and worse. Julius, too. We started robbing liquor stores, people at ATMs, friends, family, whatever we could get away with. Turns out a friend of mine," she said and drew quotation marks around the word *friend* with her fingers, "was slagging me behind my back. I didn't like that. A'all. Julius, either. We needed more money one night, and I called her to come over to get high with us." She paused, still staring at the floor. I felt the story intensifying, the crumpled circle of women staring at Marlene. "She walked through the door, and we both jumped her. Julius pistol-whipped her and I joined in 'til we were takin' it in turns."

A few of the women, Liz and Kel included, let out shocked whimpers. Jody smirked and inspected her nails. I was relieved I wasn't the only one who was shocked.

"We told her we'd let her live if she got us some money. I was so cracked outta m'mind I probly wudda killed 'er, too.

We took her outside to a bar and pimped her out. We made her give blowjobs to anyone wanting one and took the money. All night we got high, at her expense. She eventually passed out, and I don't know to this day whether she dead or alive."

The air was racked with silence, not even the wind dared to breathe. Diamond, from B cube—the perpetual snorer—broke the silence. Startled out of an illicit snooze by the unnatural quiet, she oinked like a pig. The unexpected interruption was welcomed with shattering laughter. For a second, the horror of Marlene's secrets was a bond among us—and I didn't feel so different and awkward.

I called Mam to let her know I shared my room with a wanted armed robber.

"Don't worry about it, luvvy. Just think, you'll be cured soon."

"Mam, you can't be cured from addiction. I'm not even supposed to drink again 'cos I'm probably an alcoholic, too."

"That seems a little extreme, darling! A glass of wine never hurt anyone."

"Right, Mam, and probably a rock of crack, a line of coke, a balloon of heroin wouldn't, either. So long as I just stopped at one."

"Well, now you're just being ridiculous—you can't compare drugs and alcohol—"

"I'm telling you, Mam, more alkies die than heroin addicts in detox. It's all they go on about in this place."

Marlene complained about her teeth. She spent two days in the dispensary begging for attention and a ticket out to the dentist. I saw her one of those days after I woke up with a sickness that wasn't helped by the window being left closed the night before. All the germs from all the people had stormed my body and had no escape. Every muscle ached, and I felt worse after they weighed me and I found out I'd gained five pounds in a month.

The dentist was a common excuse to get a lift into downtown LA, where it would take no time to get crack or heroin. It never crossed my mind Marlene wouldn't come back. She was court ordered. For her, the consequence was a stretch in prison, not jail. Prison meant being locked up for many years.

The night she was away, Julie filled her bed. She'd slept from the moment she arrived. I grabbed her some cereal at breakfast, but she slept. This was common for the meth heads who smoked or injected.

The county bus returned from downtown in the afternoon. There were some newcomers who hopped on the bus at Crocker Street, a place infamous for crack dealers. This was never one of the places I had been, but I made a mental note in case I was suicidal in the future. Back on Alvarado, my old dealers claimed I owed them money. If a dealer thinks you owe them money, they pimp you out until they were paid back with interest. I was learning so much in rehab.

Marlene never came back. Julie continued to sleep.

CHAPTER SIXTEEN

LIFE FLEW BY AND WAS SLOWED ONLY BY THE WEIGHT
OF TIME. The cast of characters rotated constantly. The faces I
recognized were down to a handful. It was a relief when
Psycho left. She was given permission to sing at graduation. At
last, I got to hear what she'd been draining my batteries on. She
was a good singer, but I was glad to see the back of her.

A staggering number followed in Marlene's footsteps and
her bed alone rotated characters to the point me and Donna
were convinced it was cursed. But when I thought about their
options, the families they had to return to, more felonies than
I'd had hot dinners and crack house, junky homes. What was to
be expected? It made me incredibly sad for them and magnified
the good fortune of my own life even more.

I often pictured myself standing in my room on the night of
the fire, unable to see the flames through the smoke. Swirling
tornadoes strangling every breath, crucifying my will to live.
Hearing these women share their stories was like flinging the
door and windows open in my mind. The tornadoes of smoke
unraveled and drifted away. There was a shift in my breathing,
a sprite in my walk, even with the weight I'd gained, which
was nowhere near the forty pounds we were expected to put on
at Acton, to my relief.

Me and Donna became the old timers in the cube. Our
relationship welded firm in one afternoon. I'd just picked up
my post and Mam had sent me some PG Pyramid teabags. I
also had a collection of Tetley. The envelope was thick, but I
could still feel tea that had collected into lumps in the bags,
through the paper. It was a banned item and I wondered why
Jack in the post room hadn't ripped it open to see what the
suspicious lumps were.

Spring was seeping in. The weather was scorching by nine
in the morning—at least eighty degrees. By the afternoon, it

could be ten to twenty degrees hotter, but it never stopped me gagging for a cup of tea. Mam always drank tea in summer because she said it quenched her thirst. I pictured her sitting in the back garden on a deckchair reading a book sipping out of a china mug. Mam drank tea in the same fashion my dad drank lager.

In the dorm, they kept the air conditioning pelting at full blast. To me, it seemed backward to have heat outside and the inside freezing. I could never get used to it, like I couldn't get used to iced tea, because it was so opposite to home. I pushed the door to the dorm open, pulling my hoodie tight around me. A babble of voices in the distance was getting rowdy about the temperature.

"Can you turn that thing off, I'm gettin' a headache!"

It sounded like Diamond, and when the sentence ended with the slap of a domino on the table instead of a full-stop, I knew I was right. Her and her crew, Ginny and Mole, sat around the table in the communal area every afternoon gas bagging, wheezing laughs, and playing games annoyingly loud. They reminded me of the three witches in the opening scene of *Macbeth* brewing trouble, so I steered clear.

"Fuck you and yer fuckin' dominoes!" another voice shouted back. Diamond, Ginny, and Mole cackled and a thunderous din of dominoes repeatedly hitting the table followed.

I sat on my bed and ripped open the letter. Donna was napping and the other two beds were empty, waiting to be filled. Since we were expecting Marlene to come back, Julie had moved into Jody's cube. Four tea bags fell out.

"What's that?" Donna asked. This let me know that she, too, slept with one eye open.

"Just some teabags me mam sent me. I might go and get some 'ot water and make some."

"Oh yeah? You can do that? When I go, they tell me I can't have any. 'Against the rules,'" she said, dropping her voice a few octaves.

"I tell them I'm English, and it's essential I have my afternoon tea, and if they ever feel like baking me some scones that would be wonderful."

Donna laughed hysterically. "That's amazing. Here, if you go and get us some water, I have coffee and creamer. I'll give you a cup."

I remembered Donna and Marlene making afternoon coffee and taking off for a walk. The aroma of coffee granules had become a lavish smell compared to the coffee they served for breakfast. Starbucks seemed like a lifetime ago and the smell of it deep down in the caverns of my subconscious. I was learning to be grateful for what I had.

"Nice one! Yeah, give us your cup an' I'll run over."

Ten minutes later I was back with my delabeled coffee jar and her mug filled with hot water. We loaded them with coffee and creamer. I used heaped teaspoons, the same way I made it when I was studying for A-levels in sixth-form college and had to stay awake all night—that was before I'd discovered coke or speed. It felt similar to getting my hands on a fantastic drug deal. The inside of my mouth drooled, my stomach spun, and the glory of the very first taste—like angels on my tongue— could never be recreated. But I chased it, anyway.

The caffeine rushed through me, and in a whirlwind I picked up clothes, cleaned the top of the bedside table, and organized my locker—before crashing. Donna picked up her clothes, too, but she had built up a tolerance level to the caffeine and her efforts weren't so frantic. She gave up when I was finished and flopped onto her bed.

"Man, I wish I had a gagger," she said.

"A what?"

"A gagger. Ya know. Didn't you ever do a line of coke that knocked you sick and made you heave, but spun your fuckin' head off your shoulders?"

A smile crept across my face. "Yeah, I know what you mean."

I picked up Mam's letter again, and this time pulled it out. She'd written to me with her left hand to prove to me it could be done after I'd complained to her about how I had no endurance in my right hand since I'd broken my wrist and dislocated my shoulder. *Business is picking up...*She wrote in barely legible, slanted writing. Mam could always tell me how to patch a weakness up with a strength. I was tired of that game. Wore myself down to rehab with the pretence.

I read on: *You can always call me and discuss anything you want love...*I threw the letter to one side. That clearly wasn't true or maybe I would have a healthy relationship with myself and my brothers' memory. If Donna hadn't spoken to me at that point I could have easily called Mam and woken her with a tirade of bitterness.

"Who's ya letter off, hun?"

"Me mam, back in England."

"Seems like you should be a little more jazzed than that. I can't get my boys to write, and they live in California."

I was confused. "So you think that because they live closer they should have more motivation to write to you?"

Before she could figure it out, Liz wheeled in a grey wheelbarrow.

"Hey Flip, hey Donna. I brought you gals some new roomies. This is Kath and this is Phoebe," Liz nodded at each of them in turn while still hanging on to the wheelbarrow.

"Hey."

"Yeah, hey."

Liz plonked herself on my bed, and I bounced into the air.

"Ya mind if I sit here, Flip?"

"No worries, mate."

I was surprised we got two white girls. Phoebe, an alcoholic, admitted herself but was pressured by her kids. I couldn't ever imagine telling my dad he might have a problem with alcohol and marching him to rehab. He'd laugh and go to the pub.

Kath had come from jail to get a shorter sentence. She, too, had kids and a job—the only person I knew with a job when she got out. She chatted away about her arrest and her sentence all the while taping two short pencils together and testing them as one long one.

"Wha' yer doin'?" I asked.

"Writing to my kids," Kath said.

"No. With them pencils. Why yer doin' tha'?"

"Oh," she laughed. "In jail, they only allowed us these tiny pencils but my hands are too big to hold 'em," she said and put her pencil down and held up her hand. They w*ere* pretty big.

"You wanna use a pen? This isn't jail, you know."

"You have one? For real?"

I opened my bedside drawer and pulled out a pen Em had posted to me from Australia, black and shiny. I held it out in my hand.

"Ladies and more ladies," I said. "Here we have a fo' real pen."

We all laughed—and, for the first time, I was relaxed and at home in the cube and it didn't seem so much like a jail cell.

Through my forced lunches with Jody, she had also become a friend. She would drag me out of "The Barn"—her nickname for the dining hall—to eat with her and her friends Rico and Jamaal. Jamaal was one of those who had gone to see the dentist downtown and had never returned. Me and Donna had nicknamed the compound bus "The Hearse."

Rico and Jody ordered fried chicken and sandwiches from a local eatery, and it was the best food I'd eaten since the last meal Fe had cooked. The only other place we were allowed to order from was a pizza place. I wasn't a fan of ordering pizza with American friends because they preferred pepperoni as opposed to ham and pineapple that me and our Charlie were totally addicted to.

With Jody and her friends, I shared a picnic table near the TV area. Most tables were empty because other people were eating the slop they dished out in the dining hall. I would have preferred to eat with everyone else picking through a tray to find something edible. I'd declared myself a vegetarian so I could get an alternative to processed meat with veins of fat running through it. It reminded me of the Spam that Mam put on our butties—coming out of the tin covered in jelly like a newborn baby out of the womb. The alternative was to declare yourself a vegetarian—but that meant an extra scoop of tinned, soggy vegetables. I went back to being a meat eater so I could trade it for something I might want.

No one liked Jody because of her snobbishness and boob job. She refused to participate in cleaning—instead, buying girls with contraband and hard cash, which she had plenty of. She got me with phone minutes—as many as I wanted, and I could call wherever I wanted. It was like legal crack to me. I went wild calling everyone I knew all over the world. She gave me small cans of double espresso shots, too, which had the same effect on me as a couple of grams of coke. But Jody was as false as her boobs.

Rico turned out to be The Dude to know. Anything you thought you could only dream about, he could make real. He had earned his nickname, "AM/PM," a petrol station with shop attached that sold everything you might need with a full tank: soda, ice cream, chocolate, cigarettes.

"Cigarettes! Nice. What about coffee?"

"Sure. Anything for a sweet smile like that."

I heard his comment, but I didn't know what to do with it. My face burned, so I didn't have to say a word anyway. I ignored him, which was easy to do with so much excitement about coffee and cigarettes.

"Yes!" I shouted. "I need both. When can I get them?"

"Whoah, girl. Eatcha sandwich first," he laughed.

After lunch, I ran back to the dorm where Donna immediately ribbed me for hanging out with Jody.

"I don't know how you can even stand to be around her for a second. She's so false. *Penelope, Penelope,*" she tried taking her voice off.

"If you must know, Donna," I said. A smile spread across my face, and I allowed it to linger for a moment.

"What? Tell me. Don't act like a punk."

I laughed at the thought of me acting like a punk. What did that even mean? Shin-high Doc Martins and drainpipe jeans and a shaved head?

"I know where we can get cigs and coffee."

"What? Where?"

I took from my pocket a new pack of cigarettes and slowly pulled off the seal of the cellophane wrapping. I opened the flap and the silver paper was perfectly folded like a gift. I tore it off and smelled the bouquet of the tobacco before offering one to Donna.

"Well I'm not sure now you've had your nose all over 'em."

At sixty days, I was eligible for a sixty-day chip but the bigger reward was a thirty-hour pass to leave the compound. By this point, I was ready to break free and cop lungs full of smog that streaked just below the snowcapped mountains. There were many who had gone before me and had gone for good. I wanted to smoke weed, but the threat of a pee test on my return made it too risky. I still had nowhere to go when I left and wasn't ready to sleep in a bush or in a shelter.

The time started at seven in the morning and went through until one in the afternoon the next day. The hours were set in stone and like the rest of the laws that governed the compound there was a zero tolerance attitude. I arranged with Fe that I would bunk down at Grandma's without telling Ali. But since Ali lived in the town of Acton, she said she'd pick me up from the train station and take me back to rehab. Donna said that was drug addict behavior because I was being dishonest to make the situation suit myself.

"What, and neckin' all them Benadryl i'nt?"

"Punk!"

I left at ten in the morning on The Hearse and hoped this didn't presage my doom. As we got closer to downtown LA, the skyline appeared like the magic kingdom out of *The Wizard*

of Oz, a handful of buildings in an otherwise flat landscape—spectacularly different from the rugged mountains I'd grown accustomed to in Acton. A glow surrounded the buildings and, although in this instance it was a magical effect, I knew it was probably the radiated smog.

I was turfed out at Pershing Square, where I was instantly drowning in waves of freedom—the best high I'd ever had. The air was filled with sounds and smells that I'd forgotten existed. People bustled around me, shoving and tugging in every direction. It was like the dining hall at meal times.

I fled the temptations of downtown for the safety of the bus that sluggishly edged me towards Grandma's house. I was dreading seeing Fe, though. I knew she would say I was chunky, or chunkier than the last time she'd seem me.

Nothing had changed. I blinked to make sure it was real. My life had galloped into a new way of thinking and behaving. I'd developed faith in the fate of uncontrollable circumstances. It was a new idea that the fire was going to happen, regardless of the orbiting circumstances—and I was destined to live. Thinking about my life experiences in these terms didn't make it less painful. Lost love is a persistent ache, but I could cope. The crushing weight rearranged into manageable loads. Sickening clichés made sense: *At least I'd had these beautiful boys to love—some people never get to experience even that. Mam had done her best to go on and give us a life. We'd had education, a home, a first car, holidays in the sun.* I'd experienced trust and love and friendship at Acton, and, even though it felt foreign to me, I recognized that Mam had tried to give us all of these—and when she couldn't, prodded us with a hot poker of encouragement.

I considered myself lucky for the wisdom I'd gained regardless of the circumstances that had given me that wisdom. I was a chunkier on the outside but totally overhauled on the inside. That was obvious when I walked into Grandma's house and the chill of my demons evaporated with a warm hug from Grandma and then Fe and quickly disappeared into the dark, cobwebbed corner it had slithered from.

Grandma was propped up in bed beaming a smile with her eyes sparkling. She held me and I didn't want to let her go, but Fe interrupted with a story about her latest boyfriend who had a foot fetish. He spent hours rubbing her feet, paying special attention to her toes and whispering sweet nothings to them.

"He crazy, Bloody Dude," she said. "I get bored and I leabe! He speak more to my foot than to my face."

I'd missed listening to Fe's accent, but she had nothing new to say: *Different boyfriend, different fetish*, I thought. I was thankful I wasn't trapped in the same miserable place I had been sixty days ago, grateful for a new perspective that enabled me to crush the person I was because that person was killing me.

More than anything, I was thankful that I'd been locked up long enough to recognize the changes in myself when put in the exact same environment. I felt as if I were having an out-of-body experience of what seemed a different lifetime. I had no idea that was possible.

The next morning, I left without any anxiety. I knew I could walk away for months more and when I returned it would still be the same.

I had to get to Union Station by half ten to catch the last train that would get to Acton before one. I'd arranged a time with Ali to pick me up. Everything had to go perfectly, as planned.

Before I got on the bus, I stopped for some freeze-dried coffee, laundry detergent—so I didn't have to use the county-issued crap that left me with an unbearable itch—and, of course, cigarettes. Mission Milo had asked me to get him a black and mild cigar and Donna wanted me to try and get Benadryl. Another full moon had passed and she didn't have much longer to stay, the Benadryl made her sleep and was permitted. Since we had become friends, she sent me to the doughnut meetings to scavenge them for her while she slept her way through the days. Sometimes, I jumped on the end of her bed, the only way to get her to move. I wanted her to make me laugh, which helped me get through the days.

I was desperate for a Starbucks, the crowning jewel to my time on the *outs*. I thought I deserved one, too, for my strength to stay away from all the temptations. I'd heard in meetings that this was like wanting a reward for running out of a burning building. I ignored this analogy for being too close to my truth and decided to go anyway.

They appeared like dots before my eyes. Had there always been this many? I ordered a venti coffee and poured in lashings of half and half and brown sugar. It was divine, the best coffee I'd ever tasted. I was at this point content—and content is better than fucking miserable or too-high-to-feel. I could accept that.

I thought the traffic would be reasonable when I was headed to the train station, but rush hour in Hollywood was constant. I'd forgotten that in Acton where the real world doesn't exist until leaving becomes a reality. I caught the rapid bus that didn't have as many stops but the speed it trundled at made no odds. I was starting to panic—racing thoughts, sweaty hands, incessant fidgeting. After an hour, I knew I was going to miss the train but I had to give it a shot. I jumped off the bus early and started running with the biggest bottle of Tide available, it felt like it weighed fifty pounds or more. I hoped I could run through the traffic, but the superpowers I was certain I had with the caffeine pounding through my veins didn't kick in.

I arrived at Hollywood and Vine metro station drowning in my own sweat. It was like the tube in London with several flights of steep staircases to descend and a gate to jump that was impossible with the bottle of Tide. I stopped to buy a ticket, the first honest train journey I had taken. It was a short ride to Union Station but once there, it was a cavern of tunnels leading to more tunnels. Now I was dripping anxiety, my eyes swimming in the numbers on the information board above me. I couldn't slow down my thoughts enough to make sense of it. My mind itself was like a hurtling train leaving the outside scenic blur.

I watched my train chug away from the platform, blowing me a black toxic kiss as it left.

Shit! Fuck! Fuck-shit! Aaagh! I needed a plan quick. I found a phone and called the office, and Sheryl picked up.

"Well honey, if ya not here by one they'll pack ya belongings forya!" she said in the same sweet honey tone she used to confiscate my alcohol-fueled mouthwash. I was on to Sheryl's game, and she couldn't fool me any more

"Right! So wha' shalla do? Will they let me on The Hear…I mean, the bus?"

"Uhhh. Hold on, honey."

She held the phone receiver in her hand trying to muffle me out of earshot.

"Honey," she returned. "Our bus picks up on Crocker Street, Fifth and Crocker. If you can make that, it'll be okay."

A voice in the background urged me to run, probably Dan— he was a patient working in the office with Sheryl and was having an affair with a new girl, Michelle, in my dorm but in Liz's cube. He was always trying to bend rules and turn a blind eye to give patients a second chance instead of the instant discharge rule.

I had an hour and some scrappy directions full of lefts and rights that for some reason had confused me all my life. When I was seventeen I had to draw an "L" and an "R" on the back of my hands for quick reference to pass my driving test. I was also worried that I was in possession of a rucksack full of banned items. At this point, the only thing in my favor was the Starbucks and masses of adrenaline that had flooded my brain. It was as uplifting as snorting a gagger. I think an American football team might have found it impossible to break my energy at that moment.

I found a loo and walked into a cubicle that had no other guests nearby. I remembered to grab Ziploc bags from Grandma's house, and I tore the foil back from the coffee jars. A fine cloud off bitter coffee dust exploded from the jar, but I knew I was lucky to be getting this. I split it into the Ziploc bags and taped them to my stomach. When I ran out of skin I switched to my shins. I broke the cigarettes out of the carton and stuffed the packs in the pockets and torn liner of Donna's jacket she'd loaned me. When I returned, I knew they would search me. The rule was they could check your bag and bodily fluids but not your person.

Fifth and Crocker was as grim as the myths I'd heard. I stood at the end of the block absorbing the scene. Considering this was the place with the highest concentration of crack dealers it appeared to be deserted but for the fallen few whose limbs peeked out from under bushes or from behind trees, whatever shelter could be sought. The daylight cast an ugly shadow.

The addicts I knew were chameleons. They could be high as a kite and you wouldn't notice them. If they turned to one side they could appear to be a part of a railing. The dealers would emerge as if they'd been beamed up or down, and appeared conveniently like a genie.

What if someone grabs me? I thought. *I could buy it. Will I buy it? Am I even considering this? Look where you are!* I screamed in my head. *Just one, just one.* Another voice piped in.

I started to walk. *I have to stand out. I look like a tourist. I always look like a tourist. Now they'll think I'm lost, too, and mug me. What the fuck was I thinking? How did I end up here like one of these people?*

It was shocking, it was real, it was me.

Dane from the Bible study was waiting outside a building.

"Hey Flip! Whaddaya doin' here, girl?"

I hurried over to him, as quick as I could, given the heavy bottle of Tide in my rucksack. The coffee strapped around my legs made me walk like a bandy cowboy.

"Hey, Dane. God, am I glad to see you. I missed the train to Acton, and they said I 'ad to make it 'ere or they'd kick me out. I can't believe they'd rather have me come 'ere rather than 'op on the next train. What the fuck!"

The caffeine in my body was manifesting in jittery, nervous movements and spitting words. Then I was paranoid he thought I'd taken something. "I 'ad a Starbucks and it got me wired to the max, mate, the max."

"Yeah I can see. Man, they're gonna piss test you when you get back."

"You reck?"

"I'd bet my last vein on it," Dane was a heroin addict who only had working veins remaining between his toes. Even when he had to give a blood sample, the nurse had to take it from there. I was sitting in the same room with him and bit my knuckles between my teeth when I saw the needle slide in his foot. Dane's face ripened to a fierce red and that's when I noticed he had plenty of veins left in his forehead, too. I was lucky enough to have my veins intact, and when they bulged in the heat people stared at me with envy and some pity.

"You should try a needle in them pretty veins," an old toothless bloke said.

I backed away from him and fell into a bush.

The Hearse arrived on the compound after one in the afternoon, but I had officially been on county property for a couple of hours. I was expecting the bus to pull into the car park, where I would have my bag checked and try to ignore the overwhelming coffee aroma. The driver went past reception and over the speed humps and parked outside L Dorm. I slid the door back and jumped out. This wasn't the usual procedure, but I didn't question my stroke of luck. I ran into the cube, waking Donna with the urgency in my run.

"What happened? You get caught?"

I sat on my bed, didn't say a word, and tore the Ziploc bags from my legs and stomach and wriggled out of her jacket.

"Hide it," I said legging it out of the door before I was noticed missing and the whole dorm was put on lockdown and searched for illegal items.

After all the threats, they didn't check anything or look bothered about what I'd been through to get back here. *Fuck 'em!* I thought.

228

CHAPTER SEVENTEEN

THE MOON LOOKED LIKE A NAIL CLIP SUSPENDED IN THE DARK. A quarter full, but Donna saw it as three-quarters empty.

"Gosh darn it," she had given up blaspheming since Bible study. "How long ya think it's gonna take to be full again?"

"Chill out, mate. Think of others. What am I s'posed to do when you're gone?"

"I'll send you smokes and you have more than enough coffee to make it through. Ya gonna follow me a couple of weeks after."

"Not if you leave before your time, then it'll be three weeks."

"Ya got Phoebe and Kath, they're cool. And don't forget I'm gonna pick you up after you graduate."

"Ah, yes, graduation," I said. "Just think, we'll be cured. *Cured,* I tell you!"

I'd learned to laugh at Mam's and my friends' idea that after this clean time, I'd be better and on my way to the pub in no time, so long as I didn't do drugs. It broke heavy silences and shattered tensions that grew like twisted vines through my mind.

Returning to Acton after leaving for a day pass had left me depressed and irritable. The initial giddiness of sobriety had lost its edge. I watched Phoebe and Kath unwrap their gifts of sobriety: focus, thoughts, happiness—natural highs. But as was the same with anything else, my tolerance level was shifting, and, compared to being free, it had started to get boring.

"God, Mission Milo—"

"Sweet sister! Let's not take our Lord's name in vain."

I giggled. Of course I should know that by now.

"Now, what were ya gonna say?" He was puffing on the same black and mild I'd brought him back from my pass, a few days before.

"I'm goin' crazy in 'ere! I wanna walk out, it's pissin' me off. What's the point now?" I paused. "'Cept I don't 'ave anywhere to go, still."

"Sister! You ain't ready to leave yet."

"What's that s'posed to mean?"

"Means, you walk outta here right now, you gonna fall on yo' ass. You need more tools, sister. There ain't no point in being on the outside on yo' ass now, is they? God's will, not self-will."

I felt him staring at me, gauging my reaction. Would I bolt? Even I couldn't answer that as I teetered on the edge of confusion. I could tell, though, that it would be a fall, and he talked me down from the proverbial ledge I'd crawled out onto.

"S'pose not."

"More time, more knowledge, more power. More power to you, sister."

But his words didn't stop me from trampling a few of the rules and pushing my newfound luck. In my locker, I stored a tattoo gun for a new girl, Mary. She was going to make friends and money with it but faced prison time if she was caught. Kath and Phoebe were the exact opposite to me and Donna. An invisible line separated our jungle—clothes spewed across the floor and beds, writing materials flung with half-finished letters, drawers open with Ziploc bags peeking out, full and empty—from their primly organized belongings. Phoebe and Kath had curling tongues propped in the hollow frame of their beds so when they woke they could style their hair. The cube smelled of fried hair and stale cigarettes most mornings.

They were grateful I volunteered to store their nail paraphernalia, and I kept it all for them in my bedside drawer. I left it all visible, and, in the event of a counselor raid, they would have no problem finding it and having an excuse to kick me out. The unfulfilled threat became an unfulfilled promise.

When softball season swung into action, Rico, who was leaving the next day, agreed to walk across the softball pitch holding my hand—an action with a definite, without doubt, certainty to get him and me thrown out. I held on tight to Rico. Jody had tried to couple us up, as he was best friends with Damian who she was breaking the ten-second rule with. But Damian had split on The Hearse and had never returned and now she was after Rico. I didn't mind losing Rico in that respect. He was tall and burly—he would have made a magnificent rugby player—but it was the Indian-giving principle that made me get cross with Jody. As far as Rico, I was petrified of running out of fags and having to search through the bushes like the people I'd seen on my first day.

The counselor on duty was Karen, a normy—that meant she'd had no addiction or drinking issues. She also had no sympathy or empathy and was one of those people who couldn't understand how anyone ended up at Acton. Why didn't we all just stop before this point arrived? Where was good old-fashioned willpower? If anyone could answer that, she'd be out of a job.

I was banned from using the gym because of my wrist and shoulder injuries. But I would sneak in on the tail of nagging boredom. Sometimes I managed a couple of sets of ab crunches or would pump my legs until they hurt before getting caught. Unlike counselor Billy in the library, she wouldn't ignore the indiscretion and sent me packing every time. I hoped I could use her meanness to my advantage.

"Philippa," I heard her shout. Rico was crushing my hand as we walked in front of the batter's mound. *This is it,* I thought with a smile. *I'm outta here.* "Please come over here."

I wriggled free of Rico and walked over. "Were you just holding Rico's hand?"

"No!" I was ready to put up a fight like I'd seen others do when they were being sent back to jail as defective goods. White knuckles and red screaming faces. Fingers peeled back off the metal bed frames. I was ready for it all for the kiss of freedom.

"I didn't think so."

What! Is she serious? I thought. *I was clearly holding his hand, just kick me out.* I shouted loud enough that nobody could hear. My internal voice only shattering my ears.

Half an hour later, my name boomed over the tannoy to attend the Recovery House where the counselor's offices were located. Ann was my counselor but I'd hardly seen her this whole time, and suddenly I was standing in her office.

"I need a urine sample from you," she said.

"Nice to meet you, too," I said.

"Huh?"

"Nothin'. Good timing, I just finished a liter of water."

She handed me a small container and followed me to the bathroom and then into the bathroom. It took a second to realize she wasn't going to leave. I was grateful not to have a shy bladder. I'd heard about this condition from those who had been in jail, who told me it could take hours for a couple of drops. It was humiliating enough to end my attempts to get out. Instead, I had to focus my efforts on surviving the last few weeks.

❖

I told Jody about holding hands with Rico to try and get kicked out and also to piss her off now that she was after him.

"Why don't you just walk out Penelope?" she asked.

Whenever I considered this, I could see only barriers. Where will I live? How will I live? My visa was about to expire, too. It was a work visa sponsored by the PR agency I no longer worked for. If I stayed in the country, there was every possibility that unless I found someone to marry, I would have to stay in America forever and never see my family again unless they visited me, or leave knowing I could never return. None of those choices was a choice. To me it was similar to being asked would I prefer death by needle or the electric chair. How do you really choose? Donna was determined to find me a husband and cigarettes and post them both to me.

I ate lunch alone one day while Donna was at the finance office collecting food stamps for when she left. I was about to stand up when Victor and Hector plonked themselves in the chairs facing me.

"Ai'ight," they both said.

"Hey."

"Jody been tellin' us you messin' wid her." Victor said. He was the Secretary of the cocaine recovery group and, until I handed over the cash, I had to speak to him on a daily basis as the treasurer of the cocaine recovery group.

"What? How?"

"Rico. You getting' a little too close wid Rico." Hector told me this, and there was no question in his voice.

"She fuckin' asked me to hang out with them and 'ave lunch." Now I was livid. "I didn't even wanna be with 'em! I wanted to eat in 'ere with all the other miserable fucks!"

"Look, Flip," Victor said. "Jody a Crip. She have someone blow yo' kneecap off if she turn on you."

I stood ready to leave, "Just one? One kneecap, Victor? If you're gonna threaten me, at least speak proper fuckin' English! I don't know who your little groups are and who belongs with who, and I don't care!" I held my palm in their faces as if to say, "Talk to the hand," a language I knew they understood. "Fuck Jody!"

On my way back to the dorm, I ran into Luis and told him what had happened.

"Jees, Flip! Ya gotta stay aways from them cats. They OG, girl! Original Gangbangers. They kill fo' fun. Dontcha worry, I gotcha back."

I walked away quickly, not looking around and holding my breath, which I only realized when I got back to the cube. Donna was getting ready to go to anger management, a class we had together now that we were both in the last phase of the program.

"Where've ya been? I was waitin'."

"Gettin' threatened off Jody's heavies. She's gonna blow my kneecaps off or summat, 'cos she's a Crip." I watched Donna's expression. Her face disappeared behind her eyes and tonsils. My heart sank. "Don't leave early! Please!"

❖

The third full moon appeared out of the shadows of space. The sky was glittered with stars. In LA, there was too much smog to have this much clarity when it was dark. I felt like God was showing me a view of the world through His crystal ball, a shining path dazzled with stars, should I choose to follow it.

Me and Donna were sitting in a meeting for alcoholics sliding notes back and forth across the table. The speaker was boring, talking about how she saw all these blades of grass now that she was sober. If I was around this woman, she would make me want to drink, I wrote to Donna. She replied she was going to have a large glass of wine tonight as an antidote to counting blades of grass. I laughed and winced at the same time. *How good wine would taste,* I thought. *And, after this much time, I bet it would only take a glass to fuck me up.*

Lots of people left Acton having bargained with themselves. I'll drink but not smoke crack or inject meth, I often heard. Donna was going to a sober living house, where they did random drug tests and attending daily meetings was a requirement of living there—enforced by getting a house slip signed, similar to the cards we had at Acton. It seemed the only difference between Acton and her new place was not being classed as a patient. Regardless, Donna had to stay clean, but tonight she could drink if she wanted because she wouldn't have to give a urine sample yet.

Halfway through the second speaker, Linda, Donna's sister, popped her head around the door. Donna had been distracted and was looking over her shoulder during the whole meeting. We both stood. There was no way I was going to listen to any more of these dull ex-drinker stories. Phoebe and Kath were at a meeting for druggies, but they had left early to say goodbye to Donna before she absconded into the night.

Her bags were packed, and we each grabbed one and walked to Linda's car. I looked behind me at the vision of log cabins cushioned in the dark and surrounded by trees. A comforting scene that I had envisioned on my arrival, but it wasn't my reality. We formed a circle and held hands, reciting the serenity prayer. I felt strength flowing through us like a current, which came from plugging into each other. I hugged Donna last, and I held on the longest. I wasn't ready for her to leave. I knew I'd see her again, but the emotional pain was still as deep as a death, and I had to fight back the tears—at least until the lights went out and the dark could hide my pain.

"You'll be fine, kid," she said. "I'll send you smokes right away and I'll pick you up at graduation." She pushed me away and turned to Phoebe and Kath. "Look after this one 'til I get back."

"We will," they said together.

We watched as she drove slowly and carefully away over the speed humps, a silhouette wave visible through the back window. Her other arm dangled out of the window, her cig leaving a trail of smoke. That night, I slept because I was emotionally drained, not from the usual stench of Donna's feet that somehow knocked me out. I realized it was more likely that awful smell gave me comfort that she was there, like our Mike and his snuffy blanket.

Donna's memory was swiftly replaced with Selene who was only in her twenties but was kicking heroin. There was only a handful of us that age, and I couldn't shake the feeling that maybe I'd given up drugs too soon in my life. Maybe I should have stuck with it for longer. In the meetings, I learned, from the many crack stories I'd listened to, that crack withdrawal wouldn't have been an issue had I smoked constantly. One woman told us she was on her way to make a car payment when she overheard two young lads discussing getting high. The payment was never made, the car repossessed, and her family didn't see her for six months until she was picked up for prostitution.

"I wuz too scared to stop. It wa'nt no option. I din't wanna come off it. That make me suicidal. It wuz bedder to live like a stray dawg, eatin' outta trash cans, sheetin' 'n'peesin' in alleys 'n sellin' ma body."

It made sense to me. With all the drugs, I wouldn't have cared either. That's what successful crackheads do. I shuddered at the insanity, at the idea of smoking crack for months or years on end and then quitting. I could imagine the torture, mind and body kicking and screaming at the withdrawal like a raging bull. It would take years to tame a beast like that. The beast I was dealing with was ugly enough for me, and I was relieved I hadn't had to experience anything more intense. I felt certain drugs weren't to be a part of my future. I'd learned enough here.

Selene was timid, and so shy she changed her clothes in a shower cubicle. She made no attempts to cover up her track marks. "Fossils of experience," she told me. She seemed to have lifetimes of wisdom crammed into her soul and spilling from her aura and mouth. I took her to meet Mission Milo. I knew they'd get along, so it was a pity that his time was up, too. I prayed Mission Milo would make it. He seemed strong, but so had Clarice.

Donna kept her promise and sent me a carton of fags. Before they were half gone, I was shocked to realize there were only four days until my graduation. I was asked to read the twelve steps at the ceremony, but I had to know them by heart to win five dollars. I paced Serenity Row, a dirt path with a row of trees on either side, and recited them to Michelle over and over. I was bored without Donna, and she was lonely without Dan who had worked with Sheryl in admin up until he had completed his time. They'd never been caught, not even for surpassing the ten-second rule.

This wasn't Michelle's first time in rehab, and she knew the twelve steps by heart, but she was in rehab because she wasn't applying them in her life. To me, they seemed self-explanatory. I could see that I was powerless over drugs. Before I got into crack, there were many nights I had trawled the streets of Hollywood hoping to see Ron in a queue to a nightclub or decide which one he might be in to score more coke. After university, when my friends got jobs and calmed down with using drugs, I became the local dealers' best customer, as I had become with Ron. It was a horrific fact to learn about myself. But now that I knew addiction is genetic, it made sense considering Dad's record.

I wasn't certain about alcohol. I didn't think it would do to me what it did to him because I didn't like it the way I did the drugs. Hangovers were a drag. Also, because the alcohol meeting seemed dull compared to the druggies' meetings—and especially SOS, a nonreligious group. I felt as if I'd had a spiritual awakening—that I had a purpose to having lived. Fate had intervened and, as much as I didn't like it, as long as I fulfilled my purpose I could somehow cope with my brothers' deaths—just as Dr. Snell had said all those years ago when we had read *Macbeth*. My purpose allowed me to regain an inclination of faith.

I stopped blaming God and Mam for my life. I had enough education to survive and know how to implement the first three steps. The other nine steps I would memorize and have to figure out later.

I was having to split my attention between the ceremony and what I was going to do when Donna picked me up. Where would I go? I had to return to England before my visa expired or I would never be able to return to LA. I couldn't be sure Donna was going to find me a husband that I could fall in love with and marry in the next month, as much as I wanted to believe her. I would find a way back.

The Friday of my graduation arrived, finally. I woke up with clammy hands and rattled nerves. The girls in the dorm tested me on the twelve steps and I recited them backwards and forwards, sideways, any which way I was asked. The reward was five dollars that I'd decided to give to Selene.

I had to find an outfit, too. I had to squeeze into my only pair of jeans, squishing my skin, like dough, into the leg. I lay on my bed to try to fasten the button, but the moment I stood up, it popped open, *Fuck!* I thought. They would have to do anyway. I found a long T-shirt to hide my gaping jeans. Kath and Phoebe were ready with makeup brushes to paint my face. After nearly ninety days, I was confident enough to decline and had unearthed enough about myself to know I would only ever wear makeup to please somebody else. At this moment in my life, I was getting used to myself, carving an outline of who I was, much like a chalk outline that cops draw around dead bodies. The difference being my outline couldn't be rubbed out with a soggy footprint or a street cleaner's bristles, nor could I erase myself with copious amounts of dirty street drugs. I'd learned that the incredibly hard way.

The day was a scorcher and instead of the dining hall, the ceremony was moved outside. In the morning, when we were forced to sit in a room to watch a video about relapsing, we watched as chairs were lumbered from the dining hall over to the picnic tables. I stood on the brink of excitement while others jumped in fully clothed. Today, I could feel the excitement, but it was tainted with nerves. Uncertainty was still looming all around me. It seemed as if the peaceful backdrop of the mountains now served as an obstruction into my vision of the future. So much so that when Donna picked me up I still had no idea where I was going.

My bag was packed and hidden under my bed. I'd handed back the tattoo gun. Jen hugged me and said, "Thanks. Good luck out there."

"Yeah, no worries, Jen. Try an' keep your 'ead in 'ere. Stay out of the drama, too. It's fuckin' insane what I got myself into."

Jody had left in the night. She had always told me she wouldn't participate in graduation. She hadn't been involved in anything when I thought about it. One Saturday afternoon there had been karaoke, a special treat for patients, an event complemented with popcorn and pop. Jody had picked out a hip-hop song and insisted we do a skit together. I was bored and agreed.

We practiced in the communal area, where most of the time there was a group of women playing cards or reading ancient magazines. As we practiced, Jody would pull a move and I copied. One by one, the heads bobbed up and back down again, like a Mexican wave, but eventually they stopped what they were doing to watch. Laughter rolled off their tongues, and the roar of clapping hands filled the room. Jojo jumped up, her body was fluid like a ribbon in the wind. Jody didn't like her stealing the attention and bumped her onto the sofa with her arse. On the day of the performance, our act drew cheers louder and heavier than in the dorm. I didn't know I had it in me to do that in front of a crowd of people. The positive energy was like a breath of fresh air that was absorbed by my body.

Straight after us, Jojo stood up and was break dancing the crowd into rhythmic clapping and foot stomping. Jody's smile evaporated and her eyes were like diamonds that had turned back to lumps of coal.

I met Ali at Reception. Once again, my name boomed over the tannoy, and this time a cold sweat broke over my previous cold sweat that my nerves had given me in the morning. The biggest concern at this point was with all the layers of cold sweat would any of my clothes fit? It was Ali making her grand entrance, and I knew not to expect the same from Donna.

It had been eighty-nine days since I'd seen Ali, eighty-nine days since anything mind-altering—and I could taste the outside. I saw her eyes widen and wondered if she needed to do that to fit me in the frame of her vision since I'd gained weight.

"Honey, you look great," she said pulling me towards her to hug me. Of course people would say that anyway. Who in their right mind would tell someone they look like shit after they left rehab? *Fe*, I thought.

"Thanks, I feel like an elephant."

"Oh no, you needed to gain. You were scrawny and sick-looking."

While we were talking, I saw Donna drive in. I'd never seen her car before, but when a manky, dirty car drove in and its driver waved at me through a muddy window, I knew it was her.

"When are you supposed to leave?" Ali asked.

"Monday."

"What are you going to do? You know you can't go back to Grandma's. Fe's agency won't allow that."

"Yeah, I know."

Even though it was in my imminent future, it wasn't time to think about that yet. I found her a seat and went to track down Donna. She was catching up with Kath and Phoebe, and I interrupted her *Tale of Two Nights in a Motel Room with Jerry*.

"Gross, Donna, do we 'ave to listen to this?"

"This is as much excitement as we've had in a long time, you! Now sit down and listen, you could use the advice," Phoebe said.

Donna sat with L dorm while Ali had a seat in the very front. By now, I just wanted to get out. I recited the twelve steps, the sun was burning words out of the top of my head, and I stumbled on steps six and seven, but galloped to the end with confidence.

Ashley sat next to me in the graduation group, which faced the audience.

"Ninety-eight point seven," I whispered to her. She was beaming. A total transformation I never thought possible. I recognized her sister who had a few kids along with her, and I assumed they had to be Ashley's. She couldn't be that happy otherwise.

"Philippa M," the microphone boomed.

I stood. Everything between the twelve steps and now had been choppy sounds and memories that blended into a hallucinogenic moment.

I tapped on the microphone and looked around the crowd.

"Philippa M, addict," I started and paused for the chorus of voices I knew would respond. "When I first got 'ere, like many whose footsteps I'm following in, I didn't think I needed to be here. But I'm incredibly grateful I stayed, and I'm in awe at the things I've learned and ready to continue learning." I was secretly pleased at the way this sounded coming out. I sounded as if I knew something. I didn't feel it, but when I saw Ali smiling, I knew I could kid her and everyone else if I wanted. It was partly true anyway. I didn't think I needed rehab. I thought I needed a place to stay. Turned out, I needed both. I'd learned much more than I expected. I didn't know there was that much to addiction. I thought we stopped using drugs, and that was the end of it. I felt as if I had it down, though, so I wasn't going to go to meetings all the time after my release the way I'd heard people did.

"I had no idea I was an addict. I listened to the stories of the people in here who identified as addicts and realized I was just like them. I 'ad to surrender to that idea and then God. I was living on borrowed courage, borrowed love and emotion. Today, I've been taught I can stand on my own two feet. Today, I have faith not fear, and when I forget that, I have other addicts to remind me." *Bloomin' 'eck*, I thought, *I should write a book or be a Gospel preacher*. I paused to allow for more great insights to gather for the final leg of my speech.

"I have to thank, number one, God, for that, and thank the people 'ere at Acton for giving me a second chance at life, at living. And thanks for the tools that are going to get me through it. If you're new, stay. Give yourself a chance."

The applause was loud and lasted beyond sitting down. As it wore off, so did my stoic faith that a solution would emerge as to where I would live and how I would be able to stay in America.

I shivered with nerves next to Ashley, and she nudged me and smiled before getting up to deliver her acceptance speech.

When it was over, Ali hugged me again and told me how proud she was. But I couldn't stop thinking what a bitch she was for not letting me live with Grandma. She had the final say—she was the boss of everything and made sure everyone knew it.

"Yeah, thanks, I'll call and let you know where I am."

Donna was waiting for me in the dorm. It took a second to look around one last time. That familiar feeling of something ending broke a wave of sadness over me, and I walked away through a blur of tears, a rainy day in Manchester.

❖

We drove straight to Grandma's. Donna decided for me, and I directed her. She chatted about her sober living house.

"I never did drink that wine," she said.

Little did she know I'd been thinking about it since she had written it in a message at the alcoholics' meeting. *Maybe I could be an alcoholic?*

Fe welcomed me in with, "You look chunky, Bloody Dude!"

She reached for two glasses and filled them with ice, and I watched her pour the premixed Long Island Ice Tea.

Sip.

Relapse.

Sip.

Relapse.

I never did collect the ninety-day chip.

CHAPTER EIGHTEEN

MY TIME WAS UP. I HAD TO LEAVE LA. If I stayed after my visa expired, I risked being shut out completely, since 9/11 had tightened all of the loopholes I had previously exploited. Now I would be required to leave the continent if I wanted to return. A quick trip to Mexico and back into America to be granted a tourist visa was no longer an option. Getting stranded in Tijuana, as I had with Gina and Scott the night I started smoking crack, and a grumpy but liberal Border Patrol officer like Sergeant Helland would never happen in the eighteen months that had passed since that day.

I called my immigration attorney and asked his advice. He was a Northerner, from Leeds, so I felt an innate trust. He had walked me through the process of obtaining an H1B work visa, pulling back the curtain on loopholes to ensure I could stay.

"Get married," he told me this time. I'd spoken to Donna every day since my release from Acton and she still had no leads on a husband.

"What if I fly to Mexico and get a tourist visa?"

"No, love," his hard "u" pronunciation when he said "love" sounded like an old record playing on the radio. It didn't sound the same when I heard it from my own mouth. Somehow, the prickly memories of home were soothed, anxiety frosted over with a happy memory. "You 'ave to leave the continent now. The laws are incredibly strict since 9/11."

If there was any other way around it, I knew Trevor would tell me.

When I'd first arrived in LA and was working for a public relations agency, Trevor had told me to work freelance and send my checks back to England to be cashed. Otherwise, I would have to go home and come back again in six months while the work visa was processed. With a timeframe like that, any company would surely employ someone else. Even though Mam wanted me home, she agreed to deposit my pay.

After three months, my original tourist visa ran out, and I had to leave for Cabo San Lucas in Mexico so I could leave America and return on another tourist visa. By the time that one ran out, Trevor called me with the news that my work visa had been approved.

It was after that trip to Mexico that I decided I drank too much and made a decision to find a drug dealer. I met Ron in a nightclub and he supplied me with coke for years before my next trip to Mexico after which I started smoking crack. Snorting coke got rid of my beer gut in a week, none of the diets Mam had me on could have worked a miracle like that.

Trevor had been my last chance at finding an answer. There was nothing I could do at this point. I was pissed at the counselors at Acton who told me, "Stay in today, you're powerless, you have to let go, let God." I'd tried my best to find an answer, and it seemed even God didn't know one. I was spitting mad that I'd trusted these people.

I called Mam and asked her to buy me a ticket for the day before my visa ran out.

"Oooh! I will, luvey, I will!" I'd not heard Mam sound that happy in years, *since the last time she took us to the Museum of Science and Industry,* I thought. That was a time before Tony came on the scene and way before Sammy was born.

The thought of being a prisoner in my own country left me gasping for air. There was always Europe as an option, but without the language skills or capabilities I couldn't foresee a future. My only way forward was to take a step backward and that meant returning to Manchester.

I felt I had invested too much of my life in LA to let it drop completely. Although on the surface it seemed I had screwed it up, I knew I would be walking away enlightened. My gut instinct, that I had religiously ignored, was becoming a point of direction, a guiding internal star. Besides which my lawsuit with Rock 'n' Rollers was still ongoing, the settlement could be millions, and then I could buy my way back into America. I also loved Grandma like my own and even though her image of me would become unwoven in the tapestry of her memory, I had her lodged in my heart like a wayward bullet.

I didn't have many goodbyes. I'd royally fucked up in LA. Fe, Grandma, Paul, and Donna were the important ones. Grandma was slipping away, becoming transparent. She wasn't capable of dying her own hair, and she didn't have the patience to sit and allow Fe to do it. The orange dye faded to the natural white she now was. Her laziness had affected her like rigor mortis. She was pale and hardly wore her bright lipstick and blush anymore. It felt as if in the thirty days since I'd seen her we'd unconsciously or subconsciously been drawn to a similar path. Now we stood in our own reflections as the skin and bones of who we really were. But whereas Grandma's life leaked color, mine was starting to develop brushstroke after brushstroke of new shades and patterns.

It was crippling to leave her when she'd just started dialysis for her kidneys, but her memory was stunted to that of a goldfish. Sometimes I was jealous of her ability to start each moment with a fresh, unblemished life. In the next moment, I was sad she didn't get to remember the memories and experiences that had plagued and tickled her soul, morphed her into the legacy she would leave behind and the treasures of Earth she had filled her life with.

I met with Donna before I had to leave. She was sat on a bench in Palisades Park that faces the ocean, one of the best seats in the house to watch the sunset. The best being where the surf meets the sand and the soles of your feet are rinsed and your spirit is cleansed and you can tell your sins are forgiven because the sun turns different colors from yellow to orange to red before dipping behind the infinite horizon. I knew that a light show in Vegas could not beat the one I witnessed.

From afar, I watched a bloke approach her.

"Gotta smoke?"

She reached into her pocket and pulled one out for him. I ran over, giggling to myself, and patted her on the back so she leapt of the bench.

"Gotta smoke, man? Dude? Cat? Dog? Hommie?"

It was a great way to start our visit, knowing we could laugh just as hard on the *outs* as in a set of forced, institutional circumstances. We walked down the boardwalk to Sidewalk Café, where we could eat for half price because Donna had a coupon. Right when we walked in, there were huge posters suspended from the roof advertising Stella Artois. I'd told Donna about Stella when we were in Acton.

"Loony juice, we call it at 'ome. Can make the sanest person act in the most insane ways. I had a friend who started fights, stole cars and got strangers to 'elp 'im steal 'em! His name was Mark Meehan but we called 'im Mayhem! Every weekend we had to pick him up from the police station. Really nice bloke, died of alcohol poisonin'. Totally miss 'im."

"Whatever! Beer can't do that."

"I'm not kiddin' you, mate."

A six-foot trigger dangled above our heads.

We looked at each other, then at the massive Stella bottle.

The host took us to our seats and gave us menus. We looked at them, eyes dancing from section to section. I'd not had a drink since the day I got out of Acton and I'd had no desire— until I saw that bottle. I didn't want to tell Donna I'd had a drink and felt fine because I didn't want to influence her decision. I knew her brain was whirring at a thousand miles an hour listening to a chatter, they'd told us in Acton, was The Disease.

"Can I get you something to drink," Della, our server, asked us. It was hard to figure out whether these were signs or tests. Or anything at all.

"Two Stellas, please," Donna said.

"Same," I said.

She walked away, and we looked at each other.

"Are you sure?" I asked her.

"My problem was meth, not alcohol."

"But aren't we supposed to stay away from everything?" I asked, starting to regret my decision.

"Well, yeah, but I got a job now. I got a place to stay. I'm so jazzed. Anyways, I won't drink every day."

The beers arrived, and I watched Donna glug hers down, almost in one gulp. It dribbled down her chin, and she wiped it on the back of her hand. I took a swig, savored the distinct familiar flavor and the bubbles tickling my throat as it went down. The rush of alcohol through my veins was astounding, warm and tingling, working its magic so my limbs went limp. We finished our beers without ordering food and staggered back through the sunset to Donna's car, and she drove me home. We were too tipsy for our goodbye to be sad. It was more of a lunge than an embrace followed by drooling, slurring sentiments. It wasn't over for us.

The whole time I stayed at Grandma's after I'd left Acton I'd not slept in my old room. I preferred to sleep on the sofa in the front room, where I would drift asleep to a symphony of infomercials and wake with strong desires to buy creams that would make me look young and gadgets to make the best smoothies in the world. I woke up and searched the cabinets at Grandma's, certain that I'd bought one at some point. Sleeping on the sofa reminded me of where I'd come from and that my past actions had cost me this home, so it didn't do to get comfortable.

When the day came to leave, I was heartbroken. For myself and for Grandma. But I would have to be back for my lawsuit, and I kept that at the forefront of my mind. I treated it with the same attitude I had when I was leaving Manchester, *Fuck it just do it!* That way, there wasn't room for nerves or feelings. I could cope and, as with my brothers' death, sometimes that was all I could hope for.

❖

Mam was there to meet me at Manchester airport. Waving and beating her war-cry, "Yoooohoooo!" as I dragged my luggage through the double doors. Twelve hours earlier, I'd been praying for a reprieve. A mix-up with my visa meant I had an extra six months, I'd hoped the customs officer would say. On the other hand, he could have found out I'd not worked for the company that sponsored my visa for eighteen months and ban me from returning. I thought about what I'd learned at Acton, what I'd learned about acceptance was one of my favorites and most useful, especially at this point. I felt the same release as I did after I'd been held under the water by a wave, struggling against the currents and undertows, before I was released and the oxygen gushed into my lungs, breathing life into me again.

Mam hugged me tight.

"Mam, you've gotta watch my arm."

"Sorry, love." She took a step back and examined me in her usual way. I knew she was likely to be considering my weight. "Well you don't look much like a druggie. I expected you to be really thin with all them drugs."

I was irritated this was her first comment. I knew Mam had been getting ideas off the telly about what drug addicts look like and had stuck my head on their shoulders. Then I thought about the people I had just left at Acton whose parents didn't seem to care and abused them in the most horrific ways, including incest. Mam had a good heart and gave me everything she thought I needed, not realizing that all I ever wanted was her. It was hard not to be emotional with Mam and my brothers. They just had to look at me and my tear ducts were punctured.

"Mam! I lived in a car not on the street," I blubbed and snotted.

"Welcome 'ome." She smiled and hugged me again.

On the drive home, we passed fields of snow, Mother Nature's blank canvases, and I wondered what I would fill mine with. What did I want from the future and what would it actually bring?

Mam swung the car into the driveway, and I could imagine the headlights slicing through the front room, high enough to

248

decapitate me when I was twelve, but miss our Sammy completely. It was a well-trodden routine to walk in, sling my bag against the baseboard, and run up to the loo at the top of the first flight of stairs.

I went up to my bedroom and was relieved to find nothing had changed. My bed was in the same place and had the same blanket on it. My desk still had papers scattered across it in front of the old computer where I did my homework and where I rolled my first joint. I walked over to the window from where the fireman had rescued me. It slid open easily since it had been replaced with a modern window after the fireman had put his axe through the frame. I didn't like all the new stuff that replaced the old—none of it had the character of the original building. But when I looked down at the forty-foot drop onto concrete, I knew I was lucky to be alive.

"Good as new," the builder had assured us. Problem was, I wanted it as good as old, the way home used to be. I longed for the wallpaper we used to have in the toilet with names of plants that it had taken years for me to be able to read and pronounce. A toilet basin big enough to fit an elephant's bum—more specifically, my Nellie the elephant bum. It had an old-fashioned chain flusher, too. The Victorian radiator wide enough to sit on and maybe I would have if it didn't feel like cold razor blades because it was never switched on.

"A bloody waste a money to 'ave a radiator in the loo. I don't know who the Victorians thought they were," Mam said when we moaned it was an ice box. "You kids are spoiled! You're probably too young to remember when we had an outside loo at Gilda Crescent."

Old memories washed over with fresh paint and pungent new carpets. But I couldn't go back to that frame of mind, only seeing what I'd lost. I had to push forward, write a book, envision possibilities, so I didn't have to feel the tragedy of my family was in vain.

I came back downstairs and peeked my head around the lounge door, kept closed to keep the warmth in, and slithered up next to the radiator—my old stomping ground. Every house I went to of my friends had a space at the radiator saved for me and my icy limbs and face. I had it down to an art. I untucked my T-shirt that would soon be relegated to a layer buried way below jumpers, long-sleeved thermal underwear that I would probably steal off Mam, and various T-shirts to make up nine or ten layers of clothing. With the T-shirt loosely dangling over the radiator, the heat shot up my back to my neck and it felt like warm massaging hands.

Mam put the kettle on and came in with a mug of tea for us both. It was a hot cup of happiness, the steam warming my face and from what I'd learned in LA, probably clogging my pores, too. I sat down on the sofa and put the mug on the table.

"Find a coaster for that!" Mam shrilled. I realized then that nothing changes in reality, at least people don't unless they really want to. But I was grateful that Mam was the same in that way since the rest of the house had undergone a facelift. I still wished I could be open with her, though, and talk about Mike and Sammy, the guilt I battled with. But I knew that would do no good. The blazing trumpets of the opening credits to *Coronation Street* came from the telly, the camera panned across the backyards of the terraced houses and the cat, the same cat from years ago, walked on the wall that separated the backyards.

"That cat's gotta be dead now, Mam."

She didn't answer. This was Mam's drug of choice. She was entranced from the first note of the trumpet.

Midway through the episode, our Charlie came waltzing through the front door.

"Mam? Our kid?"

I lunged for the door fiddling with the handle—nerves and excitement made me jittery. It flew open and the smell of Sarson's vinegar and fish and chips came rushing at me. Standing behind the parcel of food wrapped in newspaper was my brother, thirty years old and not looking a day over ten.

❖

Our Charlie was head of chippy runs and taping *Coronation Street* for Mam. *Corrie,* she called it. The moment Mam got home from the market with her day's takings, I made her a liqueur coffee and Charlie jumped on his bike to the fish and chip shop. Often, he would return with items missing, Mam's fish and no gravy for our Chris.

"I'm too quick, Mam! I beat the buses and everythin' and the chips come flyin' out!"

He blew his cover returning home empty-handed, stinking of cigarettes and rain.

"I lost the money, Mam. It were the buses again, I swear."

She shouted, calling him a liar, as he ran past her crossing his arms over his head to protect himself. She was too quick for him, though, and she walloped his backside as he streaked past. He knew he'd be in for it, but it was worth it for a quick puff. Nowadays, I could understand it. I took risks I never thought possible for crack.

The rain dripped down the lenses of his glasses and he stank of rain and cigarettes, still, and lager, too, nowadays. But he could afford his own cigarettes, and we all got to eat. He put down the parcel and I squeezed him tight.

"Someone's put on weight, Nelly!"

I laughed.

He tried to push me off him, but I refused to let go until I'd frustrated him and he wriggled and pushed me away. We were both laughing, and I couldn't have been happier. The void wasn't filled with an echo anymore or drugs and alcohol—it wasn't even filled—but moments like these, with my brother, kept trickling in. I clung to faith that someday it would be nearly full, but never quite full because there needed to be room for growth. After dinner, me and Charlie went to the pub, The White Horse, and met the lads—his group of friends since he was a teenager.

"Wha' yer 'avin', our kid?"

I still didn't want one. Even sitting in the pub didn't bother me.

"Nah, think I'll stick with wa'er or juice."

I could feel my accent thickening already. T's sticking in my throat, words melding together.

"You wha'?

"Wa'errajuice, our kid," I shouted in case the rumble of voices that sat directly beneath the cigarette smoke smog had made it hard for him to hear.

"I 'eard you, our kid. I just can't believe wha'am 'earin'. 'Ave 'alf a lager or summat."

"I'm pretty sure I'm not s'posed t'drink. I'm not even bothered anyway. I don't feel like a drink."

"Shot. Shot. Shot..."

"Shot. Shot. Shot..."

"Shot. Shot. Shot..."

Voices chanted all around me and hands slapped the top of the table, sprays of spilled beer splashing my face. Feet started to tap, too, and it seemed like a British version of the drum circle. My brother appeared from between a parting crowd with a shot glass that looked like a tiny pint of Guiness but was Tia Maria with Bailey's on top.

"Drink that, our kid, and there's a wa'er init fer yus."

I hesitated before necking it. If I don't really want it then maybe I'm not an alcoholic.

For five days, I looked out of my bedroom window waiting for the marine layer to clear. It took me that long to realize there isn't a marine layer in Manchester and that the darkness and clouds were the weather.

I distracted myself looking for writing courses, something short but meaningful. A Master's, one year only. With a Master's, I could probably get a visa to teach back in LA. I didn't realize the hoops I would have to jump through to get onto the course. They expected me to have knowledge of authors and writing already. The last thing I'd learned was how to rack up a crack pipe. Manchester University accepted me on a part-time basis, which meant the degree would take two years. Kingston University allowed me to attend full-time.

❖

In Guildford, our Chris's house was decorated country gentleman style. I don't think he realized how much of his taste resembled Mam's. Regal sofas and dark wood furniture, each morning he left for work in a fancy suit and an overcoat, shaven and showered. Him and Charlie were polar opposites, and I was somewhere along the equator.

We went to dinner and shared some wine.

"What do you think you'll do in the future? What are your ambitions?"

He'd had a fatherly impact on me since the night of the fire. Every night, he came into my room and rubbed my back and asked me how I felt. I knew he wanted to rub the shock and the pain out of my body. He couldn't do that but his gentle voice helped soothe the serrated edges of my heart. He'd never changed. He just wanted to help me move forward.

"I dunno. I'll see what happens with this course. Hopefully, I can be a teacher back in America. I'm not sure I like being back."

In reality, I knew I didn't like being back. The world seemed big and scary. My friends and family had moved on, got jobs, bought houses, had babies, and I didn't know if I was capable of all that or whether I was kidding myself with the book idea. I just had to devise a plan to get a visa. Donna might find me someone to marry.

"Okay, well I'll help you make a plan so you can see how you can reach your goal. It makes it easier when you look at it in steps. We'll do that tomorrow. Now, eat your dinner."

Sometimes I couldn't believe he was my brother. He treated me how I would have liked to treat Mike and Sammy had they lived and I had the opportunity to be an older sibling. I was lucky. I was lucky to have Charlie, too, just in a different way.

Chris lived next door to the police station, but it was close to Kingston. There were cameras on top of the CCTV police vans that looked into his kitchen, big, spying Cyclop's eyes. I picked up a temporary coke habit before uni started and those cameras sometimes felt like God Himself watching me, and I was freaked out enough to remember my trip to Acton and stopped before class started.

I resolved to stick to booze, which wasn't my problem I'd decided. In the meetings, the speakers droned on about how it wasn't possible to have one drink or one pill. I knew I could never do one line of coke or one rock. They told us it was the catalyst to craving and it would only get worse, a progressive disease. I thought that was rubbish. I never craved more drinks, one got me tipsy, with two I was sloshed, and I never knew what happened with three.

One night, before I left for Guildford, I went out with my friends from high school, Jane and Deborah. When the news of my brothers' death filtered through to my school, these two girls were sent by the headmaster to keep me company. We went to a pub quiz and although I said I wanted juice, whatever kind they had—buying a nonalcoholic drink in a pub was foreign to me, too—and it was laced with something every time.

That night, I lost control enough to lose my new phone. I made a police report to get a replacement through insurance. When I got home and unfolded my copy of the report, I found a leaflet for a hotline I could call because I'd lost my phone. I couldn't believe England had come this far. Sixteen years ago, when my brothers died there was no help, now if I lose my phone I can get therapy. I couldn't help laughing.

When I arrived in Guildford, I found a meeting, Since no one knew me here, I wouldn't have drinks forced down my throat and thought I shouldn't make a habit of drinking. *More alcoholics than heroin addicts die in detox,* I remembered hearing at Acton. In LA, the meetings went on twenty-four hours a day. I crumbled when I discovered the meeting I'd found was the only one each week, unless I was prepared for a long and expensive train journey to London. I didn't enjoy the meeting—there was no cheering and clapping, no hugging. I realized the American-Feel-Good-Factor really did exist in real life but was not part of British culture, as not drinking was also not part of the culture.

I never would have believed I would miss Acton and the security of the compound and the people in it. This is why people didn't like leaving, I realized—flung into a world of temptation, and we are just human. After all.

I learned a lot at Acton. I forgot most of it soon after. I forgot that addiction was a progressive disease, *One's too many and a thousand isn't enough*, I remembered much, much too late. Each night after class in Kingston, I bought a gin and tonic in a can to drink on the train home. Soon I bought two. Then I went out with classmates before getting my drinks home, one of those nights passing out in the waiting room as the last train chugged by.

I progressed.

EPILOGUE

❖

THIS BOOK REPRESENTS THE BEGINNING OF MY JOURNEY, ALTHOUGH I DIDN'T KNOW IT AT THE TIME. Since then, I have lived another book's worth of adventures and self-discovery. I did realize my purpose in going back to school and completing a Master's in creative writing, and, even though as I write this, I remain unpublished, I'm still certain it's what was meant to happen. Whether it's supposed to be a cathartic experience for me or I hope is inspiring to people who read it, I don't know. It's my purpose, that's all.

The statistics we were told at Acton, that only five percent will remain sober, turned out to be true. Most of the people I knew in there, including me, got loaded again. Even though I didn't get it at the time, alcohol does count and addiction is addiction. The substance is neither here or there.

I have no idea what happened to Scott and Gina apart from sparse information found on the Internet, which leads me to believe they left California for another state, and they are still together. In my mind, it's for the best as we had sunk too low together to be able to come up for air. Besides, I met plenty of other people to have dysfunctional relationships with, but you can read about that in the sequel.

GLOSSARY

BRITISH EXPRESSION	MEANING
76 petrol	76 gas station
Alice band	Headband
Baddies	Evil superhero or character
Barmy	Crazy
Beaten floor	Worn and scuffed
Bent [copper]	Dishonest [police]
Biro	Brand of pen
Black discs	Pupils
Blobber	Part of a car door depressrd to lock the door
Bloke	Man, dude
Bloomers	Women's large underwear
Blunt	Cigar hollowed out and filled with marijuana.
Blurb on a tannoy	Announcement on a loudspeaker
Bucks fizz	Champagne and orange juice; Mimosa
Butties	Sandwich
Car in a tip	Car in a mess
Car park	Parking lot
Chinky night	Chinese takeaway night
Chintzy	Cheesy, gaudy
Chippy	Fish and chip shop
Chippy night	Fish and chip night
[Chris's] flick	Hairstyle with long fringe sported by 1980s pop groups
Cinema	Movie theater
Coddled	Treat tenderly, pamper
Commando	Dressed without underpants or boxer shorts

BRITISH EXPRESSION	MEANING
Coppers	Small change, pennies
Crisps	Potato chips
Curling tongs	Curling iron
Div	Stupid, moron, fool
Dodgy	Questionable morality or integrity; shady, a scam
Dodgy bloke	Man who appears suspicious; shady dude, scam artist
EastEnders	Long-running British soap opera
Eight stone	Refers to weight; there are 14 lbs in every stone, so 8 stone is 112 lbs
Fag	Cigarette
Floppy	Limp
Footwell	Compartment of a car designed to accommodate feet
Full with queues	Long lines
Full-stop	Grammatical ending to a sentence; period
Gaff	Home, apartment
Gagging	Desperate desire, craving; jonesing
Gas bagging	Talking, chatting
GCE	General Certificate of Education earned in high school until 1988, when a new system was introduced
Get my kit off	Take clothes off in a sexual way; remove clothing, strip
Gigs	Spectacles, specs, or glasses
Ginger thins	Ginger cookie
Glugged	Sound of a liquid being swallowed
Goody/goodies	Good superhero or character
Greggs	National English bakery chain
Grotty	Dirty, disgusting

260

BRITISH EXPRESSION	MEANING
Guise	Under the influence
Half ten	Ten thirty (time)
Hannay	Fictional name
In a huff	Bad mood; tripping
Joe 90 gigs	*Joe 90:* Puppet TV series introduced in the UK during the 1960s where Joe, the main character, wore spectacles with a black rim
Jumper	Sweater
Lashings	Large quantity of something; heaps of, loads of, mountains of
Legging it	Run away, escape
Liter of petrol	Liter of gas
Loo	Bathroom, restroom
Loons	Crazy, loony
Lounge	Front/living room
Lumbered	Moving heavy objects awkwardly and slowly
Maccy D's	McDonald's international burger chain
Manky	Dirty, disgusting
Mod cons	Modern conveniences in terms of household appliances and latest tech equipment
Morris Ital	Medium-sized car from the 1980s built by British Leyland
Neckin'	To swallow
Nick[ing]	Steal or burglarize
Nob	Jerk, dick
Nugs	Bud or nugget of marijuana
Nutted	Head butt
Nutter	Crazy
Petrol	Gas
Petrol station	Gas station

British Expression	Meaning
Phone box	Phone booth
Post box	Mailbox
Post room	Main room
Post[ed]	Mail[ed]
Prick	Jerk, dick
Proper sad	Extremely sad
Queue	Line
Rabble	Disorderly crowd, a mob
Revising	To study
Rhyl	Popular tourist town in Wales
Right turn Clyde	Reference from a Clint Eastwood movie where the monkey (Clyde) sticks his arm out and knocks people out
Routing through	Rummaging
Salopettes	Garment for skiing that consists of quilted pants reaching to the chest held up with shoulder straps
Scallyness	Scally is the lowest form of the British youth culture that frequent council estates drinking or smoking, creating trouble
Scarpered	Legged it, ran away
Scrap yard of fag ends	Junkyard of cigarette butts
Scrapped	Fought
Scrappy	Vague
Shag	Have sex
Slagging	Put down, deprecate the reputation of someone or thing; fuck over
Slice of porridge	Thick oatmeal
Snuffy	Personal name of my brother's baby blanket he slept with even beyond babyhood

BRITISH EXPRESSION	MEANING
Sod	Politer version of bastard or fucker, e.g., lucky sod instead of lucky bastard; can also mean fool or idiot
Sodding bums	Foolish transients
Softball pitch	Softball field
Some bollocks	Some bullshit
Spliff	Rolled cigarette with both tobacco and marijuana; joint
Summat	Colloquial slang meaning something
Suppliers for nets	Lace curtain wholesalers
Sweets	Candy
Tail of his cloak	Edge of his raincoat
Tannoy	Loudspeaker
TCP (brand)	Antiseptic
Telly	Television
Tenerife	Largest of the Canary Islands
Tosser	Jerk-off, loser, dumbass
Tracky bottoms	Sweat pants
Trawled	Sifted through
Treacle	Molasses
Trolleys	Shopping cart
Turfed out	Dropped off
Turned houses over	Robbed, burglarized
Waggers	People who cut school or class
Wagging	The act of cutting school or class
Wanker	Jerk off
Windscreen	Windshield

ACKNOWLEDGMENTS

Thanks to all the people who have helped me along the way, including but not limited to:

John Rechy for his faith and encouragement. My classmates from John's class, Chris Rice, Dan Loughry, Jeff Moskowitz, Len Leatherwood, Donna Blass, Robert Rifkin, and Soniarita for their exceptional critique and inspiring work.

Thanks Yolanda Evans for introducing me to the works of John Rechy and telling me about the classes. Also for taking turns with Chuck babysitting so I could get there.

Jill Schary Robinson and the Wimpole Street writers for all their encouragement and great dinners.

To Beth for encouraging me to do a writing course that lead to a Master's at Kingston University, where I also met some great writers who helped me enormously—Jan Simpson, Lisa DiVito, Louise Johncox, Alice Thurling, Andie Vickers, Maureen Notestine and OJ Dagistan (I assume I beat you?). The great teachers Mick Stephens, Paul Bailey, Carole Burns, and Meg Jensen.

To my anonymous friends for your spiritual guidance and without whose help I may be in a gutter.

ABOUT THE AUTHOR

Philippa Mayall was born into her own gritty northern drama in Manchester, United Kingdom, in 1973. Her penchant for writing was discovered by her mother at an early age. She kept switching the lights on to write down nuggets of sentences and phrases she thought of in the night and didn't want to forget. This made her very unpopular with her brother who shared the room (they remain good friends today).

She moved to Los Angeles in 2000 and her time in America is enormously influential on her writing, as are her roots in Manchester. After realizing her real dream of wanting to write about her experiences, she moved back to England, where she studied for a Master's in Creative Writing at Kingston University.

Phoenix is her first book. In the future, she hopes to write more. Philippa currently lives in Los Angeles, California.